INVESTIGATIVE REPORTING

Advanced Methods and Techniques

INVESTIGATIVE REPORTING

Advanced Methods and Techniques

John Ullmann
University of Wisconsin, Eau Claire

ST. MARTIN'S PRESS ■ New York

EDITOR: Suzanne Phelps Weir
MANAGER, PUBLISHING SERVICES: Emily Berleth
PUBLISHING SERVICES ASSOCIATE: Kalea Chapman
PROJECT MANAGEMENT: Omega Publishing Services, Inc.
TEXT DESIGN: Gene Crofts
COVER DESIGN: Rod Hernandez

Library of Congress Catalog Card Number: 92-62728

Manufactured in the United States of America.
98765
fedcba

For information, write:
St. Martin's Press, Inc.
175 Fifth Avenue
New York, NY 10010

ISBN: 0-312-06270-2

Acknowledgments

David Armstrong on scanners, from *The Newsletter,* May, 1992. Reprinted by permission of the author.
Scott Clark on CAR information, from *The Newsletter,* June, 1991. Reprinted by permission of the author.
Rob Daves on cleaning data, from *The Newsletter,* November, 1991. Reprinted by permission of the author.
Stephen Doig on CD-ROM, from *The Newsletter,* February, 1992. Reprinted by permission of the author.
Dan Eggen on methodology of the "Free to Rape" series by Allen Short and Donna Halverson, from Nov. 10, 1991 issue of the *Star Tribune.* Reprinted with permission of the *Star Tribune,* Minneapolis–St. Paul.
Ettema and Glaser, "Narrative Form and Moral Guilt through Investigative Journalism," © 1988, *Journal of Communication.* Used with permission of Oxford University Press.
Egon G. Guba, "Investigative Journalism," from *New Techniques for Evaluation* by Nick C. Smith, ed. © 1981. Reprinted by permission of Sage Publications.
Kathy Hansen on Folio VIEWS, from *The Database File: The Newsletter of News Research,* January, 1993. Reprinted by permission of the author.
Lou Kilzer from *Afterwords,* a newsletter on writing and editing from the *Star Tribune* newspaper in Minneapolis, MN. Reprinted by permission of the *Star Tribune,* Minneapolis–St. Paul.
Lou Kilzer and Chris Ison, "A Culture of Arson," from Oct. 29, 1989 issue of the *Star Tribune.* Reprinted by permission of the *Star Tribune,* Minneapolis–St. Paul.
David Protess et al. *The Journalism of Outrage.* New York: The Guilford Press, 1991. Reprinted by permission of the author.
Adrian Tilley, "Chapter Three: Narrative," from *The Media Studies Book,* edited by David Lusted (London: Routledge, 1991). Reprinted by permission.

to Wendy S. Tai,

the best journalist in my home

PREFACE

I've told thousands of journalists over the past 14 years at least part of what's included here. I figured I'd reach the rest of you in one fell swoop.

This book simultaneously addresses two common problems: Reporters taking themselves too seriously, while not taking the process of producing good projects seriously enough.

Here's what's in the main chapters:

Chapter 1: This chapter explores the barriers to investigative reporting and foreshadows ways around them.

Chapter 2: The subject is how to become a better detective. Some of the tips come from within journalism, but most come from other investigatory crafts and professions.

Chapter 3: This chapter demystifies computer-assisted reporting, with plenty of examples. Coupled with the two sidebars, it offers some surefire ways to get started.

Chapter 4: Here are some tips on how to get sophisticated database searching done at no cost whatsoever to you or your organization, plus some ideas that do cost.

Chapter 5: How to use social science methods to elevate your projects is the subject matter. Don't be frightened. Read it and leap into this kind of reporting.

Chapters 6 and 7: In these last two chapters, there is a lot of advice about how to increase the odds of finding and producing better projects.

Concluding each chapter are sidebars illustrating important aspects of public policy and investigative projects. Several of these sidebars were contributed by practicing journalists. Steve Weinberg illuminates the careers of Don Barlett and James Steele, two of the best investigative reporters ever to ply the craft. Jerry Uhrhammer shares tips of his and those of Mary Hargrove, Olive Talley and Mary Neiswender on various aspects of the investigative interview. Anne Saul shows how anyone can get started doing computer-assisted reporting by using local voter registration records. Tom Hamburger illustrates how social science methods elevated a classic investigation of the Minnesota Public Utilities Commission and the large companies it favored. Joe Rigert gives valuable advice on organizing and keeping track of the immense amount of data an investigation produces.

Appendixes One, Two and Three: These three extras examine what we can learn from several observers of investigative reporting who toil in the academy.

Sometimes the advice in this book is for editors, sometimes reporters and all of it for students who wannabe.

The underlying premise of this book is that investigative reporting—project reporting of any kind—is too important to leave just to editors.

That is, the toughest, most difficult barriers for a reporter to overcome are those hurdles placed in his or her path by the people in the newsroom.

Without question, and with few exceptions, the current crop of editors/managers at daily newspapers will be judged in decades to come as being generally bad for journalism and probably bad for newspapers specifically.

If this were another kind of book, I could cite many chapters in verse, or even iambic pentameter. Perhaps two examples will suffice.

■ There are more than 1,750 daily newspapers in the United States. More than 1,200 have created some kind of telephone service where their subscribers can call for information. At the very time newspapers are beginning to face stiff competition from the various kinds of old and new electronic media, especially the telephone companies, newspapers are training their readers away from finding answers in the newspaper to getting them over the phone.

■ Throughout the United States, management in newspaper after newspaper is requiring shorter articles, heavier graphics and lighter topics while paying less and less attention to the kinds of articles for which a First Amendment is needed.

It's a kind of dumbing down to compete with television.

Part of this trend is to "accommodate the reader," and part of it is to accommodate the attention span of the current crop of editors. Everywhere I go on my speaking or consulting jobs, reporters say it has become harder to get ambitious enterprise articles in the newspaper.

What newspapers should do is capitalize on the two strengths they have over all other media—60 million readers trained to pick up the product and, yes, read; a talented, motivated, already blooded pool of reporters who can seek out and package information no one else in the competition can get, not to mention understand.

Contemporary reporters comprise the greatest army of information getters and spreaders ever assembled in time and space.

As the managing editor of the *Charlotte Observer*, Frank Barrows, says, "The future of newspapers is breadth and depth."

Depth, of course, is the provenance of project reporters. And this book will help you do better projects.

If you try the tips, adopt the strategies, employ the tactics, talk the talk and walk the walk, you can do better projects at your newspaper or television station whether or not they want you to.

One last reading aid: A few things are repeated in this book, because a particular treatment of an idea would be incomplete without the repeated advice, even though it also fits elsewhere. Don't be dismayed by the few times this happens. Blame it on John Dewey, who counseled that anything worth saying once is worth saying many times. As you know, if you've gotten your education in the United States, this is the one piece of Dewey advice every teacher knows and follows.

Finally, when your professional life has ended and you are sitting on your porch swing, granddaughter attentively on your lap, war stories at full flow—yours not hers—what exactly will you be proud of most? (1) "I gave good budget at the 4 o'clock huddle"? or (2) "I could whip out a nine-inch, non-jump story in only four hours"? or (3) "I once wrote or edited a project that created conditions for change that meant a great deal to a few people"?

I'm not saying that everything in the newspaper should be investigative. There is a place for bulletin-board reporting, for features, for sports, for the comics—but none of these is why you, or I, or even they, got into the business. If you've read this far, I'm pretty sure I'm describing you when I say that, at least once, you want to participate in a stellar piece of journalism. If you've done this work before, you want to overcome the barriers that either keep you from doing more or keep you from doing it better.

This book has lots of advice on both counts. Because most of my experience is in print, most of the examples are from the print media. But most of the book is of equal value to print (newspapers and magazines) and broadcast reporters.

Your only obligation after reading this book is to do some journalism that counts, then train or help others to do it too.

Acknowledgments

If television had reported the issuance of the Ten Commandments, the 10 o'clock news reader would have done it like this: "God gave Moses the Ten Commandments today. If we follow them, we will have everlasting peace. If we don't follow them, we will suffer eternal damnation. Here are three of the more important ones."

I had a lot of help producing this book. Here are some of the people who were important in helping me get it right. (Where it is wrong, it represents utter failure on their part.)

You and I are indebted to the journalists who shared their techniques in this book, including Tom Hamburger, Mary Hargrove, Mary Neiswender, Joe Rigert, Olive Talley, Jerry Uhrhammer and Steve Weinberg.

The journalism educators who read early versions and suggested changes were especially helpful: Margaret J. Patterson, Duquesne University; David Protess, Northwestern University; Sherry Ricchiardi, Indiana University–Indianapolis; and Carl Sessions Stepp, University of Maryland.

My editors at St. Martin's Press saved you from my early, unfettered humor and would have done even better had I let them: Cathy Pusateri, Jane Lambert, Nancy Lyman, Suzanne Phelps Weir and Elizabeth Toomey.

Rich Wright, president of Omega Publishing Services, and copyeditor Laura Starrett translated my prose into English.

And Bob Greene, assisted by hundreds of IRE members, panelists and officers, along with former colleagues at the *Star Tribune,* taught me everything I know.

I thank you one and all.

John Ullmann

CONTENTS

6 From Ideas Through Reporting   144

7 From Writing Through Publication   164

1

Beginnings

There are a number of barriers to good investigative reporting. All can be overcome, and it's well worth the effort.

There are still some among us who assert that all reporting is investigative reporting. That is, all reporters "investigate" what they write about. This
view, in which the term *investigative reporting* is redundant, works fine until
we read the first newspaper we come across. Or watch the nightly newscast.

Somehow the weather report, the feature on how to macrame in the dark
and the front-page in-depth report on the political make-up of the incoming
state legislature don't seem very "investigative."

Our suspicions are heightened when we compare these stories (and all
the others that day) to the lead front-page piece about the mayor "double-
dipping" on travel expenses that were paid for by others. That article lays out
how the mayor extracted $22,000 from the hometown treasury for expenses
already paid by the private interests who invited the mayor to speak.

That story seems to take a certain kind of ability and a lot more work than
the others.

Stated another way, if all reporting is investigative, why is there such a
difference between what is called investigative reporting and nearly all other
kinds of reporting?

Must we conclude that investigative reporting, like pornography, is one
of those things we can't define but that we know it when we see it?

Not at all.

The best definition is that offered by Robert Greene, the former assistant
managing editor of *Newsday*.

> It is the reporting, [primarily] through one's own work product and
> initiative, matters of importance which some persons or organizations
> wish to keep secret. The three basic elements are that the investigation be
> the work of the reporter, not a report of an investigation made by some-
> one else; that the subject of the story involves something of reasonable
> importance to the reader or viewer; and that others are attempting to hide
> these matters from the public.[1]

The example most commonly used to establish the difference between
public policy and investigative reporting is the comparison between the Pentagon Papers project and Watergate reporting.

The Pentagon Papers, published by *The New York Times* and other newspapers, shed important and disturbing new light on the U.S. government's
actions during the Vietnam War. *Times* reporters spent months analyzing the
report, putting it into context and comparing its findings with what was put
out by government spokespersons at the time. It was a valuable public service. It was not investigative reporting but a public policy project. The Pen-

tagon Papers itself was the work of the government, which produced the report in the first place.

Watergate reporting, however, was mostly the work of reporters who pieced together the facts related to the Watergate break-in and the events that followed. All of the elements detailed by Greene are present.

Most newspapers do both investigative projects and public policy projects. In fact, they are more likely to do the latter than the former.

Why? Many of the skills needed for investigations and public policy projects are the same: a willingness to work long hours, to become expert on the subject, to develop sources related to the topic; the ability to unravel and explain complicated matters, to form hypotheses,—whether generated by a tip, a report, or just careful observation—and test them against all the relevant facts and opinions.

Investigative reporting, however, has the additional element of exposing wrongdoing, of uncovering violations of law, regulation, codes of standards, or even common sense or decency. Here we are focused not only on institutional wrongs, such as why U.S. farm policy does not work or why our students test more poorly than students their age in other countries, but we are focused additionally on the persons who commit the wrongs.

Editors or reporters who are clever, read widely and think clearly and penetratingly can brainstorm public policy projects into being. What's wrong with education in our city? Is our water safe? Are property taxes assigned and collected fairly? These questions can lead to excellent public policy projects.

Investigative reporting projects, however, must start with a reason to believe that something is wrong, that someone has done something wrong. These are rarely dreamed up in the newsroom. They come in from the street. That is, a tip, an indictment, or a series of observations by a beat reporter starts an investigative report in motion.

Moreover, investigative reporting can be much more hazardous than public policy projects and the magnitude of harm caused by errors in reporting is much greater. Consequently, newspapers and television stations usually reserve these stories for their more experienced reporters, and it's right that they should. You can imagine how a series on organized crime in your community could cause problems, while a series on your community's air quality might cause fewer potential problems for you and the people you are writing about.

However, public policy projects are a good training ground for reporters who want to be investigative journalists.

This book gives tips and techniques that will help you with both kinds of projects and, usually, both are referred to here as projects.

In particular, this book is designed to improve reporting and editing skills that help you hurdle the biggest barriers to projects.

Barriers to Investigative Reporting

Unfortunately, the barriers to investigative reporting are many and need to be confronted and overcome:

■ Access to information. It is indeed difficult to find people who will talk about wrongdoing either on the record or for background only. Moreover, the printed record is often difficult to get, and, on occasion, impossible. Successes often take months and cost more than we like or can easily afford.

■ Learning to use sophisticated tools. Some reporting tools that used to be considered a luxury have become a de facto standard in much of the field of project reporting. The reporter ignorant of computer-assisted reporting skills, at negotiating the release of sequestered documents through the Freedom of Information Act or its local counterpart, who is unused to collecting and organizing whole forests of documents and notes are at an increasing disadvantage—one that will continue to worsen.

■ Topical ignorance. Acquiring knowledge about the issues we report can be a serious roadblock. We usually start a project knowing little, if anything, about the subject, the key players in the arena, what the rules are, how they've been manipulated or even the standards that are appropriate for gauging whether something is worth investigating. Said in another way, by what measure will we judge the facts, opinions and disputed material that we will inevitably find?

■ Pressure. The two most common types of pressure—to abandon or to quickly finish the investigation—are the flip sides to the same stress-bearing barrier. Complaints to editors, publishers and station managers by persons or organizations under investigation are real. I've talked to hundreds of project reporters in my 15 years in investigative journalism, and these complaints are common. And every reporter who's ever been assigned a project has been under daily scrutiny and prodding to finish up, finish up now, get it published or aired.

■ Time. Time is the enemy of all projects. Reporters are not only under constant internal pressure to show results, but events outside the journalist's control often conspire to add urgency to the project's completion date: You might get competition from a rival news organization; events in the state legislature or within an inspector general's office may moot the entire effort; the focus of the investigation may be indicted, or may decide to hold a news conference about your investigation in an attempt to blunt its impact. These are all serious concerns for those of us toiling in daily journalism. Your newspaper or television station makes its mark on readers and viewers by publishing *news*—journalism that is timely and exclusive—rather than following up the news of others.

■ Legal issues. Project reporters and their editors report and write with the ever-present expectation of adverse legal scrutiny—for libel, slander, invasion of privacy. And it must be constantly in your mind also, lest you harm yourself, the people you are reporting about and your fellow reporters, who lose a little more freedom, a little more credibility every time a colleague loses a lawsuit or publishes a correction or retraction.

All of these points are examined in greater depth in subsequent chapters in this book. Specific tips and techniques are offered on interviewing, computer-assisted reporting, managing time and data, getting the project into a publication in its best possible shape in the shortest possible time, dealing with your bosses better and how to relate to lawyers reviewing your copy.

But one barrier in particular needs more amplification.

Boss Barriers

Most newspapers are not set up very well for producing projects. Part of the problem is that the newspaper is event driven and preoccupied with putting out that day's newspaper. This in turn often makes supervising editors unreceptive to longer-term project ideas offered up by their staffs.

Consider this hypothetical example of a project idea's treatment at the hands of a city editor. The problems illustrated are common in every newsroom, but fortunately, rarely are all experienced at the same time.

Step One. The education reporter attends a national conference of education researchers in San Francisco—on her own time and at her own expense because the newspaper saw no benefit in sending her. At one of the panels, the education reporter hears experts suggest that longitudinal test scores were higher among students in de facto segregated schools than in schools that had been forced to integrate. She is stunned by this and, rightly, suspects this would be a good project.

Step Two. After returning to the newspaper, the education reporter proposes to the assistant city editor (ACE) a project to localize the researcher's findings and flesh them out with compelling anecdotes featuring real-life educators, parents, readers and students, along with quotes from national experts she sourced at the conference.

The ACE, who is skeptical, nevertheless passes the idea along at his morning meeting with the metro editor. The metro editor, though skeptical, promises to bring it up with top editors sometime later that month, which he does. Following that meeting, the ACE is instructed to tell the education reporter that she cannot take the time off from her regular daily routine to chase the project idea.

Step Three. Undaunted, the education reporter pursues the story over the next three weeks in between her regular production of daily stories and on her own time. She is lucky. She stumbles upon three state education researchers who have been analyzing the very same topic for two years and are about to write up their results. Excited and pumped up by this unexpected bonanza, the education reporter comes in on a Saturday and crafts a detailed, 10-page memo about the issue, along with an outline of 20 stories that could be published in a three-day series. She asks for two weeks of full-time effort to produce the project, knowing it will take four. She enthusiastically gives the memo that Monday morning to her ACE who, though skeptical, gives it to the metro editor who, though hostile, promises to show it to the top editors, which he does.

Step Four. The metro editor takes the education reporter to lunch, explaining that in his rigorous schedule, lunch is the only time he has to really "talk it over" with her. While waiting to be served, the metro editor asks a dozen questions about the proposal (of which 10 already are answered in her memo and the other two are, frankly, bizarre and off-point). He then explains that the newspaper just can't take the time nor spend the money to allow her to leave her daily assignments. This entire exchange takes fully eight minutes of the hour-long lunch. On the walk back to the office, the metro editor thanks the education reporter, by the way, for the energy and initiative she has shown in her proposal. He wonders aloud if maybe they shouldn't regularly have these luncheon meetings, which, he says, has thoroughly invigorated him. He laments that he ever left reporting for editing.

Step Five. Thoroughly frustrated and demoralized, the education reporter shelves the proposal and returns to her preparation for the next school board meeting.

Step Six. A month later, the three state education researchers announce their findings, which are controversial, to a state legislative committee. The story is covered by the newspaper's capitol reporter, who makes three fact errors in his 25-inch report and clearly fails to grasp the implications of the researchers' findings and conclusions.

Two days later, a citizen's group pickets the local superintendent of schools, who said in a TV interview that the researchers' findings "merited review." The demonstration is covered by one of the newspaper's general assignment reporters, who also fails to talk to the education reporter and focuses completely on the political aspects of the demonstration, stating that clearly the superintendent's popularity is waning.

The findings that sparked the controversy are summarized in two paragraphs at the end of the story, one of which is cut to make the story fit. Both stories run deep inside and are missed by the education reporter in her not-so-daily perusal of her own paper.

Step Seven. Eight of her regular beat sources upbraid the education reporter for the slipshod, misleading and error-riddled way the newspaper handled the issue. One of the most vocal is the superintendent of schools, who looks wan, perhaps even waning. The education reporter goes back to read the two stories, is appalled, finds her old memo, updates it and drastically scales it back, then resubmits it to her ACE who, though horrified, agrees to give it to the metro editor.

Step Eight. The metro editor, incensed, sends the following electronic memo to the reporter, after first upbraiding the education ACE: "We've already run two stories on this issue, which is probably one more than our readers care about. You are not writing for your sources. As I thought I explained at our hour-long meeting last month, we have no money or time for projects and, anyway, readers are much more interested in the issues that affect them, such as the waning popularity of the school superintendent. Can we please drop this subject now and get back to the kinds of stories you professed an interest in when we put you on this beat six years ago? Of course, I'd be happy to talk to you about this, if you'd like. I'm known for my open-door policy."

Step Nine. Within the year the education reporter takes a job on the personal staff of the superintendent of education whose popularity, it's been frequently reported, is waning. This defection completely flabbergasts the metro editor and the top editors, who don't know what else they could have done for this reporter. After all, the education beat is a coveted beat, one where a reporter can really strut his or her stuff.

You'll find specific advice on the problem of editors too busy to look kindly on your project ideas and how to handle them and get them on your side in chapters 6 and 7.

Arming Yourself

Knowing that these barriers exist, that they exact a toll and that they must be dealt with are important steps in the life of a successful project. Ignoring them can prove needlessly costly. And the rewards for dealing with them are enormous—for you, your news organization and, most especially, for readers and viewers.

Investigative reporting has earned an important role in our democracy. Its historic predecessor, muckraking, is responsible for numerous safeguards built into everyday life. It played a major role in undergirding the realization of the need for regulatory agencies, a government tool invented in the United States.

To this day, much of what we know about how things work and don't work can be traced in many ways to the enterprise and hard work of reporters—working on both investigative and public policy projects—who went beyond the public relations handout to see how things really were.

To see how you can fit into this picture, and to illustrate the "advanced" in advanced investigative reporting, let's take a brief look at four reporters who exemplify most of the positive attributes outlined in this book.

Four of the Best

If all investigative reports and public policy projects go below the surface, unearth facts that were hidden, unexamined or not understood, what is it about some of them that makes us say, "Wow, what a story"?

We can answer that by scanning the careers and journalism of just four people—Jim Steele and Don Barlett, Robert Greene and Lou Kilzer, each of whom has won two Pulitzer Prizes.

If you were to make a chronological listing of the four best investigative reporters of all time, first would be Ida Tarbell and last would be Jim Steele and Don Barlett. (Feel free to place your own fourth anywhere in between. I have six or seven candidates myself, some of whom are still alive.)

Because they are among the very best ever to toil in the field, you can read an engaging profile of Barlett and Steele at the end of this chapter. But some of the characteristics of their work are worth highlighting here.

Steele and Barlett tackle big, tough issues—the kind of justice administered by judges, the fairness of the Internal Revenue Service, the legacy of nuclear waste, how special interests get favorable treatment from Congress with laws that save them, and cost us, millions of dollars, and, incredibly, what went wrong in America.

Certainly Barlett and Steele have benefited enormously by working since 1970 at the *Philadelphia Inquirer,* the preeminent newspaper in the country for the ongoing production of stellar projects. That newspaper routinely devotes the time, money and editorial energy that allows a legion of reporters to produce outstanding journalism.

But Barlett and Steele produce journalism that answers fundamental questions ignored by almost everyone else and demonstrate what can be best about U.S. newspapers—the willingness to connect to their readers' lives by really exploring issues that directly affect people in fundamental ways.

Bob Greene's career, most of which, until his recent retirement, was spent at *Newsday* as a reporter and assistant managing editor of projects, is a collection of superlatives. He has always been active in the margins where the mainstream is defined.

Consider:

- He is the father of team investigative reporting[2] and, in 1967, set up *Newsday*'s permanent investigations team, the first in U.S. journalism history.
- He is the author of "The Stingman," a riveting book (and which contains the best description ever written about offshore banking scams).
- He and his team have won numerous national and regional awards, including two Pulitzer Prize gold medals—one in 1970 for exposing massive political corruption on Long Island that snared, among many others, a top *Newsday* editor; and in 1974 for "The Heroin Trail," a year-long probe of how heroin gets from the poppy fields of Turkey into the veins of Long Island children.
- He is one of the two or three most important people central to the creation and success of Investigative Reporters and Editors (IRE), the nation's most important resource for working journalists.[3]
- He was the chief person responsible for the unprecedented reporting effort of IRE, the Arizona Project, which was published following a six-month investigation stemming from the assassination of *Arizona Republic* reporter Don Bolles.

These last two credits, inextricably interwoven, deserve amplification.

IRE was born in 1975, in part with help from Greene. In 1976, Don Bolles, a founding member of IRE, was assassinated. What should be the proper response from IRE, the nation's only organization of investigative journalists? Greene argued then and now that the IRE response should be something that would help give all journalists a life insurance policy by sending the message that you cannot kill the story by killing the journalist.

He argued that IRE shouldn't go into Arizona as an avenging angel, but only to do a job of investigating corruption and the peddling of influence at a depth that a single reporter could not. And then, only if invited by Arizona news media. IRE was invited and some three dozen journalists from dailies, weeklies and broadcast outlets spent up to six months in Arizona under Greene's direction.

The series, run in part or whole all over the country, was controversial, won national journalism awards and is generally credited by people in Arizona for the increased awareness of political corruption and the massive increase in police activities designed to thwart it.

Without exception, every one of the team's members I have talked to say the project couldn't have been done without Bob, not someone *like* Bob Greene, Bob Greene himself.

Greene was the team's boss, father confessor, memory, organizer, spokesman and one of its top reporters.

Following publication of their findings, IRE was hit with six lawsuits. In the end, only one went to trial; IRE lost none of them and paid out no money in damages, in major part because Greene and his team had been so thorough and their documentation so believable that potential and actual juries couldn't side with the plaintiffs as juries usually do.

Greene spent most of his weekends for more than a year running around the country giving speeches and raising money on behalf of the IRE defense fund, collecting more than $75,000 in these and other efforts.

When IRE came to the University of Missouri, Columbia, in 1978, a move spearheaded by Bob Greene, it had only a few hundred members and its sole educational role consisted of a national conference. That alone was a tremendous contribution to journalism education. At these conferences, scores of the most famous journalists in the United States explained to hundreds of reporters how, exactly, they could do these same stories following these same strategies and tactics. The educational effort was unprecedented in journalism.

IRE has since grown to more than 3,000 members, has regional and specialized topic seminars, produces a journal, has an electronic library containing thousands of investigative reports, produces a steady stream of literature, and provides reporters and editors, students and teachers with other services. It has truly grown to become the most useful single resource for anyone interested in serious reporting.

Many people share in the accolades for starting, nurturing, spurring and maintaining the organization, but if you were to cite the single person most responsible, it would be Bob Greene.

Because of his skills, stature, and the sheer quantity and quality of his work and counsel on behalf of IRE, the organization has prospered.

Lou Kilzer never took a journalism class. They apparently don't offer reporting courses at Yale, where Kilzer studied philosophy and, briefly, continued an avocation he honed while in high school—competitive debating.[4]

I know Kilzer because he worked for me during my last three years at the (Minneapolis–St. Paul) *Star Tribune*. I've come to appreciate that he is simply the best detective I've ever worked with, met or known about.

It's one thing to understand that something is wrong when it's handed to you, it's another thing altogether to find out what's wrong when the clues are minuscule.

No one is better at that than Lou Kilzer.

Why? Part of the reason is the way Kilzer thinks about things—circular instead of linear, skeptically, analytically. In another age, Kilzer would be president-elect of the contrarian society, but only president-elect. After the election, he'd have second thoughts about accepting the job.

Here's how Kilzer describes the ways he approaches an investigation.

Remember Lt. Columbo and how he got all that great information from the bad guy right off the bat?

He could just take out his trusty notebook and ask perfectly appropriate questions. After all, there was a dead body to puzzle over.

And remember how Columbo kept coming back to the bad guy with further polite and perfectly appropriate questions? And remember how the perpetrator got more and more irritated the more he visited with the detective, until he wised up and kept his mouth zipped? And remember how by then it was too late?

In the projects office, Peter Falk is our paradigm. We not only adopt part of his style, but we hold fast to the dead-body rule. To explain:

Often, in extended projects, where someone may eventually be accused of serious shenanigans, the tendency is to wait until the end of the research and then "confront" the person with a fistful of evidence. This is what I used to do, until I discovered a couple of problems.

First, I sometimes was flat wrong.

Once I thought I had Denver's parks czar—Joseph P. Ciancio—on the ropes for a series of business deals with people who held concessions contracts at municipal golf courses.

All my volumes of real estate records turned to dust when an amused parks czar pointed out that the Joseph P. Ciancio whose name appeared on the records was a second cousin. My editors were not happy campers.

I began to think that if there's a chance for an innocent explanation, it's better to find out early.

The second problem with waiting too long to talk with the subject of your research is that it gives him all the advantages, and you gain none.

In 99.9 percent of the cases, the subject will know all about your investigation by the time you march into his office. If he is guilty, you will have given him weeks to concoct a scenario and you will have missed the chance to lock him in early to a story that can actually be checked out.

Here are a couple of rules of thumb, though they're certainly not engraved on tablets:

If a person is truly guilty, he's not going to admit it. He'll lie. The quality of the lie is directly proportional to the length of time he has had to prepare it. Columbo nursed those bad early lies into murder indictments.

On the other hand, if a person is not guilty, he tends not to lie. His story will check out and you'll have saved yourself a lot of work and your subject a lot of aggravation.

This is where real-life Columbo work differs from the TV series: Not every subject is guilty. Going early to your subject is equally good at determining innocence as guilt.

This does not mean you burst through your subject's door at the first whiff of scandal. The dead-body rule comes into play, like this:

You should approach your subject as soon as possible after you have a substantial allegation or appearance of wrongdoing that would make an ordinary person—i.e., a newspaper reader—want to hear an explanation.

We go in and say: "Hey, these records say such and such or this person says this and that, and it strikes us as curious. I'm sure you can understand why our editors want us to find out what gives. . . ."

Reporters should approach their subjects the way Chicago voters visit the polling booth: early and often.[5]

Outstanding detection is an attribute of advanced investigative reporting.

To be sure, the art of detection is an amalgam of skills, representing a synergy of intellect, training and years of experience. But many of these skills and techniques, mostly ignored by journalism books, can be acquired or sharpened, and need to be employed to produce this kind of superlative journalism. Suggestions on how to do that begin in the next chapter.

NOTES

1. Robert W. Greene, foreword to "The Reporter's Handbook: An Investigator's Guide to Documents and Records," John Ullmann and Steve Honeyman, eds. (New York: St. Martin's Press, 1983.), vii–viii.

2. As a consultant, Bob was asked to help the *Boston Globe* set up its investigative team. The *Globe* won a Pulitzer Prize after their first year and sent Bob a telegram saying, "Thanks teacher."

3. Gene Roberts, former editor of the *Philadelphia Inquirer* and the person most responsible for making that newspaper the envy of journalists everywhere, said it best recently at an IRE conference in San Francisco: "I now wonder how journalism ever managed without you [IRE]. You're providing training, instruction, reporting techniques and methodology that would not exist if you did not exist. . . . In short, you are taking the long view in journalism, a profession in which increasingly publishers and editors are having a difficulty seeing beyond the next quarterly earnings report." Quoted by Olive Talley in *News Library News* (Spring 1992), 1, 18.

4. They have the odd idea in the philosophy department at Yale that students should read the original works of the philosophers, rather than books about the original works of philosophers. Going back to the originals, researching and marshaling facts for debate contributed, I am sure, to Lou's detective abilities. Without question, those skills contributed to the chagrin of editors engaged in making changes to his copy.

   5. This is excerpted from *Afterwords,* an in-house *Star Tribune* newsletter on writing and editing put out by Ron Meador, now assistant managing editor, projects. (March 8, 1990, p. 1.) The "we" Kilzer uses is the editorial we. In *Star Tribune* projects I supervised, we used both the methods he describes. He refers to the Columbo method as the honest broker approach. The more familiar way is usually called the concentric circles approach. However, I can't ever remember using Kilzer's approach until Kilzer demonstrated its value. Neither way is the only way for all situations.

Profile: Donald Barlett and James Steele

by Steve Weinberg, University of Missouri-Columbia

Donald Barlett and James Steele began work at the *Philadelphia Inquirer* on the same day in September 1970. They did not meet immediately. They were thrown together one day when *Inquirer* executive editor John McMullan asked them to check into alleged abuses of a Federal Housing Administration (FHA) program to renovate homes for occupancy by low-income families. By choosing Barlett and Steele, McMullan was exercising a sensible option to get the investigation done properly.

It hardly seemed like a match made in heaven. Steele was Midwestern, an urbane-looking college graduate, soft-voiced but gregarious, smooth with people. Barlett was from an East Coast state, without a college degree, taciturn, a sometimes standoffish loner, fierce-looking and balding, with an incongruous squeaky voice that no source or editor ever forgot.

It turned out to be a perfect match. Within four years, Barlett and Steele had won their first Pulitzer Prize. They had, by 1993, won virtually every other major hard-news or investigative prize, plus a second Pulitzer.

Yet when Barlett and Steele won their second Pulitzer Prize in 1989, their names were still pretty much unknown outside the *Philadelphia Inquirer* newsroom—even though they are almost certainly the best team in the history of investigative reporting, Woodward and Bernstein included.

In an age of investigative journalist as hero and celebrity, Barlett and Steele have a dry-as-dust image, perhaps the inevitable fate of reporters who look into the genesis of tax loopholes rather than White House wrongdoing. They lack charisma, and they know it. "As two of the more boring people in journalism, little has been written about us," Barlett says. Unlike Woodward and Bernstein, Barlett and Steele never have been portrayed by famous movie actors. As Steele says, "We're not very exciting material, except for the work." That is certainly the perception inside the *Inquirer,* where one long-time quip is that the team's idea of a good time is spending an hour at the Xerox machine.

To those who have never met them, the duo's identities are not separate, with the names pronounced in one breath as "BarlettandSteele." At times, they, too, submerge their individuality to think of themselves as a unit. Steele is fond of saying they have stayed together "longer than most marriages last in this country."

Part of the glue is that they both possess the controlled outrage so vital to sustained, quality investigative reporting. Barlett says their foundation is "an old-fashioned brand of idealism": They believe people really should be treated equally, that the playing field should be level, that government should not favor one group over another, that private-sector entities should be watched as closely as the public sector.

They have something else in common—total absorption in their reporting. They have no diversions except their wives and children.

Year in and year out, Barlett and Steele happily spend the work days of their lives together in an office just off the *Inquirer* business news department. A Swedish journalist who visited them described their work area with detached amusement in an article later published in a Swedish magazine:

> In Sweden they would be nearly a case for industrial inspection. In a little wretched corner with heavy boxes stacked one on another up to the ceiling, two old gray steel desks are taking up, for the most part, the floor surface. The rest is occupied by a worn document cupboard, crammed book cases and computers. Every square millimeter of the floor surface is utilized, except for a narrow entrance for Barlett and Steele to meander toward their cluttered desks. There rise stacks of paper beside powerful calculating machines; [there are] also piles of yellow archive folders to swallow new documents. In front there is a smaller room with yet more document boxes, also up to the ceiling.

From that office they have pursued a range of topics—some assigned by their editors, some of their own choosing, all eventually agreed upon unanimously. The ideas never come to them in plain brown envelopes or during clandestine meetings in parking garages.

Underlying it all is Barlett and Steele's fascination with how businesses, government agencies and other institutions function or malfunction to the benefit or detriment of society.

The oeuvre that produced their numerous prizes flowed from the FHA investigation assigned by McMullan. "He asked us to look around Philadelphia for evidence of abuses in the FHA 235 program for the renovation and sale of old houses to low-income families," Steele says. "Philadelphia had been cited in a report by Wright Patman's banking committee in Congress. We spent a few days looking at local real estate records to see what was there. We suggested to the editors that it would take a long time but that the research would be fruitful, so they let us go ahead."

It turned out that the U.S. Department of Housing and Urban Development (HUD) had a foreclosure problem: Low-income buyers would quickly discover the supposedly renovated houses were in lousy shape, so they would walk out. Nobody else would want to buy after that.

"It took us six to eight weeks before we were ready to write our first story," Steele says. "We had to go through deeds and mortgages to see what the speculators were doing and who bought houses from them. We went out to see the houses and interview the families living in them. We had to decide how many houses we had to see before we would have enough back-up stuff to prove our thesis."

The published series exposed fraud in Philadelphia, showed Barlett and Steele they could work smoothly together and demonstrated that the *Inquirer* was making a commitment to in-depth journalism.

Barlett began to believe he had reached journalistic nirvana. At one point during the series, "I received a telephone call from one of the city's real estate brokers who said, 'I guess you won't be writing about us any more.' I asked him what he meant and he said the brokers had pulled their ads until publication of the stories was stopped. That was rather significant since the *Inquirer* at the time was only marginally profitable. I will never forget the day that I went in to see McMullan. When I asked him if it was true the ads had been canceled, McMullan—a man who gave new meaning to the word *acerbic*—looked up and growled, 'Yes, but that's my problem. Not yours. You just continue to write.' The paper lost several hundred thousand dollars. But the only thing Jim and I were ever told was to keep the stories coming."

The FHA series also led to the now legendary court study. During their research on FHA renovation scams, Barlett and Steele had heard about judges letting the bilkers off easy. So the *Inquirer* duo decided to examine dispositions of those court cases. They ended up doing a lot more than that as other types of cases began to catch their attention.

After discussion with *Inquirer* editors, Barlett and Steele decided to look at the handling of a wide range of violent crimes. "There was a lot of debate in Philadelphia at the time about the criminal justice system," Steele says. "How was justice being meted out?" Barlett and Steele set out to find the answer.

In an isolated alcove nestled under one of the domes of Philadelphia's City Hall were the records of violent crimes committed over the past quarter-century. Those records were contained in rows of legal-sized file folders stacked on dusty metal shelves eight feet high. Using castoff desks and broken chairs, Barlett and Steele spent the hot summer in a room without air conditioning, going through thousands of complaints to police, warrants, arrest sheets, bail applications, indictments, court hearings, psychiatric evaluations and probation reports. From that, they culled the completed cases of 1,034 criminal defendants charged with murder, rape, robbery or aggravated assault, then methodically recorded 42 pieces of information about each case—including race of the accused, prior criminal record, length of sentence and the like. They coded the information onto IBM cards and ran the cards through a computer, uncharted technologic territory in American newsrooms at that time. Their guru was Philip Meyer, a Knight Newspapers correspondent who had thought about computer-assisted reporting while on a Nieman fellowship.

From the resulting 4,000 pages of printouts, plus their courtroom visits and interviews with crime victims, prosecutors, defendants, defense lawyers and judges, Barlett and Steele wrote about criminal courts routinely dispensing unequal justice.

As they explained later, "The data we developed on individual judges did not always square with the conventional wisdom around City Hall, which had neatly pigeon-holed judges into 'lenient' or 'tough' categories, often for political reasons. For example, one judge, a political foe of the district attorney, had long been accused of being soft on criminals. If pressed to support their charge, the district attorney's office would eagerly cite a handful of her rulings to buttress their claim. Naturally, this judge was one of those whose cases we studied. As the months passed, a picture of the judge began to unfold that was somewhat different from the one drawn by the court's knowledgeable sources. Far from being lenient, the judge was, if anything, tough. Though slightly more likely to impose probation than a jail term compared with other judges, the jurist imposed much stiffer jail sentences than her counterparts."

Word of the series, and the computer's role in it, spread through investigative reporting ranks. Then Philip Meyer showcased the series in his groundbreaking 1973 book "Precision Journalism: A Reporter's Introduction to Social Science Methods." The techniques of Barlett and Steele were beginning to trickle down.

The court series marked a turning point for the *Inquirer* and Barlett and Steele. After McMullan's broom had swept the newsroom clean, Eugene L. Roberts, Jr., entered from the *New York Times,* hired to build the *Inquirer* into a national model.

Roberts's ascension was the beginning of a shift to subjects of national interest. The oil industry came first, an obvious institutional topic at a time of alleged shortages.

During their preliminary research, Barlett and Steele began noticing the overseas expansion of the multinational oil companies. "By reading the annual report of one company, Mobil, for example, in 1972, covering such operations as refining, sales and exploration abroad, one doesn't learn too much," Steele says. "But if you cull statistics from the previous nine reports, a dramatic picture begins to unfold. In the early 1960s, most of Mobil's operations were based in the United States. By 1972, Mobil was refining and selling more oil abroad than in the United States."

Barlett and Steele inspected shipping records at Lloyd's of London to determine that during the Arab embargo tanker sailings from Middle East ports to the West increased. They compared oil company advertisements in U.S. and foreign newspapers to document the different lines to different audiences.

Their series contradicted the conventional wisdom, concluding the "oil crisis" was more the consequence of oil company manipulations of supply than of the Arab embargo. Members of Congress and other policymakers began citing its conclusions during debates.

For their next project, Barlett and Steele decided to turn to one of the most powerful federal agencies, the Internal Revenue Service. They chose the IRS because during the oil series they had become fascinated with why that bureaucracy was settling claims against huge corporations for much less than what was owed.

"Government agencies regularly issue all kinds of information about their operations. You would be astounded at how much information they do in fact release," Steele says. "People have asked us, how do you read the annual report of the IRS and make sense out of it or see the seeds of a story? If you read one report of the IRS, you don't get much out of it. You have to read about 10 or 20 reports covering a long period of time, then chart selected trends within that agency."

The published series focused on the agency's tendency to concentrate its enforcement efforts on low-income taxpayers rather than upper-income individuals and corporations, a conclusion borne out by the statistics in the annual reports.

Barlett and Steele's research took on new meaning because they compiled a chronology, standard procedure for them. When pulling together information from different sources, a chronology allows them (and many other journalists who have followed their example) to see the totality of someone's activities in a way scattered notes never allow.

In the IRS series, one of the key figures whom Barlett and Steele profiled was declared bankrupt in Chicago. It seemed he had few assets of interest to the IRS. Yet, the day before declaring bankruptcy he had bought a $200,000 house outside Washington, D.C. They ran across that dramatic juxtaposition because of their chronology of his business life.

The series won the 1975 Pulitzer Prize for national reporting. The award stressed how Barlett and Steele had "exposed the unequal application of federal tax laws."

After winning their first Pulitzer, Barlett and Steele began producing a book-length *Inquirer* series (which were later published as books) about every two years. The next topic was waste and fraud in the spending of U.S. foreign aid.

To begin, Barlett and Steele compiled briefing books on individual aid projects. They reviewed congressional staff reports and committee hearings, plus executive branch documents at the State Department, World Bank, Export-Import Bank, International Finance Corporation, Asian Development Bank and Overseas Private Investment Corporation.

Then Barlett and Steele split up to travel, visiting sites in Peru, Colombia, Thailand and South Korea. They found money intended for low-income housing going to luxury homes and apartments. Barlett surprised the director of the Agency for International Development's (AID) Thailand office with the extent of his knowledge, thus eliciting an admission that AID had done little to see whether its money was being spent as intended.

During the foreign aid investigation, Barlett and Steele had a rare experience in a craft where discovery is usually incremental: A dramatic finding jumped out of a document.

The team had made a request to the State Department to review the files for a large U.S.-backed housing project in South Korea. After a delay of weeks, they finally got a call to visit Washington. A bureaucrat directed them to a small room piled high with bulging files.

"For a week, we sifted through them," Steele says. "Slowly, a picture of waste and mismanagement began to emerge from the bulky record. Then, on our last day, we came across a document tucked into the files which illustrated dramatically just how far the housing program had strayed from the goals set by the U.S. Congress. Supposedly built for Korea's poor, the houses were nearly all occupied by bureaucrats and army officers in the employ of South Korea's dictatorial president, Park Chung Hee. Rather than serving as a symbol of U.S. concern for the downtrodden, the Korean homes had been used by an autocratic ruler to reward those who helped him enforce his antidemocratic rule."

The much-profiled Howard Hughes, one of the world's richest and most mysterious persons, became the centerpiece of the next series. Barlett and Steele, as always, did things differently. As the *Inquirer* said in a contest entry at the time:

> While the personal habits of Hughes, whether in fiction or fact, may often have been more fascinating, it was his business dealings which had a profound impact on the operations of government agencies. The series, we believe, recorded for the first time, with an abundance of detail and

documentation, the wide-ranging power and influence of the Hughes organization. The series focused attention on the corrupting influence exercised by businesses not generally subject to monitoring by independent or governmental agencies.

The lead of the series said the average daily take of the Hughes empire from the federal government was $1.7 million, and had been for ten years.

Hughes was so important that, after his death in 1976, Barlett and Steele expanded the newspaper series into a model investigative biography, "Empire: The Life, Legend and Madness of Howard Hughes." The book begins with Hughes's death, then moves backward to his birth. After that, it is largely chronological.

The book's acknowledgments are fascinating for what they say, implicitly, about the way Barlett and Steele operate. First they give thanks to anonymous sources. Next come librarians at 39 public, private and university repositories, ranging from the Library of Congress to the Scotland County (Mo.) library. Many of the librarians receive thanks by name, including nine at the *Philadelphia Inquirer.* Then come clerks in 12 courts, public information officers at six federal agencies and, finally, a tax analyst.

In the sources section, Barlett and Steele give special prominence to three cases arising from Hughes's takeover of Air West; two lawsuits involving Robert Maheu, the former Nevada operations chief for Hughes; two lawsuits stemming from Hughes's alleged mismanagement of Trans World Airlines; hearings from the U.S. Senate and House of Representatives; and four categories of internal records from the Hughes organization.

After publication of the Hughes book, Barlett and Steele turned to a topic eventually published in 1980 as the series "Energy Anarchy," the story of a government planning to spend billions of dollars developing synthetic fuel plants even though that same government had been abandoning similar plants for three decades, of a government giving incentives to drill for oil in the wrong locations, of a government working hand-in-hand with multinational corporations to export a dwindling energy resource for less than half the price paid for imported Arab oil.

As they often do, Barlett and Steele provided perspective so that readers could see the whole forest, not just one tree. The first part opened like this:

> The future looked ominous. The nation was running out of energy and, at the president's request, Navy ships steamed at reduced speeds and homeowners and businesses turned down their thermostats to save fuel. Rep. Richard Welch (D-Cal.) expressed a concern shared by many in Washington about the nation's dwindling oil reserves. "The American Petroleum Institute estimates that the oil reserves from known petroleum

deposits at the end of the year amounted to approximately 20 billion barrels of crude oil," Welch told his colleagues in the House of Representatives. "Consumption was then at the rate of 1.75 billion barrels per year and is steadily increasing. This means our known reserves will be exhausted in less than 12 years."

That was in 1947.

In the years since, the United States has produced 92 billion barrels of oil—nearly five times the oil that the industry said was in the ground in the first place. Today, industry and government alike put this country's oil reserves at 27.1 billion barrels—7.1 billion barrels more than in 1947, not even allowing for the 92 billion barrels pumped out of the ground.

If this seems to suggest that estimates of the nation's oil reserves have little to do with how much oil truly is in the ground, that is precisely the case.

From oil, Barlett and Steele turned to nuclear energy. The series, which appeared in 1983, took 18 months to complete, involved 20,000 miles of travel, distilled hundreds of interviews and assembled 125,000 or so pages of documents. Requests for reprints topped 40,000, from at least 40 states and foreign nations.

As in the case of other Barlett and Steele series, the nuclear waste articles, while generating praise, also provoked criticism within the affected industry. But critics have never proven any factual errors, nor has the *Inquirer* been compelled to publish any corrections.

The series was the genesis for the book "Forevermore: Nuclear Waste in America." The book's opening shows how compellingly Barlett and Steele, with help from the main editor Steve Lovelady and other *Inquirer* staffers, can explain arcane matters:

The turtles that creep along the banks of the Savannah River, near Aiken, S.C., are radioactive. So is the water in a well that serves the borough of Lodi, N.J. So, too, a drainage ditch that runs along a street in an industrial park in southeast Houston. The turtles, the water and the soil were once free of radioactivity. They are now contaminated because of the ignorant and careless handling of radioactive materials. More important, they are a symptom of the inability of government and industry to control nuclear waste, a catchall phrase for scores of the most deadly and long-lived toxic substance ever manufactured.

Barlett and Steele won their second Pulitzer Prize for a 1988 series on hidden Congressional tax breaks for multimillionaires.

At first glance, the topic looked like it would be boring. Even after nearly two decades of investigating complex subjects no other journalists would dare tackle, Barlett and Steele found the tax favors to be their most arcane story yet.

"We felt like Egyptologists half the time, just trying to crack the code," Steele says. But through their unflagging doggedness, combined with their techniques that have filtered down to countless journalist-disciples, Barlett and Steele indeed cracked the code.

The duo began their daunting inquiry with a U.S. Senate Finance Committee list naming about 650 beneficiaries of so-called "transition rules" woven through tax overhaul legislation. The rules exempted certain businesses and individuals from complying with the tax law.

No other investigative reporters looked systematically behind the list's obscure names, like North Pier Terminal and La Isla Virgen Inc. No one else compared the committee's list with the 900-page law, to see whether it was complete.

It wasn't. By the time they were through, Barlett and Steele had found thousands of wealthy individuals and hundreds of well-connected businesses designated to profit from the hush-hush tax favors.

To uncover the identities of those people and businesses, Barlett and Steele deciphered legalistic jargon with no help—indeed, with sometimes open hostility—from the congressional tax-writing committees.

A more or less typical provision reads: "The amendments made by Section 201 shall not apply to a 562-foot passenger cruise ship, which was purchased in 1980 for the purpose of returning the vessel to United States service, the approximate cost of refurbishment of which is approximately $47,000,000."

It turns out that that paragraph, inserted into the tax code by a member of Congress, gave wealthy investors in the SS *Monterey* an $8 million break. At the beginning, of course, Barlett and Steele had no idea which ship was involved, who and how they had succeeded in obtaining special treatment.

To determine the concealed identities, Barlett and Steele searched at the U.S. Securities and Exchange Commission, corporation records in state capitols, lawsuits, bankruptcy proceedings, financial disclosure statements of members of Congress and computer databases covering thousands of newspapers, magazines, newsletters, government reports and the like. After 15 months, Barlett and Steele had the pieces in place to write the series.

Even with all the research, it could have been an important, yet boring, series. It was anything but boring. Part One begins:

Imagine, if you will, that you are a tall, bald father of three living in a Northeast Philadelphia rowhouse and selling aluminum siding door-to-door for a living. Imagine that you go to your congressman and ask him to insert a provision in the federal tax code that exempts tall, bald fathers of three . . . from paying taxes on income from door-to-door sales. Imagine further that your congressman cooperates, writes that exemption and inserts it into pending legislation. And that Congress then actually passes it into law. Lots of luck.

The story then profiled one rich, influential person after another who had received special treatment. Each case study was a mini-masterpiece, beyond the skills of most journalists. The series reprint—44 tabloid pages—drew more than 50,000 requests for copies.

Unlike most investigative efforts, it even changed the world a bit. A newsletter published by the accounting firm of Arthur Andersen & Co. said when the congressional tax writing committees began to think about placing more favors in a later law, they worried about additional Barlett-Steele scrutiny. As a result, not a single tailormade provision was included the second time around.

In 1990, Barlett and Steele took a renewed look at Congress' penchant for helping the wealthy. The latest federal budget act was being hailed for its fairness in raising the taxes of the rich. Unlike so many politicians and journalists, Barlett and Steele read the 1,000 plus–page legislation, compared it with the Tax Reform Act of 1986, and concluded that in fact it imposed tax increases on the middle class, with the increases at the top being illusory in the longer run.

Today, Barlett and Steele are working on another *Inquirer* project. They also have signed a contract with the publishing house of Simon and Schuster for a biography of Nelson Rockefeller. He first tugged at their interest during their 1974 series, when they discovered he was conducting his personal foreign aid program to Latin America.

There is no end in sight for the team. "We've always tried to just split it down the middle as best we could, both reporting and writing," Steele says. Barlett adds, "It is important to have a partner to bounce ideas and information off as a long-term project proceeds. Another advantage of two reporters is in dealing with uncooperative officials. If in the quest for some record I get worn down by recalcitrant bureaucrats or corporate executives, Jim moves in and seeks the information from another angle."

Steve Lovelady, who has edited Barlett and Steele's copy at the *Inquirer* almost from the beginning, hopes they go on forever. He marvels at their relentlessness, their understanding that it's a long road to the truth, their encyclopedic knowledge about a subject before they conduct key interviews. Their preparation is an example for all journalists to follow. "Like a good lawyer," Lovelady says, "Don and Jim live by the maxim 'never ask a question you don't know the answer to.' "

Barlett and Steele's Distilled Wisdom for the Ages might read like this:

■ Always collect far more information than can ever possibly be used. In fact, the backup information should be in a geometrical proportion to each paragraph written. The trick is to know when enough documents have been collected, when enough interviews have been conducted, to prove a point.

■ In dealing with masses of information, a computer helps you store and analyze data. But hand-drafted forms work better for extracting key indicators from one document after another. That said, as many backup documents as possible should be photocopied. You never know what might become important to your investigation. Sometimes key documents have a way of disappearing later from a source's files, or getting misplaced within agency repositories.

■ Some subjects will never be simple to decipher. As Barlett and Steele said about their nuclear waste research,

> Our task was complicated not only by the complexity of the subject but also by the sharp division of opinion among the experts on such critical matters as how waste should be isolated and the amount of radiation the public should be permitted to receive. In addition, the subject is wrapped in strong feelings aroused by all things nuclear. Like abortion, gun control and capital punishment, radioactive waste is an issue on which views are solidly fixed. . . . Sorting out the extremists, as well as the vested interests in science, politics, industry and the government bureaucracy . . . is an arduous process.

■ Up to 95 percent of the information you use can be found in the public record. The challenge is to find it, analyze it, then try to make sense out of it. The work is rarely glamorous. You sit in an office building, looking through mountains of files that make little sense to the uninformed. What keeps you going is the realization that eventually the pieces will begin to fall into place. The day-in, day-out work normally does not leave you on the edge of your seat. But analyzing performance of major societal institutions must come from a personal examination of the public record.

(Steve Weinberg, author, editor and University of Missouri educator, is a former executive director of IRE.)

Being a Better Detective

*Most of the skills you already use—observation, inter-
viewing, listening, even thinking—can be greatly im-
proved. This chapter and the sidebars detail a number
of ways to hone your detection abilities.*

All detectives are investigators, but not all investigators are detectives.
The investigator needs a trail of investigative factors leading to further
investigative factors and to a successful conclusion of [the] inquiry. But if
there are no investigative factors, [the investigator] is finished.

That's where a detective comes in, a [person] who can paint a land-
scape he has never seen from inside a darkened room. It's the difference
between the craft and the art.

—James Barnett, quoted in an FBI handout to investigators

Like most investigators in any of the detection crafts, investigative reporters usually find out what happened because, in the end, someone decides to tell us. Occasionally we stumble across the whole thing recorded in some documents, such as court transcripts or Internal Revenue Service settlement agreements, but usually we need someone to tell us.

But what if nobody's talking?

Or suppose everybody's talking, but no one has the picture to give us because they don't have it themselves? Can we still get it?

Finding and drawing conclusions from numerous facts is the heart of detection. Consider: It takes some 180 logs to make a log house, but a pile of logs in the yard is not a log house and never will be until someone with determination and craft molds them into a coherent and useful pattern.

Thinking and Drawing Conclusions

Thinking is a very natural act. What is unnatural is its scarcity.
—Karen Rosenblum-Cale, "Teaching Thinking Skills: Social Studies"

For journalists, drawing conclusions is a particularly difficult task. For starters, we've been given little academic training in thinking. We're too busy inverting the pyramid in reporting classes, verting it back in features classes, memorizing who invented type and other journalism history nuggets, designing the hell out of a mock aspirin ad, learning the difference between nominal and ordinal Ota, developing photos and deconstructing published or broadcast journalism to find out how badly the mass media have screwed up society. (Pretty badly, it turns out.)

In fact, we're trained *not* to draw conclusions about the information we gather. The facts are enough, thank you. This remains de rigueur even after landing our real-life jobs. Again we are told, this time with force, that the facts are enough, thank you, especially if you can get them into a nice, tight-and-bright, 12 inches. Or, nowadays, 8 inches.

Traditionally, and to this very day, the only two topics where interpretation is regularly allowed are sports and politics. Commentary in political reporting is a relatively recent development, arising after it dawned on us that these political shenanigans are just another game that spectators can't understand without interpretation and analysis.

In this kind of reward system, thinking about what things mean is not a luxury. It is a handicap. Those who can't shed the habit leave for the big bucks in other industries, or stay and drift into those sections of the newspaper where thinking is rewarded. Being that this is a book about thinking, as opposed to one about making money, let's see what professional investigators in journalism and, especially, those in other crafts, think the best detectives are all about.

Let's start with a 1952 description of detection and detectives by William Dienstein. (Complete citations for the authors and the books I quote are listed at the end of the chapter.)

Having, I am sure, journalists in mind when he wrote his book, Dienstein lists perseverance, intelligence and integrity as his first three attributes of detection. By integrity, he also means that the investigator must have "a sincere desire to arrive at a conclusion based upon facts. . . . He [or she] must be honest with himself as well as with others." His fourth requisite is a knowledge of people—an ability to understand motivation and a skill that persuades people to confide in you. And finally, Dienstein warns that even if we possess all the above, it still might not be enough. "An investigator must be 'sold' on his job, and if he is an individual who likes to work regular hours, he [or she] cannot hope to become a good investigator. Investigation requires thinking and acting, acting based on continuous thinking."

So now we know what it takes. We've got to be honest, work hard and hone an atrophied skill—thinking.

But what do we think about?

And how do we go about thinking about it?

Having read scores and scores of articles and books on detection and investigative techniques, and toiling in investigative reporting activities for more than a decade, I can reduce the answer to one (very long) sentence. We've got to see all the trees in the forest, then the forest as a clump of trees, then return to seeing the individual trees, then back to the overarching forest concept. It's amazing, actually, that the best books on detection weren't written by the U.S. Forest Service.

They weren't. But there are some excellent suggestions offered by experienced investigators in other fields. All of the suggestions involve sharpening and honing skills we use all the time—reading, looking, listening, fact gathering, fact marshaling and, throughout, thinking, thinking, thinking.

Reading for Evidence

The historian quickly learns that the words *evidence* and *evident* rarely mean the same thing. —James Davidson and Mark Lytle, "After the Fact: The Art of Historical Detection"

One of the very best "investigations" books was written by historians James Davidson and Mark Lytle, who dedicated a whole book to showing how historians go beyond conventional wisdom to find out what really went on and why.

For instance, let's look over these historians' shoulders as they do something most investigative reporters take a great deal of pride in being able to do for themselves—follow the paper trail. Take one of this country's founding documents, the Declaration of Independence, one we surely can't find anything new to say about. Not so. For more than 25 pages Davidson and Lytle detail how skeptical and rigorous examination of a document and the events preceding its production can lead to some anti-intuitive interpretations and conclusions:

- Although we celebrate our Declaration on July 4, that's not the date the colonists declared themselves free from England. The actual deed occurred July 2, with paperwork to follow. Two days later.[1]
- The colonial congress wasn't voting on the actual paper enshrined in the National Archives Building. It was voting instead on a motion made June 7. The Declaration is merely an explanation of the reasons for the colonies to go it alone.
- Remember the famous painting by John Trumbull showing all the Continental congressmen present to sign the Declaration, all together or they'd be hung out to slowly twist in the wind, separately and all that? Never happened. These wily politicians probably weren't ever all in the same room at the same time. And at any rate, the Declaration appears to have been officially signed on August 2, not July 4.
- As you might expect would happen if one of your stories was passed around to a convention of editors equipped with pens, Thomas Jefferson's draft was heavily edited.[2] Some one-fourth of the original was trimmed. Also, 86 additional edits were made, including those by Jefferson himself—struggling, I'm sure, to ward off all the perceived damage done by these would-be copyeditors.[3]

Davidson and Lytle offer four "tactics of interpretation" for examining critical documents:

- Read the document for its surface content. The authors note, for example, that a diplomatic historian will look for things much different from what a political theorist will look for, and both might miss things because of their biases or professional emphases. So it makes sense, the authors say, to step back and approach a document first as an uncritical listener might. "Having begun with this straightforward reading, the historian is less likely to wrench out of context a particular passage, magnifying its importance at the expense of the rest of the document."

■ The context of a document may be established, in part, by asking what the document might have said, but didn't. For instance, in an earlier draft Jefferson blamed the King of England for slavery in America. That was deleted. Nor does the document strike out at the English parliament, which, after all, was the source of most of the colonies' problems. The "what's not there" provides insight into the document and the men who wrote, edited and ratified it.

■ A document may be understood by reconstructing the intellectual worlds behind its words. This advice is to seek understanding about the forces working their will on document preparers. "By understanding the intellectual world from which a document arose—by tracing, in effect, its genealogy—we understand better the document itself."

■ A document may be interpreted according to the way it was used for its specific function. Why does the Declaration say what it says, the way it says it? Through examination and backgrounding, it may become clear who the audiences really are. For instance, the Declaration had sections aimed at the French (it's okay to help us now); the English citizenry (we still like you but your government made us do it); lawyers (here's the legal justification for this illegal action); the King of England (if you don't think we're going, just count the days we're gone); and so forth.

An overall point is that the document itself may be a lode of information if we go beyond just the text. Reporters who have struggled to ken the story contained within any semiannual inspector general report already are philosophically aligned to heed this advice.

And, as Davidson and Lytle point out elsewhere in their book, the facts are not enough. You must find the connection between them, then make sense out of them. Interpretation and analysis are critical. (That's the difference between a reporter and a recorder.)

So much for paper trails. Let's look at different aspects of detection, such as observation, listening, memory and judgment, to learn from others in and out of journalism.

Thinking Clearly

The brain is an organ that balances behavior to the complex environment. It is an organ that also has limitations. We expect ever more of it as societies become more complex and as demands increase and personal and societal aspirations rise, but still the brain cannot simply see truth. . . . We can see others err conspicuously while remaining quite blind to their own shortsightedness, and we sometimes can even see our own shortsightedness in hindsight. We are unalterably prone to illusion, plagued by degrees of self-deception, vulnerable to suggestion and peer influences, easily misled by beliefs and language, provincialized by ego, and blinded by the false security of species of common sense that are only normally satisfactory. —Philip J. Regal, "The Anatomy of Judgment"

Although there are many books available on how to think better, quicker, deeper, longer, more creatively and so forth, you need go no further than Rudolf Flesch's 1951 book, "The Art of Clear Thinking."[4]

This is, of course, the same author who gave us the abominable Flesch Test, whereby any writer can learn through a simple formula how far we are writing above the heads of our audience, which, according to the Flesch Test, is always the case.

But this book is a small, wonderful, albeit discursive, discussion about how to reason clearly.

Flesch eschews formal logic the way most of us learned it in college (but plugs, as he should, Boolean logic for other purposes), and suggests that all the logical fallacy concepts can be found out by asking "So what?" or 2) "Specify."

Here's an example, which I've shortened slightly, of analyzing a piece of prose using Flesch's two fog penetrators.

The following excerpt is from an article challenging certain applications of the Fair Labor Standards Act (which forbids the employment of children under sixteen, especially near heavy machinery). The author is a small-town printer and publisher who was caught violating the law. He complains that he has been forced to replace children with an expensive machine. To make it easy for you, I put "So what's" and "Specify's" in their proper places.

> Recently . . . a man with a face like a beaked eagle [So what?] and with a bulging brief case [So what?] edged in [So what?]. . . . He was from the Department of Labor to check . . .
>
> The office door crashed open, and in roared twenty-six kids ranging from nineteen years down to seven. . . . He asked: "What are these?"
>
> I started to tell him. . . . A gang from the high school always dropped in after school, and we usually let five or six [Specify exact number, ages, and frequency of employment] join the folding party [Specify at what wages] and gave them cider, cookies, radio programs and lots of chatter

[So what?] for two or three hours, two days a week [Specify exact periods].

"It's sort of a private youth movement," my wife explained. [Specify what it consists of.] "When they're not in here, many of them are running loose in the streets, getting into all kinds of trouble [So what?]. Here they earn some money and . . . have a good time [So what?]."

It isn't always possible to go beyond "So what?" and "Specify" and supply the facts missing in the argument. In this case, however, the data were available and so I could rewrite the excerpt for you, leaving out all the irrelevant stuff and specifying what wasn't specified. Now it reads like this:

Recently a man from the Department of Labor came to make a check. . . .

The office door crashed open, and in roared twenty-six kids ranging from nineteen years down to seven. He asked, "What are these?"

I started to tell him: A gang from the high school always dropped in after school, and we regularly employed ten boys under sixteen to fold papers. One of them was eleven, two were twelve, three were thirteen, and four were fourteen. Their wages ranged from 16 cents to 35 cents an hour. One fourteen-year-old worked in the evening until 11:30, another thirteen-year-old until 11:00.

Now it may be that you would restore most of the adjectives challenged by Flesch once you get around to writing a story. However, it is still abundantly useful to challenge each of them as we try to figure out what is important and what is not in determining what really happened.

Discerning Details

Once, months before, he'd talked to me about "paying attention," explaining that it was the only difference between a master detective and a bungler, and also the only insurance policy most of us would ever get. "Paying attention" meant things to him it didn't mean to me. For me it meant keeping my eyes open—really listening to what a witness was saying, always asking why if some expected piece of information didn't show up in a records check, staying alert to the changing mosaic of neighborhood sounds and movements on a surveillance. —Josiah Thompson, "Gumshoe: Reflections in a Private Eye"

How come cops, public and private, are so good at describing people and we aren't? Is it because cops are so much smarter?

No. It's because they've taken the time to acquire the skill and most of us in journalism haven't.

Cops can recount that a person was five-foot-two, eyes blue, hair brown, weight around 110, jeans blue, plaid shirt red, green and black, shoes brown and scuffed, and distinguishing features include . . . whatever. Can you?

Try this test.

On a piece of paper, write down a description of the room you are now in. Make it so detailed that any reader would instantly recognize the room should they wander in for the first time. But do it without looking up.

Pretty sad description, isn't it?

Or try this. Write down a detailed description of what your significant other looks like, including the clothes he or she is wearing today. Again, do it without looking.

Same results? These are the easy assignments. You've been in this room more times than you can forget and your significant other is, well, your most significant other.

Observation is a skill, just like writing or riding a bike, and none of these skills gets developed without practice, failure, practice, critique, practice, success, practice, practice and practice.

And practice.

The next time a colleague wanders over to your computer terminal to regale you with how good his or her latest story is, stop typing and actually study them. Closely. After your colleagues leave, more than a little nervous about your sudden intense interest, type a description of the colleague on the screen. Later, look him or her over again and match it against what you wrote.

Do this at least once every day and your observation and description skills will bloom. And people will stop bothering you at your terminal.

Moreover, *thinking* about what you see is also important. As Flesch and others point out, the key to solving problems is finding and making use of obvious clues that are lying there in plain sight, known as "common knowledge". But to actually see the clues, we have to look at what everyone else is looking at in a different way.

Here's a problem repeated by Flesch. You are put into a room with a table and three small boxes. In the boxes are a few short thin candles, tacks and matches. On the table are paper clips, paper, string, pencils, tinfoil, ash trays and other things. Your task is to put three of the candles side by side on the door at eye level. How do you do it?

According to Flesch, "The answer is very simple once you know it. You empty the three boxes and tack them onto the door as platforms for the candles. Now why is this so difficult to think of? The answer is clear: the three boxes are 'fixed' in the problem situation; to solve the problem, you have to 'pry them loose'."

Flesch gives two guidelines: 1) Look for what at first may appear an irrelevant key factor in a situation; 2) find any unsuitable patterns.

Improving Your Memory

One day you come into a room. Let's say the room is white, although the color of the room suggests an absence of color to you. A man appears through a door and stands before you. He asks, "What does this mean?" and proceeds to voice the following four musical notes: da, da, da [pause] dum—the last spoken lower than the rest.

"Come on," he urges, "what does it mean?"

You shrug. You say: "It means nothing."

He laughs. "Nothing? Then you have no ear for music."

You try to defend yourself: "You gave only four notes—da, da, da [pause] dum—the fourth note lower than the rest. How can that mean anything?"

The man smiles. "You need imagination to hear music." He then clears his throat and runs the same four notes by you, only this time the first three come all at once and the fourth, lower than the rest, benefits from no pause: "Da-da-da-dum." Instantly you recognize it as the beginning of Beethoven's Fifth Symphony.

The room, suddenly, is full of color and meaning. —Anecdote retold by H. L. Goodall, "Casing a Promised Land: The Autobiography of an Organizational Detective as Cultural Ethnographer"

Did this ever happen to you? You and two other reporters go to a meeting with the top editors to discuss the project you've modestly produced as a svelte, lean and mean 450 inches.

The editors explain to you that "War and Peace" was published as a book, not a newspaper series, and for good reason. They tell you and your partners that your project must be cut. By two-thirds. Maybe more.

Then they make trim suggestions over the next 40 minutes or so.

You and your partners reconvene in the cafeteria to grouse about the decision and divvy up the work. It quickly becomes apparent that the three of you can't begin to agree on what was said, especially where it concerns your own particular part of the reporting or writing effort to be gutted.

In fact, selective and erroneous recall happens all the time and is probably the source of most disagreements at the office and in the home.

Like observation, really listening and really hearing are also skills—hearing something off key from the actual tune is common to us all.

The tape recorder, of course, ends debate. It can also be used as an aide to improve your memory.

After the next taped interview you conduct, return to the office and write up the interview without listening to the tape or looking at notes, including even quotes that you think you remember accurately.

Then check it against the tape.

Over a relatively short period of time, you will be amazed at how good your memory becomes.

For a reporter, there's more to listening than accurately recording and regurgitating. Interviewing is supposed to be a controlled conversation with you asserting control.

Because interviewing is an active participation sport, the tape can also be used to see how well you performed your part at facilitating the exchange and getting the most out of it.

Listen to the tape to see how well you did. Did you interrupt once when it was just getting good? Did you fail to discern a response from an answer? Did you muff a follow-up that might have produced some insight or needed explication?

You can also run this drill with an actual human being.

Take a colleague along to an interview. Give him or her a question or two to ask, but remember that your colleague's real purpose is to watch you and take notes on how you did. Then, when you get back to the office, you can have a useful discussion that will lead to an improvement of your interviewing skills. (You should pick a close friend who promises not to squeal on your performance to others, unless it is to brag about your prowess.)

Thinking Big

Investigation is a process of reasoning before it is a series of discrete tasks. —David Binder and Paul Bergman, "Basic Investigation: From Hypothesis to Proof"

Just sitting down to puzzle through a problem, by yourself or with colleagues, is a good place to start with a project idea.

Although there are numerous celebrated projects born of a simple, but powerful question, my all-time favorite example was told in the first edition of "The Reporter's Handbook: An Investigator's Guide to Documents and Records."

In 1976, *New York Times* reporter David Burnham asked a deceptively simple question that was ultimately to produce a highly illuminating story.

One of the central arguments issued by opponents of the development and use of nuclear power plants is that the fuel might be hijacked by terrorists and used to blackmail governments or, worse, to make nuclear weapons. Government spokespeople routinely discounted the danger, but Burnham wondered if any amount of the fuel had, in fact, ever turned up missing.

He called the Atomic Energy Commission, the forerunner of the present Nuclear Regulatory Agency, and asked them. None of your business, was the reply.

Undeterred, Burnham filed a Freedom of Information Act (FOIA) request with the agency and then began the long process of prodding and using follow-up letters, timely bursts of outrage, appropriate kinds of pressure and appeals. His persistence paid off: Expecting the missing amount to be measured in ounces, he was thunderstruck to learn that it was measured not in ounces or even pounds, but in tons.

Thinking Long

Critical thinking means "distinguishing between verifiable facts and value claims; determining the reliability of a claim or source, determining the accuracy of a statement; distinguishing between warranted and unwarranted claims; distinguishing between relevant and irrelevant information, claims, or reasons; detecting bias; identifying stated and unstated assumptions; identifying ambiguous or equivocal claims or arguments; recognizing logical inconsistencies and determining the strength of an argument." —Barry K. Beyer, "Improving thinking skills —practical approaches," *Phi Delta Kappan,* April 1984

It's become the most common refrain in U.S. newspapers: We need to make the newspaper more reader-friendly. By this, editors usually mean that 20-inch stories must be cut in half. Ten-inch stories become the norm. No stories may jump. Pace (i.e., shortness) reigns supreme.

Keep this in mind. In 1992, Don Barlett and James Steele published a massive, multiday project in the *Philadelphia Inquirer* titled, "America: What went wrong?" Circulation went up 10,000 copies each day. They received more than 200,000 letters. The topic? United States tax policy. This example obliterates once and for all the claim that readers won't stay with breadth and depth. They will. You need to pick projects that touch people's lives and pursue the project in ways that are compelling.

Newspapers are for readers. Length is not the main ingredient when determining palpability. Story is.

Reporters who work under conditions where length decides everything live in an atmosphere that penalizes thinking. At these places editors must be taught to think again, minus the prop of the electronic scissors, so that their reporters can start thinking again.

Thinking Exercises

Critical thinking will take some work for individuals to understand and apply well. We need to better understand the ideological forces in science and academia, and the higher educational system lacks coherence and is usually not too helpful. . . .

Pyramid Films' *A Private Universe* begins with the scenes at Harvard University graduation. Graduates are asked why it gets hotter in the summer and they answer incorrectly that it is because the earth gets closer to the sun. The educational film proceeds to demonstrate how people, even an educated elite, can fail to grasp something as simple as a physical model of the solar system because they interpret straightforward information in terms of incorrect basic assumptions.

Whether or not one's parents, peers, and educators believe that responsible individuality and individual objectivity are possible as more than slogans can affect the direction and strength of one's personal aspirations and confidence in oneself. Individuality is a sacred word in our culture, so we always give lip service to it, and there is no shortage of egoistic mythology. But unfortunately, much of what we hear, expect of each other, and are taught actually discourages the cultivation of independent thinking and acting. —Philip J. Regal, "The Anatomy of Judgment"

Let's take advertising as our everyday laboratory for practicing the art of thinking critically, or seeing through deception. Here are two examples:

■ I've drunk beer all over this planet—in homes, bars, restaurants and virtually everywhere else it's offered. Often they are the brands most advertised on television. Not once has drinking a beer made me pretty and sexy, in my own eyes or anyone elses, contrary to the message in beer commercials. Never has my selection of Budweiser caused a beautiful woman to suddenly take notice of me, as the advertisements explicitly imply. In my younger days, I will confess, when my consumption was much larger, bordering even on social abuse, I did notice that those around me became more beautiful and more interesting as my consumption increased, but never on the scale portrayed in television advertising. Beer advertising is a visual, antilogical hypothesis.

■ If I bought a pair of Air Jordan shoes, I would still be unable to walk through the moves that Michael Jordan used to do effortlessly in the air. Not without hurting myself. And I used to play basketball, back during a time when jumping and shooting simultaneously were interesting concepts best left to others.[5]

I could consume breath mints from dawn to dusk, wear the most popular brand of suits, shirts and ties, gird my loins with Fruit of the Loom and still be no more popular in any newsroom than I am now—which is to say, without that visitor's pass, I'd be just another interloper waiting to be escorted out. But that's not the message we get, nor the one we act on when we part with our money at the mall.

As with all the skills discussed in this chapter—observation, recall, thinking clearly—we need not wait for those rare journalistic moments to improve them. We can't afford to, nor need we artificially reduce the chances to improve. We are bombarded daily, even hourly with opportunities that, given a little attention and method, will improve us for the next chance to practice our craft.

Forming Hypotheses

Hypothesis is the most important mental technique of the investigator . . . [an important function of the hypothesis] is to help one see the significance of an object or event that otherwise would mean nothing. For instance, a mind prepared by the hypothesis of evolution would make many more significant observations on a field excursion than one not so prepared. Hypotheses should be used as tools to uncover new facts rather than as ends in themselves. —W. I. B. Beveridge, "The Art of Scientific Investigation"

The best project reporting has much in common with the best of the scientific tradition—hypotheses are formulated, databases are searched to see what's been published, interviews are conducted and paper trails followed (the experimental phase), the negatives and positives to the hypothesis are weighed, conclusions are made about the evidence mustered, the project is published.[6]

I bring this obvious observation to you to make two points:

1. This is still the best method to seek out "what happened."
2. Project reporting starts and ends with a point of view. That is, a good investigation starts from a premise, a hypothesis, a notion or tip that something is wrong and should be checked out. We fool only ourselves, not our readers and certainly not the plaintiff's bar, when we say that we don't have a point of view or, worse, that our articles are somehow neutral. They are not, nor should they be. We set out to investigate a notion. We report on what we found and go to great lengths to explain what it means. It is good science and it is good journalism and we shouldn't shy away from it.

When editors go before the public to say their newspapers only tell the facts, they are setting up an expectation that is never met, not even in the shortest article about the latest library board meeting, which can be a fantastically value-loaded piece of opinion: it is much shorter than the actual event; the quotes are only fractions of what people uttered; the lead, which trumpets to readers what is important, often is different from what those who participated would chose—any report involves distillation process permeated with the value judgments of the reporter, who was there.

This does not mean we needn't be "right" in our projects. We must be right about the facts and we must work just as hard on the antithesis as we do on the thesis.[7] And then we let the reader in on why we arrived at the conclusions we do, so that they can agree or disagree.

Testing Hypotheses

Fechheimer knew all this. He knew the detective is no hero of reason. That's why he'd been so amused by my early attempts to figure out a case by reading and rereading the file. He knew the detective's world is not the sunlit world of the eighteenth-century philosophers, but a nightmare world where hunch and chance are more important than logical acuteness. —Josiah Thompson, "Gumshoe: Reflections in a Private Eye"

Hypothesis testing is done in three places—the mental exercises we perform in the office, on the streets where we check what people have told us against what others will say, and in the paper trail that corroborates or debunks.

This is just plain hard work. It is an effort to see what reasons there are to believe or disbelieve what we are told. It is the lengthy part of an investigation and one we shorten at our peril.

Seeking Skeptics

Discussing a problem with colleagues or with lay persons may be helpful in one of several ways.

A. The other person may be able to contribute a useful suggestion. . . .

B. A new idea may arise from the pooling of information or ideas of two or more persons. . . .

C. Discussion provides a valuable means of uncovering errors.

D. Discussion and exchange of views is usually refreshing, stimulating and encouraging. . . .

E. The most valuable function of discussion is . . . to help one to escape from an established habit of thought which has proved fruitless, that is to say, from conditioned thinking. —W. I. B. Beveridge, "The Art of Scientific Investigation"

Back at the office, there are two excellent ways of testing the value of what we are finding out—talking and writing.

There's a tendency among project reporters (especially rookies) to avoid sharing their findings until they near the end of the project. This is a mistake. It is wiser to talk out the findings with your editor or selected others in the newsroom on a regular basis, which can lead to new insights and help avoid error or oversight.

Our journalism is always helped through confrontation with intelligent skepticism, even outright, angry and partisan negativism. We are always helped by knowing the negatives before something is published, rather than afterward. Better yet is when we adjust or, where appropriate, "correct" our presentations beforehand. (See Sidebar 5.1 by Tom Hamburger on page 130.)

Writing Early and Often

A useful aid in getting a clear understanding of a problem is to write a report on all the information available. This is helpful when one is starting on a investigation, when up against a difficulty, or when the investigation is nearing completion. Also at the beginning of an investigation it is useful to set out clearly the questions for which an answer is being sought. Stating the problem precisely sometimes takes one a long way toward the solution. —W. I. B. Beveridge, "The Art of Scientific Investigation"

Another common error is to wait to write until you think the project is finished. It is in the writing that we often find what is missing and what is finished. Writing is what journalism is all about and waiting until the end is always a mistake.

Moreover, these early drafts are excellent tools to see if what we think is important and the way we are telling it comes through to readers. (The value of periodic memos is detailed further in Chapters 6 and 7.)

Reaching Conclusions

For me truth is not a place to come to through a simple accumulation of facts or through narrow definitional debates. . . . For me, truth is always partial, always dependent on where you are standing when you perceive it, and tangled up in the language you use to describe it. —H. L. Goodall, "Casing a Promised Land: The Autobiography of an Organizational Detective as Cultural Ethnographer"

Nearly all journalism starts from this condition: We weren't there and we didn't see it, so we have to piece it together.

Too often we offer our articles as if they are the only sustainable versions of truth. We should perform at such a level that any other trained investigator with the same access to documents, records and sources would find the same things we did, find we overlooked nothing and inescapably come to the same conclusions we did.

Conclusions, however, are the key component for discussion.

Sometimes the same set of known facts can lead to competing conclusions, and the best journalism deals with them by acknowledging their existence and explaining to the reader they can be discounted or championed.

Sometimes it's even important to tell readers what conclusions you are *not* reaching. Here's the front-page portion of the main article from "A Culture of Arson," my last project at the *Star Tribune* and one that won Lou Kilzer and Chris Ison the 1990 Pulitzer Prize for investigative reporting.

A multimillion-dollar industry profiting from arson and suspicious fires is flourishing in St. Paul with the assistance of several key firefighters. And much of the money has flowed to two men linked to Fire Chief Steve Conroy.

A year-long *Star Tribune* investigation shows that Conroy has contributed to a culture in which arson has thrived. He has tolerated shoddy fire investigations and allowed firemen to moonlight for a firm that has represented alleged arsonists in fire insurance claims.

In addition, two convicted arson conspirators appear to have had ties to both Chief Conroy and his brother.

"I've never seen such a pattern of impropriety as in the St. Paul Fire Department," says Elden Boh, a fire investigation expert hired by the *Star Tribune*.

Fire has so permeated St. Paul that Conroy, his brother and 15 of their friends and associates have suffered 51 fires in the past 25 years. Nearly half of those were clearly arson, although it is not known who set them. In another 24 percent of the cases, investigators did not determine a cause.

Millions of dollars in insurance money from St. Paul fires has flowed to two companies:

The first firm, Public Adjusters Inc., was financed by Conroy through a series of loans in the 1960s shortly before Conroy was promoted from captain to fire chief. In return for a commission, the firm helps fire victims collect as much as possible from their insurance companies. Headed by William J. (Billy) Whelan, the firm has used hustle and connections to attain a near-monopoly in the business in St. Paul. Whelan has employed two men who were later convicted of arson conspiracy, and within the past year alone has represented several people who were found to have set their own fires.

The second firm, Conroy Construction Co., is run by the chief's brother, Pat. This nearly invisible company has had more than a million dollars in fire repair contracts steered its way by Whelan in the 1980s.

Chief Conroy says he has no financial interest in either company, and his brother and Whelan agree.

Of the more than 100 fires from the past six years in which the *Star Tribune* was able to determine that Whelan or Pat Conroy became involved, 32 percent were labeled arson; another 25 percent of the fires were suspicious or undetermined. Who set the fires was seldom determined.

One factor contributing to the success of the industry is the St. Paul Fire Department itself.

Several St. Paul firefighters, including three of Conroy's district fire chiefs, have worked for Whelan—sometimes testifying for people their own department suspected of arson.

Also on the front page was a box refering to a separate inside article highlighting the main disagreements: "Conroys respond: Steve Conroy says he has no connections to an industry profiting from arson and suspicious fires. He defends his fire department, calling its arson investigators among the nation's best. His brother, Pat Conroy, says the *Star Tribune* is trying to make something out of nothing. And the chief's friend, William Whelan, says he has succeeded as a public adjuster through hard work, not connections, and that he doesn't knowingly represent arsonists." The separate story inside was more than a column long.

Displaying Courage

Last, there's one other ingredient: Courage.

It takes a great deal of courage to see things as they are when so many have a vested interest in having you and others see things as they are not. It takes a great deal of courage to subject your journalism and journalistic techniques to the standards espoused in this chapter. And it takes a great deal of courage to publish the results.

At the 1991 computer-assisted–reporting conference held by the National Institute for Advanced Reporting at Indiana University in Indianapolis, a *Los Angeles Times* editor was explaining an impressive, creative and lengthy campaign finance project he'd directed. After illuminating the kinds of problems he had with a federal database—dirty data, incomplete data, time frame issues—he discussed the "problem of libel":

> A friend of mine used to say that he viewed his role as an editor dealing with lawyers and his impression was that they were supposed to defend him when he got into court. Well, that was a while back. But where I work, their job is to keep us out of court. And I had lawyers line-editing the copy before it went into the paper to make sure that we didn't get ourselves sued by the people who we were now going to claim were in violation of election law when the federal government hadn't charged them with that crime.

What's wrong with that picture? Many things.

First of all, the only foolproof insurance against being sued is to not publish, because in the United States, anyone can sue almost anyone over almost anything.

What the best media lawyers can do is to tell you the odds—the odds that this phrase, that sentence or those paragraphs will incite a lawsuit, the odds it will go to trial and the odds you will win or lose. That's it. They emphatically cannot keep you from being sued, except with electronic scissors.

It's okay for lawyers to make suggestions about your copy related to legal issues, but you should always keep in mind whatever shortcomings the lawyer may bring to the task.

For instance, lawyers aren't trained to know about fairness. They've never had a course in it, nor do they practice in a craft that honors it. Law is not about fairness, it is about power and those with it usually win in the end. And, as for lawyers, they win when you win and they win when you lose.[8]

The picture of a lawyer actually sitting at a keyboard and altering copy is the "Apocalypse Now" of modern journalism. The way it is supposed to work is that lawyers advise journalists, but journalists make journalistic decisions.[9]

In modern America, investigatory projects should be shown to lawyers—it's now almost a legal standard of care in a libel suit, almost reckless disregard if you don't. But don't look to lawyers to libel-proof your work. They can't, because there is no such thing.[10]

NOTES

1. According to the authors, John Adams wrote home to his wife, Abigail, that July 2 would be memorialized as "the most memorable Epoca in the History of America. I am apt to believe that it will be celebrated, by succeeding Generations, as the great anniversary Festival. . . . It ought to be solemnized with Pomp and Parade, with Shews, Games, Sports, Guns, Bells, Bonfires and Illuminations from one End of this Continent to the other from this time forward forever more" (Davidson and Lytle 61).

2. Thomas Jefferson had a character trait very similar to many reporters who later recall the editing process. Oh, they say, there were some minor editing changes, but not much. However, Davidson and Lytle write, "Jefferson's 'original paper'— which he endorsed on the document itself as the 'original Rough draught' " went through heavy editing.

3. Apparently it wasn't lawyered, although some in attendance were lawyers. Today's libel lawyers point out that if the Declaration of Independence had been lawyered, its publication might not have led to war and lots of money would have been saved, except for some legal fees here and there.

4. Rudolf Flesch, "The Art of Clear Thinking" (New York: Harper & Brothers, 1951).

5. I grew up in Indiana. In that state, if you can't play basketball by age 4, you must move to Kentucky. Consequently, most of us learn to play quite well by age 3.

6. "The following is a common sequence in an investigation on a medical or biological problem. A) The relevant literature is critically reviewed. B) A thorough collection of field data or equivalent observational enquiry is conducted, and is supplemented if necessary by laboratory examination of specimens. C) The information obtained is marshalled and correlated and the problem is defined and broken down into specific questions. D) Intelligent guesses are made to answer the questions, as many hypotheses as possible being considered. E) Experiments are devised to test first the likeliest hypotheses bearing on the most crucial questions." W. I. B. Beveridge, "The Art of Scientific Investigation," rev. ed. (New York: W.W. Norton & Co., 1957), 12.

7. "A danger constantly to be guarded against is that as soon as one formulates an hypothesis, parental affections tends to influence observations, interpretation and judgment; 'wishful thinking,' is likely to start unconsciously. Claude Bernard said: '(People) who have excessive faith in their theories or ideas are not only ill-prepared for making discoveries; they also make poor observations.' Unless observations and experiments are carried out with safeguards ensuring objectivity, the results may unconsciously be biased." W. I. B. Beveridge, "The Art of Scientific Investigation," rev. ed., (New York: W.W. Norton & Co., 1957), 49.

8. At the *Star Tribune* I was privileged to work with one of this country's great media lawyers, Pat Hirl Longstaff. She had a personal code of honor to limit her remarks to legal issues and would read stories in printout form, not at the computer keyboard. She has since gone into private practice.

9. And did letting the lawyers line-edit this series have an effect on what was reported? Of course it did; it always does. Here's how.

After exhaustively checking the data, the newspaper decided to go the extra mile and let the people in "gross violation" of the campaign contributions law double-check the figures obtained by the newspaper. (I applaud the decision.)

> In each case we faxed to them a date, amount of every contribution that we thought they had made and said if you find a problem with this you let us know.
>
> We originally found 20 people, not 10, and we ended up in the story naming 10 who were in a) gross violation and b) offered no excuse and therefore were clearly in violation, and then we had a second group which I will refer to as the guilty with explanation—those people who were in violation but essentially said, gee, I didn't know.
>
> "[A contributor], his lawyer said, well, it really, even though [my client] signed the check, it really wasn't a contribution from him. It was a contribution from his Dad. That his Dad was in a virtual coma and we knew that, but we went ahead and accepted that explanation because we wanted to err on the side of caution. Maybe that's a mistake, I don't know. I don't think so."

A better way would have been to report the facts, along with the explanation. Leaving that information out is not erring on the side of caution, it's just plain erring.

10. I do not mean to imply that great care for accuracy need not be employed. In Chapter 7 I detail a methodology for accuracy checking in both detail and overall implications of a project. Moreover, I think project reporters should conduct their business 1) as if everyone was taping their interview, whether the reporters knew it or not, and 2) that a judge will be able to compel them to produce their notes. This keeps reporters from being sloppy or reckless.

Further, I agree with those project reporters and editors who insist that their notebooks be transcribed into the computer system as soon as possible and then discard the notebooks. These script notes have no value once they are transcribed and double-checked, and they may have some value to the plaintiff's bar if they are left lingering.

However, whatever method you use, be consistent.

Investigative Interviews: Part One

by Jerry Uhrhammer, Independent Journalist

Here's an example of an interview that went bust because of lack of preparation.

Mary Neiswender, a crackerjack investigative reporter for the *Long Beach Independent Press Telegram* before she bought an all-news radio station in Palm Desert, Calif., and then retired to write books, was trying for an interview related to the Charles Manson family murder cases.

"One of Charlie Manson's first 'girls' had his child and the grandmother had taken over rearing of the boy," Neiswender recalls.

"The grandmother was brought to the trial as a potential witness, and I had gotten a detective-friend of mine to convince her to talk to me.

"He had done a good job of building me up and even brought her to the women's restroom, where I waited.

"We started talking when I casually mentioned that one of my chain's newspapers was her hometown paper. I thought it would cement the bond.

"It didn't.

"She jumped from the chair, screamed and ran out the door.

"I didn't know she hated the paper and everyone associated with it.

"She was on the next plane out of Los Angeles.

"In that case I should have prepared better by talking to the staff of the newspaper to see what they had done. All I knew was that she wouldn't talk to them.

"I never asked why.

"I should have. . . .

"You should find out everything you can about the person. A newspaper morgue is the easiest way. Public records are another way."

We like to think that interviewing somebody is second nature to most journalists. We talk to people and ask questions about them, about others, what they know or what they believe. We listen to what they tell us and, if the quotes or the ideas are good, include it in our stories.

But for investigative reporters—those who systematically dig out and expose matters that governments or powerful people would like to keep hidden—the techniques of interviewing are more rigorous and demanding.

The basics of interviewing remain the same: Thorough preparation, asking good questions, listening carefully to the answers.

But there are significant differences between the traditional interviewing practiced in daily journalism and investigative interviewing.

It's like competitive diving. The more complex the dive, the higher degree of difficulty. So it is with investigative interviewing. Investigative stories tend to be complex and difficult to piece together. And the people you have to talk to often would rather remain silent.

In the traditional interview for a news or feature story, the reporter usually deals with a subject who is willing to talk on the record without fear of retribution.

But in investigative interviewing, the stakes are usually much higher. Investigations frequently involve wrongdoing, malfeasance and other improprieties—the stuff of which cover-ups are made. And the subject of the interview who may have knowledge of such things may also have a lot of reasons not to open up to a reporter.

The interviewee may be someone at risk, with something to lose by speaking out. This risk factor creates an underlying element of fear—fear of the reporter who is asking those tough questions, and fear of the consequences when the interviewee's remarks appear in print.

Indeed, many subjects interviewed in journalistic investigations have valid reasons to worry. A whistleblower in industry or government, for example, could lose his or her job. So, too, could a midlevel government bureaucrat who leaks sensitive documents. In more extreme situations, such as an organized-crime or mob-related investigation, the person who says too much to a reporter could lose his or her life—or so the person might believe.

Such understandable reluctance to talk is one of the biggest obstacles an investigative reporter has to overcome.

The fear factor also exists for the people at the center of our investigations. Word travels quickly over political and bureaucratic grapevines when reporters begin nosing around, copying documents, talking with people. And those who are being talked about usually become aware of it. Moreover, assuming they have something to hide, they probably have a pretty good idea what you're looking for.

It is easy to understand why they may be apprehensive, hostile, fearful. Their reputations and livelihoods may be riding on the outcome.

Investigative interviews come in all shapes and sizes. Some may last only minutes. Others may run for hours. Some are scheduled days in advance, allowing time for extensive planning. Others are impromptu, dictated by unexpected circumstances.

Investigative interviews generally fall into two categories: the information interview and the interview with people at the heart of the investigation.

In the information interview, the reporter talks to someone who, because of his or her position or associations, possesses some knowledge of the subject under investigation. The purpose is to elicit information that will help prove or disprove the investigative hypothesis.

There are no hard and fast rules for how interviews should be conducted. Each reporter has his or her own way of doing things. Interviewing is an art, not a science, and some reporters are more artful than others.

While no one does it exactly the same way, most investigative reporters agree that the most important part of the interviewing process occurs before you face the interviewee: the preparation.

The Information Interview

At first glance, the term *information interview* appears to be the ultimate redundancy. Getting information is what interviewing is all about.

But the redundancy is used here to distinguish this particular kind of interview from the interview with the subject of the project, the other mainstay of investigative reporting.

Actually, the information interview is almost exactly like the standard interview used in daily journalism. You sit down with someone, or talk to them over the telephone, and ask them questions.

There are some important distinctions.

Investigative stories, by their nature, tend to be sensitive, if not downright risky, and they frequently involve some degree of risk for those who become involved.

A person with knowledge of wrongdoing in high places, for example, may be understandably reluctant to share that knowledge with a reporter, worried about being caught up in controversy. Some are willing to speak out on the record. But others, fearful of retribution, want some protection. For such reluctant interviewees, establish the ground rules early.

Will the interview be off the record? If so, what exactly does that mean? Can the information be used without attribution? Or is it for background only? What if the information surfaces elsewhere? Can you use it then?

Before you agree to any arrangement, know your newspaper's policy. Talk to your editor. Some senior reporters accustomed to dealing with such situations are given pretty much of a free hand to cut their own deals. But it is a murky area. Proceed with caution.

What kind of information can these insiders provide? Direct eyewitness knowledge? Or secondhand reports? Do they have documents or access to documents? Will they be willing to provide them? If they are unable, can they tell what the documents are and where to find them?

Generally, I have found reluctant witnesses are more wiling to talk if they are being asked about documents and what those documents mean. This approach has an added advantage: If you get good documentation, it often obviates the need for a human source, named or unnamed, in the story. This can appeal to someone who may have key knowledge of what's happened, but doesn't want to be publicly associated with the story.

In most cases, the decision on whether to allow somebody to go off the record or on background depends on their role in the affair. Are they central players? If so, and if their activities are likely to be exposed in your stories, be wary about allowing them to go off the record. They are among those you'll want to interview, for the record, during the final stages.

Persons out on the periphery, who may know some of the details but aren't culpable, are better candidates for speaking on background or not-for-attribution, because basically, you're not going to hang a story on them anyway.

My approach in interviewing them is that I'm looking for insights, guidance, advice and direction on where to find things. Sometimes you need someone to explain why something is important. These persons, while starting out nervous, sometimes get caught up in the investigation and become extremely helpful. Sometimes they will agree to shed their anonymity and go on the record.

Being Prepared

Before a reporter begins the investigative interviews, he or she should be well-versed in the subject.

That's usually no problem. You've checked the computer databases. You've run the paper trails, you've reviewed the documents and you've built a chronology of key dates so that you've got a good mental picture of what happened and when it happened.

You've also reviewed the applicable laws and governmental regulations that tell you how the system is supposed to operate, so you'll recognize when it hasn't.

When I review documents and court records, I look for names of people on the periphery who may know something about what happened. Victims and enemies, especially. Those are usually the people I interview first. It is sometimes a hard call to make, but I try to avoid those who I suspect might tattle immediately to the subject of the investigation.

I also get a better sense of the questions to ask when the interviewing begins.

Mary Hargrove, former managing editor for projects at the *Tulsa Tribune* usually begins the interviewing process at the same time she and her colleagues are following the paper trail.

"I try to do it concurrently because people lead you to paper," Hargrove says. "The more I can do both, the earlier I can decide how I'm going to outline the deal and what the scope is."

Doing Research On . . .

During these information interviews, don't tip your hand about the story you're working on. Be guarded in what you say you're looking for. Instead of telling someone "I'm doing on a story on . . ."—in truth, you may never do a story if your investigation fails to pan out—simply give a very general explanation of what you're doing. I've always found that "research" is a nice nonthreatening term that doesn't immediately raise a lot of red flags.

I also ask people if they can "verify" or "confirm" information that I've gotten elsewhere. People seem less reluctant to talk if they have the idea that other people also are talking about the same things.

In interviewing people on the periphery, I avoid telling them that I'm "investigating" so-and-so.

There are good reasons for using benign, noninflammatory phrases during the early stages of an investigation. The biggest reason is that people talk. And if the people you're interviewing get the slightest whiff of scandal in what you're asking them, the odds are good they will tell others.

When that happens, you can expect the ripples to reach the subjects of your investigation. By that time, given the permutations of gossip, any resemblance to the questions you asked in your interview may be entirely coincidental.

Olive Talley, investigative reporter for the *Dallas Morning News,* has a similar strategy. "Almost every story I work, I formulate what is going to be my standard explanation of what the story is about, and I tell everybody the same thing: 'What I'm trying to accomplish here is blank,' 'Why I am doing this story: Blank.' That way, if people you talk to compare notes, they will have heard the same story."

Testing the Answers

When you're planning your line of questioning, set some traps to see whether the interviewees are telling the truth, or even know the truth.

Olive Talley did that when she interviewed U.S. Bureau of Prisons officials about the poor quality of medical care in prison hospitals.

"In the prison project, I learned that one of the surgeons working at the Bureau of Prisons main medical facility in Springfield, Illinois, had never completed his training in cardiovascular thoracic surgery. Yet that was the kind of surgery he was performing at the hospital on a daily basis," she says.

She planned her questions for Bureau of Prisons officials so that the questions built on one another.

"For instance, I asked questions about the general training of the staff. In essence, they assured me that each doctor had to have training in the area in which they were practicing," she continues.

Next question: "If this is the case, can you explain why Dr. Swanson is doing cardiovascular thoracic work when in fact he has not received that training? Well, they were caught. And one of the chief medical doctors said . . . he told us he had had training and—quote—we took his word for it."

By admitting they had hired a doctor without doing proper background checks, Talley says, an essential fact was established. "By letting him continue to do these procedures that were beyond his capability, they proved a lot of critics' points that the prison locations were not receiving the quality of care the bureau had claimed. So they were whammied."

Talley said she had learned from hospital staffers earlier that the doctor in question's practice had already been limited by the bureau because of his lack of qualifications. "They didn't see it coming. And I set up on the very belief they would answer those questions that way. . . . They were lying to me. . . . They reinforced the belief that the bureau was hiding bad doctors."

Often what happens in an interview is that people tell you "truthfully" what they think happened—they are not lying to you—but they can still be wrong.

It is important in these information interviews to ask questions that test the veracity of the answers, not just the veracity of the person you are interviewing.

Did the person actually see what he or she is talking about or was it hearsay? If it was secondhand information, was the teller describing something he or she saw or heard? Are there any documents—such as memos, interrogatories, letters—that substantiate this version? If so, how can you get them?

Usually people who are telling you things do so because they think it is important that the story come out. But if they aren't primary witnesses the information isn't going to make it until it comes from a better source. Often, you can explain that to the people you are interviewing and enlist their help in getting verification.

For instance, who were the people in the room who saw it happen? Do you think any of them would talk? Who? How can they be approached? Can your informant help?

The same series of questions, or general approach, can be used to track down the critical parts of the paper trail.

About Your Demeanor

The demeanor of the reporter can be the make or break element of an interview. There is a place for being firm, even tough, in an interview. But the reporter who comes on too strong at the beginning may never get out of the starting gate.

The whole idea of an interview is to get someone to talk, open up, give you information. Veteran investigative reporters will tell you that the best way to accomplish this is to be polite, courteous, mannerly.

Getting that interview off on the right foot means treating the interviewee as you would like to be treated. Being rude, brusque, nasty or otherwise obnoxious is likely to get you nowhere.

As Olive Talley says: "I would not appreciate it if somebody ambushed me for an interview, if someone woke me up or came to my home or scared my children or my family. I really think we all get along a lot better if we treat people like we would like to be treated. I know that's not always true but I think it works 99 percent of the time."

Be yourself. Don't try to be someone you're not. In investigative interviewing, it is important to instill in the interviewee the confidence that you are a person who can be trusted. The best way of doing that is to be honest about yourself and what you're doing.

This is especially true for interviews with people on the periphery of investigations such as employees or exemployees who have knowledge of how things worked and why they worked that way. These are people who often are at risk, and they are unlikely to be forthcoming unless they are convinced the reporter can be trusted.

In Talley's view, there is a great deal of overlap between the art of interviewing and source development.

"It's very, very hard to separate those two issues because what you're doing, in accomplishing a good interview, is getting those people to trust you. You're convincing them that your motives are good, that you have the best intentions, that you want to do the right thing, that you want to tell the truth . . . that you're not just trying to do a quick, dirty hit. . . .

"You have to persuade them that you are genuine," Talley continues. "You have to sort of size up their character and they've got to size up your character. . . . I think there is a certain degree of vulnerability you must project, hopefully sincerely, that you are willing to put some things on the line for them to earn their trust.

"If appropriate, I like to get on a first name basis as quickly as possible because that's where I'm most comfortable—and I think that sense of comfort in most cases is communicated to the subject. Interviews tend to be less stilted if the two parties are on a first-name basis. But sometimes such informality is not appropriate; that's a judgment call you have to make."

In the early stages, make your questions clinical, matter-of-fact, nonjudgmental and nonthreatening. Feel your way along. Get a sense of where the person you're interviewing comes from, how far they are willing to go and what they have to offer.

This approach is vital for the information interviews when you're dealing with persons who may know a lot but aren't sure how much they want to tell you.

"In the information interview, I try to get them relaxed, to tell things that are easy to tell, facts about themselves, literally vital statistics," says Mary Hargrove. "People are pretty comfortable about that. 'You grew up in Chicago? Oh, that must have been pretty cold. What did your dad do?'"

Being Direct

Hargrove, now associate editor at the *Arkansas Democrat-Gazette,* believes in a direct approach for dealing with tension, whether interviewing persons central to the investigation or in information interviews: "I've walked in on interviews where I thought, 'God, this guy is really tight and he doesn't want to talk to me. Or he doesn't trust newspapers or whatever.' It will just start real rocky.

"And I'll say, 'You're not comfortable with me, are you? Is it me? Have you had a bad experience with a newspaper? You and your wife have a fight this morning? Is there something I can do to make you comfortable? Or do you have a problem with this interview I'm not aware of?' [I'll do that] so that we can start on ground zero.

"I've had people tell me the damndest things: 'I came to work this morning and my wife and I aren't talking. It's not you. Or my mom's real sick. Or I don't like reporters.' I've had the whole range."

Hargrove suggests that it is a good idea to explore such tensions up front so that the interview can begin with a better footing.

Defensive Interviewing

Investigative reporting is a high-risk business. The threat of potential legal action—libel or slander suits, invasion of privacy—hangs like a shadow over investigative stories.

Yet, some newspaper lawyers say, investigative stories generate fewer libel suits than daily run-of-the-mill news stories that are hurriedly reported and written on deadline.

The reason is that investigative stories tend to be thoroughly researched, scrupulously reported and carefully edited, thus minimizing the grounds for a lawsuit. Careful interviewing is a key part of that process. Call it defensive interviewing.

You ask all the questions you need to ask. But you also avoid situations or saying things that could be construed by others as evidence of bias or malice—statements that could come back to haunt you in a courtroom.

"I try to approach every interview as if I would be called to the witness stand to testify about my frame of mind," says Olive Talley.

Some reporters tend to make statements with the expectation that the interviewee will verify or deny what is said.

Avoid making statements that someone—usually the target's lawyer—could later say were slanderous.

It's easier, and more direct, to simply ask questions. Be certain that every question ends with a question mark.

Instead of making a statement, "So the mayor took money from the developers," ask the direct question, "Did the mayor take money from the developers?"

By the same token, be careful about what you say to third parties. You probably will be interviewing friends, acquaintances and business associates of the person you're investigating. You can be certain that statements you make and questions you ask will get back to the person at the center of the investigation, often in distorted form: "You know what that reporter said about you?"

Be careful about what you say to your own colleagues. Journalists love to gossip, they know a lot of people and sometimes they end up talking to associates of the people you're investigating, if not the targets themselves.

The leaks may be inadvertent. And maybe not. In one highly sensitive investigation I conducted years ago, the person I was investigating claimed he was getting inside information leaked to him from someone at my newspaper.

"I try to never make any comments to the people I'm interviewing or to an unknown caller or even to my colleagues about how I'm feeling about a particular story," says Talley. "I certainly let them know when I'm happy or excited or when I'm angry, but I don't go around saying 'I'm going to get this bastard.' I don't go around accusing people of things.

"I've really toned down a lot of my offhand remarks. When people ask me what I'm doing I tend to give them pretty clinical answers."

When Mary Hargrove investigated Tulsa evangelist Oral Roberts, she developed a rule: When you talk to somebody who really doesn't like your subject, you have to also ask what he or she does well. And when you talk to somebody who really likes the subject, you have to ask what he or she doesn't do well.

Since then, she has made this a rule for all investigations.

By asking both kinds of questions, she says, you get a more balanced picture of the subject you're investigating. Second, by asking what the subject does well, you display a lack of malice, which helps you legally. Third, Hargrove says, her strategy gives the reporter an opportunity to assess the objectivity of the person being interviewed and whether they are at one end of the spectrum or the other.

"You're trying to find shades not only of the person you're looking at, or the company you're looking at, but the people you're interviewing so you know whether to trust their information, or at least how to gauge their information."

Hargrove says she avoids using information from the "nutsies" at either end of the spectrum and tries to stick with those who are middle of the road.

Of course the heart of any investigation is what the people at the center have to say, and suggestions on those interviews follow in the next case study.

(Jerry Uhrhammer, a veteran of 40 years in the news business, is a former president of IRE.)

Investigative Interviews: Part Two

by Jerry Uhrhammer, Independent Journalist

Even when you get the final interview, all the hurdles aren't over. Sometimes you have to answer for your past stories before you can get to the current one. Mary Hargrove, associate editor at the *Arkansas Democrat-Gazette,* tries to anticipate the problem. She takes along copies of previous articles.

She remembers one subject who began an interview by complaining, "I read a story you wrote about me and everything in it was wrong."

"So I reached in my suitcase and said, 'This is great, because I have a copy of it.' I even had a red pen and I said 'You circle everything that is wrong and we'll discuss it.' That really shuts them down. 'I've got all day, let's go over it. If I'm wrong you show me where I'm wrong.'

"This was the funny part.

"I'd written that this guy had embezzled something like $300,000. So he's reading and reading and reading—obviously he's read a long way and he hasn't circled anything—so I'm feeling pretty good when he says 'Here, here!'

"You know how your stomach sort of hits the pits. He was so delighted. 'You said I embezzled $300,000. I embezzled $500,000.'

"I said 'Okay, I'll fix it.'

"I had a photographer with me who just keeled over. He couldn't believe it."

Those final interviews can make or break an investigative project, and how to prepare and conduct them is worth careful planning.

Conventional wisdom has it that you wait until your investigation is virtually complete before you interview the person or persons you've been investigating. That way you know what questions must be asked.

But many investigative reporters say it is sometimes better to conduct these interviews during the early stages of the investigation.

Olive Talley, investigative reporter at the *Dallas Morning News,* likes the idea of doing a friendly interview first, rather than waiting for an interview at the end. "I find that if you know you're going to be doing an investigation on a particular person that it's very, very helpful to do a friendly interview with them first and have them tell you all the things they consider to be the facts right off. Then you have some basic framework in which to operate knowing what their position is."

Later, at the time of the last interview, the reporter can return and say, in effect, "I've done some other interviews and I find some things that don't make sense here."

Talley once used an early interview with the main subject of an investigation in a different way.

The *Morning News* was investigating the mayor of a Dallas suburb who was involved with a failing bank. Reporters were trying to determine whether there were any sweetheart deals or misappropriated funds.

But, in the middle of this investigation, the mayor decided not to run for another term. So an interview was scheduled to ask the mayor about his decision to retire. After the interview began, however, the questions shifted to the bank failure.

"He suddenly became very defensive and then became hostile. He realized exactly what we were focusing on, which was the bank as much as him," Talley says.

Talley also emerged with another story. She had heard from bank employees that the bank had purchased hunting dogs and paid for their training out of bank funds. But she had been unable to verify the reports.

"So when we were in this interview with the mayor, I just acted like I knew it and said, 'Jack, what about these dogs that the bank owns? Does that seem like an appropriate expenditure for the bank?' "

The mayor acknowledged that the bank bought the dogs, trained the dogs and furthermore he thought it was perfectly legitimate, Talley says. "He acknowledged and basically gave me all the information I needed."

With businessmen and other white-collar people, says Mary Hargrove, it is better to be up front and go for the early interview. "If they hear from 12 other people that you're looking and you're not talking to them, you really make them skittish."

Getting Ready

If you're readying yourself for the interviews with the people at the heart of the investigation, the planning process becomes more prodigious.

Write down every question you need to ask. Don't rely on memory. There are too many things to think about during the interview.

Assemble the questions in the order you want to ask them. If you have adequate time, conventional wisdom is to ask the softer questions first, saving the hardball questions for later. But that system isn't always foolproof.

Mary Hargrove recommends preparing two sets of questions—one full-sized set, plus a stripped-down version—in case the unexpected happens.

She remembers what happened to an interview in 1984 with a state health commissioner after a 100 plus degree heat wave hit Oklahoma and people died in state-licensed room-and-board facilities for the mentally ill.

The state health commissioner had been vacationing in Alaska and, when she returned, Hargrove and another reporter drove to Oklahoma City for an interview. They had talked on the way about easing into the topic. But it didn't work out that way.

"She had promised us an hour," Hargrove said, but when the reporters walked into the commissioner's office, "she was just nasty . . . very, very angry and scared. And she said, 'You've got 15 minutes.' So instead of saying, 'How's the boat on Grand Lake?' I said: 'Why are people dying in state-licensed facilities?' My partner almost fell off the chair. . . . If they want to walk through it with me, I'll walk. If they want to play hardball, I'm walking out with what I wanted, or at least asking about it."

And remember, it's not always what you ask but how you phrase it that's important.

Ask yourself as you prepare your questions: How is this going to sound from the witness stand if I'm called upon to justify my methods and actions in getting this story?

It is not unusual for the subject of an investigation to be accompanied by his or her lawyer during the interview. Assume the lawyer will be looking and listening for anything that might help the client in a subsequent lawsuit.

Getting There

Every so often, the subject of your piece gets cold feet. They agreed to an interview but by the time you show up they have changed their mind.

What do you do then?

"At that point you say 'Fine, that's your prerogative,'" says Mary Hargrove. When this happens to her, she makes a suggestion: "Let's do this. Listen to the questions. You can refuse to answer them all but I've got a series of stories ready and they say the following things. Okay. Now I don't think anybody looks good not responding in print. But that's your option again. I think there are questions you can answer here and can answer easily. These are the questions. If you want to answer them, fine. If you don't . . . but here they are.

"And they'll usually listen because most everybody wants to know where you're going. It's very hard to sit there and not make any comment. That's fine. Once you say to them, 'That's fine, you don't have to answer,' there is a visible body reaction because they think you've agreed and that they're in control. So then you start doing questions again."

Olive Talley also testifies to the virtues of being direct with nervous interviewees. She remembers an interview with a media-savvy doctor who wasn't sure he wanted to talk to her.

Talley told him: "You have that prerogative. Nobody is forcing you to talk to me now but . . . I think it will behoove you to talk to me. . . . At any point you don't like what I'm saying, you can say 'Out of here, bitch.'

"He chuckled at that and said, 'You're pretty direct, aren't you?' And I said, 'That's what I'm going to prove, that I'm going to be direct with you and I hope you'll do the same with me.' I've never had anybody in my entire life stop an interview on me. I've never had anybody say 'That's it, get out!' Never."

Talley got her interview. The doctor answered questions for three and a half hours.

At the end of the interview, the doctor told her he'd never had an interview like that before. Why? Because he'd had the feeling in previous interviews that reporters hadn't really listened to what he had to say.

"He said they mostly come in and you have the sense they have something in mind that they're looking for . . . and as soon as they get the answer to that one or two questions they lose interest and they're antsy and distracted and they're impatient and they want to wrap it up," Talley said.

Sometimes it's not cold feet, it's cold storage. You've called, and called, even tried contacting the subject's lawyer, but still no agreement for an interview.

Send a letter—preferably a registered letter so that you'll get a receipt showing that the letter was delivered. Explain in the letter what you are working on and the questions you want to ask. Make it clear that you want to interview the subject to get his or her side of the story.

Mary Neiswender, a former *Long Beach Independent Press Telegram* investigative reporter, was highly successful at sending letters.

"Angela Davis, the black activist who was arrested by police in a Marin County, California, courtroom shootout, wouldn't talk to anyone when she was arrested," Neiswender remembers. "Yet she talked to me following a letter I sent to her and her attorney.

"I knew she would be tried in California and was trying to get the venue changed to San Jose. We not only had a paper in San Jose (*The Mercury News*) but we had other papers throughout the state. She could get no better coverage.

"In my letter I mentioned a few things that would bring her to that conclusion on her own. And I'm sure she thought she could manipulate the interview.

"I thought I could do the same thing."

Another time, Neiswender wanted to get an interview with a mass murderer—one of California's many—and wrote to him in jail.

"The letter was returned as 'rejected,'" she says. "I knew that that was bullshit but I could do nothing; jailers are not the cream of law enforcement.

"So my next approach was the murderer's attorney.

"All I wanted, I said, was to figure out what kind of a guy this 'monster' was—he must have had a family, friends, a dog in his early life.

"I got his okay as long as I didn't talk about the murders he had been involved in—the torture murders of five teenaged girls.

"The interview went well. He talked about his early life, his adoptive mother, his many problems with women, etcetera. I didn't ask about the killings, as promised.

"My story was an honest profile of a killer. But it wasn't the story I wanted.

"Within a week my phone rang.

"He was calling from jail and wanted to see me again—this time I had made no promises to anyone.

"In that second interview he laid out the crimes, confessing to his part, even allowing me to read his hand-written 'journal' about the rapes and torture, the mutilations and killings and even how they dumped the bodies. I even reminded him several times I was a reporter and was taking notes, lots of notes.

"The story ran the next day. It would end up being used in court to send him to the gas chamber.

"As he sits on death row in San Quentin, he still writes to me. He still tells me about his problems with women; he married in prison and was accused of molesting his stepdaughter in one of his 'contact' visits with his wife.

"But he didn't know when to shut up in the interview.

"But then a lot of people don't, including reporters."

Friendly or Not

Olive Talley tends to take the friendly rather than challenging or antagonistic approach in these interviews because it fits her personality.

"Something everyone should do is operate with honesty," Talley says. "I tell people they should never, ever be surprised by anything I write about them because, hopefully, I will have discussed all those points with them beforehand."

She recalled an interview with a doctor about possible misappropriation of funds and questionable spending at a nonprofit corporation. The man was nervous. "He was anticipating that I was out gunning for him.

"So I told him at the beginning, 'Look, I've heard a lot about you. I've heard a lot of criticism about you. I've heard a lot of good things about you. I'm here to have you tell me what you consider to be the truth, what you consider to be what really happened. I've talked to a lot of people but I'd rather hear it from you.'"

The doctor told Talley a lot of things she didn't know. To test him, she threw in some questions to which she already knew the answers "and on most of those he came clean. So I had to give him the benefit of the doubt on some of the other things I didn't know about yet because he was pretty candid and forthcoming with me."

Talley believes a direct and honest approach pays off.

"I often find, even when there's a target I'm going after, I tell them I'm here to find the truth, no matter what it is, and if I feel there's a problem with you, I'm going to tell you and give you an opportunity to respond. I feel that people tend to be a little more forthcoming than they normally would be."

Listening Up

It is sometimes said that each reporter has his or her own bag of tricks for interviewing. Perhaps. But usually it's best to forget about trickery. It can easily backfire.

Honesty, directness, simplicity are still the best ways to get an interview off on the right foot and keep it that way. However, for that final interview, the investigative reporter also needs to be a practicing psychologist.

The subject is likely to be someone who would rather be doing something other than sitting across the table from a reporter who has been trying to dig up unsavory things that the subject would rather keep hidden. The subject may waffle, weasel, evade and otherwise attempt to avoid answering the questions.

The reporter cannot compel the subject to talk or even to answer truthfully. The success of the interview is likely to depend on how well the reporter can read the psyche of the person being interviewed, manipulating the person's anxieties and discomfort to elicit answers.

Call it technique, not trickery. Veteran reporters develop special skills for coaxing unwilling subjects to talk.

Here are several examples.

■ The pause. You've asked a question and the subject has answered. But instead of immediately asking another question, you wait expectantly, giving the impression that you're waiting to hear more. Nature abhors a vacuum.

And human nature cannot stand silence in an interview. Many times the subject, uncomfortable with the silence, will resume talking, telling you more of what you wanted to hear.

"I just sit there and look and let them fill the silence and they are going to," says Mary Hargrove. "Usually you're in their office to start with. . . . So they're the 'host' and it's very hard for people to just stare. Being in their office there's the thing in the back of their minds that they are supposed to break the silence."

■ The tease. Another useful tactic is to unobtrusively drop in little pieces of information gleaned in the investigation that will mean something to the interviewee.

The purpose is to let the subject know, in a subtle way, that you've done all your homework. That leaves the subject also wondering how much else you might know. This uncertainty about what you already know makes it more likely that the subject will tell the truth rather than risk being caught in a lie or a half-truth.

During an investigation of an Oregon district attorney's outside activities years ago, I dug up information that he had made thousands of dollars in speaking fees while traveling across the country and into Canada on behalf of groups promoting the decriminalization of marijuana. His county travel vouchers falsely indicated the airline fares were to be reimbursed with federal grants. What was actually happening is that he was operating a mini–speakers' bureau out of his public office, using the county's credit to finance his travels. By double- and triple-charging sponsoring groups for his travel expenses, he was able to reimburse the county for his travel expenses and still turn a tidy profit.

During the interview, I let drop isolated little bits of information—such as the names of his contacts in cities he had visited—and finally asked him how much profit he made from his journeys. "Oh, about $5,000 or $6,000," he answered. That was twice as much as I had been able to document.

Mary Hargrove: "There's another way, too. If you don't know the figure, just say 'I've heard it was as high as $10,000.' If you have a figure, they will correct you, fill in the blanks." If the subject wants to know who gave you the figure, just say it's something I heard.

■ The best. The most simple question to ask is why. Again and again. Why? Why? Why?

The simplest question is usually the best question because it prompts better answers.

That may seem rudimentary but it is something reporters should keep in mind because they can easily fall victim to the complexities of their investigations.

"No matter how much experience you have it is always harder to ask simple questions because you have so many thoughts going through your own head and you want to cover so much ground," says Olive Talley. "You're trying to think for the moment and then think ahead of yourself too.

"It's very difficult sometimes to say 'Why?'

"Frankly, it's the simple questions that get the better answers. Rarely does a statement elicit an answer. Oftentimes a subject will just nod. And then what do you have? That may be fine for TV but it doesn't help you in print.

"I try to make sure I don't get caught up in the interview to the point where I lose the simplicity of the question. I do that by trying to maintain the focus: What are we trying to get at here?"

Another reason why simple questions are best: They offer less room for evasion. A sharp interviewee can take a complex question and twist it into an unrecognizable form. The answer is likely to be irrelevant or meaningless.

■ The point. When you frame your questions, make them direct, concise, to the point. Such questions are more likely to produce direct answers.

After reporting how Tacoma, Wash., city officials threw away a half million dollars on a loan to a shaky developer who immediately defaulted, I got a tip that a federal grand jury was investigating the transaction. I knew the federal prosecutors would neither confirm nor deny, so I called the city official responsible for the loan. "Tell me about the federal grand jury subpoena," I asked. Up to that point, the official had refused to comment about the loan fiasco. But assuming that I already knew, he confirmed that the city's loan files had been subpoenaed and also provided other details.

Moral: Let them think you already know everything about it; you want their side of the story.

What Did I Just Hear?

During the interview, keep pressing to have the interviewee clarify what they're telling you or elaborate on what the documents show.

Sometimes you restate the obvious and they will agree. That happened to me during a key interview on the Tacoma loan fiasco.

In the files of a civil lawsuit, I found an internal memorandum from the city's community development director to the city manager that outlined the entire scenario of why the loan was made and why it failed so quickly.

It was clear in the memorandum that the loan began as a way to help a former city councilman-turned-developer get out from under a federally guaranteed loan he had obtained several years earlier for redevelopment of a downtown building. With great haste, city officials arranged for an unusual "transfer" of the loan to another developer who went belly-up within months.

When I interviewed the former city councilman, I let him read the memorandum and then asked him, "They were doing you a favor, weren't they?" His answer, "Yes, that's what it was."

That admission from a former city councilman that he got a favor from his former city hall cronies was a major element of the lead paragraph when we broke the story on the botched loan.

"I think that's part of advanced reporting, not only listening to what they're saying but interpreting what they're saying and then getting them to explain," says Mary Hargrove.

"I do a lot of things like this: 'This is what I'm hearing you say, now tell me if I'm right. You just told me that you really don't like what Mr. So-and-so did. Am I right? Did I get that right?' "

She tells her reporters to stop and paraphrase the information they're getting back to the interviewee. "Give them a chance to correct it then . . . you're making a flat statement and they'll respond to it, yes or no, but, or that's correct, that's how I feel."

Don't Be All Ears

Being a good listener is the essence of good interviewing. But watch closely, too. The two go hand in hand.

"Truly listening allows you to hear what is said and, most important, what isn't said. Inflections, eye contact, hand signals, body language all fit into the interview," says Mary Neiswender.

"Oftimes, the person you are interviewing starts to lose control. This may be vital in television, but not to a newspaper or magazine story, so you have to stop it.

"You can hear the voice crack if you're listening. That is a signal.

"You can see the corners of his mouth twitch or his eyes tear up. That's another danger signal.

"But it's important not to let him fall apart completely.

"When that point comes many times the interview comes to a screeching halt, never to resume. You don't want that.

"So at that point I change the subject delicately, not so they know I'm doing it, if possible.

" 'You know, you've got a lot of guts,' sometimes works.

"They want to believe it and the falling apart stops."

Hargrove also believes in watching the subject's face closely for clues. She provides a hypothetical example of how this can work:

"When you told me that piece of information, Mr. Smith, you made a face. What does that mean? Your voice sounded positive but you didn't look positive. Is there something else here that we're not exploring?"

Have You Heard This One?

A technique used by Mary Hargrove is to get the interviewee to agree that people are talking about him.

She used it to advantage in an interview with Richard Roberts, son of evangelist Oral Roberts.

"What do you say to the little old lady who sees that you're driving a Corvette?" she asked him. "You have to get the same calls I do: 'Those people live in million dollar homes and here I'm sending them all this money. I didn't know they were rich. I was sending them my Social Security money and I feel betrayed.'

"I said to Richard, 'What do you tell those people? You hear that, don't you?'

"Well, yeah, I do," was the reply.

Hargrove still remembers Roberts' answer: "You can't please everybody."

"That was part of a feature, but it really told the readers a lot about him," Hargrove says.

By getting the interviewee to admit that the question's topical, that "people" are talking about it, you avoid the charge that the newspaper is raising the issue.

If the reporter doesn't want to be in the position of raising the question, Hargrove says, say that "people are saying . . ."

Another possible tactic: "I've heard that you've done this. Have you heard it?"

Confronting the Facts

Mary Hargrove allows only a few "errors" in these final interviews before she challenges them with the opposing information.

"If they fail two out of three, then I'll go back and correct them," Hargrove says. "Usually the first time they lie to you, or you perceive they lie to you, I let it go. Then the second time they do it I start to pin them real hard and then the third time I say, 'Wait a minute, there is something wrong here. My information shows X clearly.' "

But she doesn't accuse interviewees of being liars. Instead, she is likely to say: "I've got a problem here, you've got to help me. . . . My problem is you just said this, but I have information or paper (that says otherwise). Why the two versions here?

"That's much easier to get an answer from than 'That can't be that way?' "

Interviews can often turn into a battle of wits. And the amount of information the subject will give up usually depends on how much the reporter has been able to dig up.

There's Dumb, and Then There's Dumb

Talley, who describes herself as a basic Texas country girl, says one of her techniques is to sort of act dumb.

"I have a dumb routine and then I have a routine where I let them know how well prepared I am and it just depends on who I'm interviewing as to what I imply. Lots of times I can get more out of appearing to be a little dense as opposed to trying to impress them with how much knowledge I have."

If the reporter comes on too strong, giving the impression he or she already knows everything, the subject may wonder why he or she is being interviewed. Talley learned the hard way.

'I made the mistake of doing that on a very critical interview," she says. During the interview, a former employee of a foundation Talley was investigating began describing the details of a particular board meeting.

"I forgot what I was doing and wasn't paying attention," Talley says. "I jumped in and got caught up in the story myself, and she literally said, 'It sounds like you know all this stuff so why do you need to be talking to me?' "

Talley says she tried to recover by telling the subject that she had heard the details previously but wanted to make sure they were true.

"But the interview changed as a result of that. She then assumed that I knew things and she didn't tell me as much as she had been telling me. . . . It was a reminder that obviously I needed to tell myself, Hey, let them tell you the story. . . .

"It was a good reminder because the next interview was even more crucial. It was such that I was able to sit back and do my 'Oh . . . oh really . . . why? No shit? Yeah, tell me about that. No, really? Tell me everything that happened.'

"Sit back and let them tell you the story."

Intimidation, Part One

One of the most difficult situations that can arise in attempting to arrange an interview is when the would-be interviewee demands that the reporter submit written questions. Usually that means the interviewee wants to provide written answers.

Written questions and written answers, of course, do not constitute an interview. They are more like lawyers' written interrogatories, a poor substitute for a free-flowing exchange of questions and answers conducted on a face-to-face basis or over the telephone.

Mary Hargrove says she sometimes will go along with the demand for written questions.

"We'll do that just to show that in fairness we tried to get someone and tried to include their response. But it's got to be a really exceptional thing before we start screwing around with that."

And she lays down some conditions of her own.

"You do a little negotiating," she says. "I say, if we do it this way, I have a right to edit the answers. Or I may not use them at all. The problem is if I send you a list and I have another question to ask, I won't have a chance to ask it.

"I also say, if we're going to do it this way, I want you to answer every one of my questions, too."

Intimidation, Part Two

Sometimes the people you need to interview finally consent, but agree to an impossibly short interview.

Olive Talley encountered that problem during her year-long investigation of medical care in the federal prison system that ended up as a finalist for a Pulitzer Prize.

Federal prisons officials had put off an interview several times. Finally, they told Talley she could have one hour with them. But she ended up getting two and a half hours.

"And the way I did that was, I just said 'If you want to end this, that's fine. But I'm going to have to say in the paper that you did not take the time to even listen to my questions on this subject matter. That you chose not to even deal with these areas. And I'll be happy to put that in the paper, that this stuff wasn't important enough to you to hear my questions and comments, and that will not look good for you. . . .' "

Adds Talley: "The thing I have been most successful in doing in extending interviews is either to impress upon them the need for accuracy and the need for fairness, and showing them that it will benefit them to at least take the time to hear the questions."

Intimidation, Part Three

Not all subjects submit meekly to interviews. They practice intimidation tactics.

Sometimes it is oral.

Other times the intimidation is more overt.

In the mid-1980s, my partner and I traveled to a posh conference room in a Beverly Hills law office for a final interview with the president of a troubled Southern California savings and loan association.

We were armed with a single tape recorder. It was like a pop gun compared to the heavy artillery on the other side of the table.

The S&L executive's lawyers had a stenotypist present to take down every word. They also tape-recorded the interview, with a technician present to make sure the recorders picked up everything.

The lawyers wanted to videotape the session but we refused.

There were two lawyers representing the S&L president—one a well-known criminal lawyer, the other a libel specialist who won a huge judgment against a tabloid newspaper that suggested actress Carol Burnett had been tipsy in public.

There is only one thing to do in a situation like that: Pay no attention to the extra attractions and go ahead with your interview as originally planned.

The intimidation tactics didn't end with the interview.

For months afterwards, there was a steady stream of threatening letters from the libel lawyer.

Mary Hargrove says she has never been confronted with a stenotypist but she's familiar with tape recorders and secretaries taking shorthand notes. "It shouldn't be any more intimidating to us than it is to them, so it doesn't bother me unless they make a big production thing with a camera. That's a bit much."

She encountered the video camera gambit while probing Medicaid reimbursements to Oklahoma nursing homes—an investigation that included a trip to the Oklahoma Supreme Court to open the records.

It took a year, Hargrove says, and when she finally got the records she found that nursing home operators were using Corvettes as company cars.

"So I went to Oklahoma City to sit down and talk to some of these guys. It was one of those big boardroom deals. I was only supposed to talk to one or two but there were like six men in there. They made a big deal out of having a videotape camera there, setting it up in front of me and trying to put it just a few inches from my face. . . . The way you react is to go ahead and do the interview as you normally would."

Hargrove says she didn't let the video camera bother her because she had her own tape recorder running. "The effect is the same as if they have their own tape recorder so I don't really care."

Conclusion

It's important to remember why you are there.

This is the climax of the investigative process when you confront the person or persons you plan to write about, lay out what you've found, and ask them: "How do you explain that? What is your response? Why did this happen? What do you have to say about this?"

But they must be given the opportunity to respond.

You do it for fairness.

You do it for accuracy.

And you also do it because this interview—which must be on the record—is the most important and challenging phase of the entire investigative reporting process. It can generate great quotes, startling admissions, amazing explanations and, most important, confirmation or denial of your basic investigative conclusions. If everything clicks, these interviews can turn a good investigative story into a great investigative story.

3

Computer-Assisted Reporting

Off-the-shelf software has made it much easier to use your personal computer to perform the tasks that used to be left to the mainframe. This chapter shows how to take advantage of this development, either to handle the data you accumulate or to analyze the tapes you acquire from local, state or federal government offices. In addition, dozens of examples are offered from newspapers and television stations across the country.

In December 1991, KOMU-TV in Columbia, Mo., aired a series over five days by David Hinchman that found "that despite government claims to the contrary, government records for the past five years show that in Missouri, the Occupational Safety and Health Administration (OSHA) discovered only 39 percent of the workplace fatalities that fall into its jurisdiction. The world's largest privately owned company, Cargill, runs a turkey processing plant that routinely crippled its workers. The agency had been largely unsuccessful at forcing change. In St. Louis, a local prosecutor was not interested in investigating a workplace death even though OSHA found six willful violations." (This example, along with the other examples of computer-assisted reporting quoted in this chapter, are excerpted from "A selection of computer-assisted investigations from the IRE Morgue" prepared by Investigative Reporters and Editors in 1992.)[1]

Here's what computers (and specialized software) are good for—math, including arithmetic, and finding patterns. That's it.

It is, however, quite enough, provided you do your part. Your part is to learn enough to make use of that machine on your desk for more than word processing and games. Don't panic. Journalists all over the country have been flocking to this technology in recent years, proof that the software has gotten cheaper to buy, easier to use and that data have become more generally available.

Chapter 4 describes how to make sophisticated use of commercial or government text databases containing articles, speeches, books, or at least their citations. This chapter gives you tips and examples of how to use your own computer to create and/or analyze data you've obtained elsewhere, usually from local, state or federal government agencies.

In April 1986, the Ft. Lauderdale *News and Sun-Sentinel* ran a three-day series by Fred Schulte showing that "the quality of medical care at Veterans Administration (VA) hospitals is substandard (even by its own standards). Thousands of patient deaths and injuries at VA hospitals were revealed as well as flaws in credentialing of VA heart surgeons and lax disciplining of doctors. Hospitals in small, remote areas were found to be especially bad."

Types of Databases

Computer-assisted reporting, or CAR, involves using one or both of two kinds of databases—those kept by others (local, state and federal governments) or those created by you:

1. Government computer databases contain information such as criminal records, liens, traffic citations, census data, judicial decisions and thousands of other kinds of records.

Reporters ask the government agency to copy the entire file (group of records) off its nine-track, reel-to-reel tapes (just like you see in the movies) and onto yours. (You can get blank tapes from your own computer operators at the newspaper or television station, or you can ask the government where they buy their's and get some from the same place.)

Bring the copies back to the office and get someone in research or marketing to load the tapes onto a mainframe so you can find the answers to your questions with their help.

Or, load the tapes into your personal computer (PC) after copying the data to disks or using commercial hardware dedicated to translating nine-track data to PC-readable data.

Or, open an account at the local college computer center, load the data on its mainframe and use its software that you access through your PC via modem to analyze the data.

2. You can create databases from such sources as government records still kept on paper, plus your interviews, readings and anything else, by loading it into your PC and using off-the-shelf software to help organize and make sense of the data by, for instance, finding patterns or relationships.

> In June 1988, the *Birmingham Post-Herald* ran a five-day series by Thomas Hargrove that showed "widespread incompetence in the way elections were administered in Alabama. In 11 counties there were more registered voters than the actual adult population and registration lists got longer from 1984 to 1988 despite a law ordering all voters rolls to be cleaned up. The worst areas were shown to be rural, disadvantaged counties. Counties that paid their probate judges per registered voter were far more likely to have inflated voter rolls than counties that paid judges flat salaries. Counties with suspiciously high levels of absentee voting were shown to have inaccurate voter rolls."

Types of Software

A database, then, is merely a collection of records from the same or disparate sources—such as names, addresses, phone numbers, voting records, tax payments—loaded into your computer. Computer software finds and sorts the information in ways you direct it to—alphabetically, by date, by address, by specific legislation—creating a new list.

> Throughout 1991, *Newsday* ran a series of articles by Penny Loeb and Tom Braden based on an "analysis of New York City finance records (that) revealed that residents were being over billed on real estate, water and sewer taxes to the tune of $275 million. Some of the city's largest and most politically connected

developers shortchanged the city at least $50 million because they got unde-
served property tax cuts."

There are four basic types of software commonly used for this kind of
work:

1. A flat-file database, such as Microsoft Works, sells at street prices for
about $100.[2] A flat file is the simplest of all database programs. That is, it
does the fewest things and requires the least amount of learning and work. It's
basically just a bunch of lists. Your Rolodex is a flat file.

2. A relational database, such as Borland's Paradox, sells for about $300.
This software can take a bunch of flat files with some kind of interrelation-
ship and create lists that show relationships in many different ways. For
instance, you might take the files of elected officials in Congress, a file of
PAC contributions, a file of their voting record on bills related to the interests
of PACs, a file of speaking fees and a file of contracts the legislators had with
businesses and individuals before being elected. The commonality to all these
flat files is the legislator. The relational database can integrate the lists in a
variety of ways for you to view the data, thereby highlighting patterns of
behavior worth reporting.

That is, the database will find any correlation between money and votes.
However, it will not show you causation. Correlation is not cause. The database may show you that your elected official received $500,000 from out-
of-state trucking firms, that he received another $150,000 in speaking fees
from trucking firms and that he voted in favor of trucking interests 95 percent
of the time. It does not show, nor can it, that your congressperson is on the
take or if he votes that way because he gets the money or if he gets the money
because he votes that way.

Nevertheless, it will show you a terrific road map that deserves detailed
exploration.

3. A spreadsheet, such as Lotus 1-2-3, sells for around $400. Although de-
signed primarily for accounting use, this is a powerful database that can easily
be used to analyze such files as Census data, property tax assessment and
other issues not requiring the sophisticated abilities of a more fully developed
relational database.

4. A statistical package, such as SPSS PC+, sells for around $200 for the
base package, with specialized modules running hundreds of dollars extra.
Although developed for people needing sophisticated statistical manipulation
of data, the stats packages also can be used as relational databases.

For example, David Pearce Demers, an assistant professor of journalism
at the University of Wisconsin in River Falls, used SPSS PC+ to analyze
5,508 property sales in Minnesota for an alternative weekly in Minneapolis.

His analysis showed "that as a group, people who own high-priced properties are paying less than their fair share in taxes, while many of those with low-priced properties are paying too much. The analysis also found that owners of business and farm property are paying substantially less than they should. Homeowners and renters are, in essence, subsidizing them."

The distinctions between these four types of software continue to blur as software designers race to increase their program's abilities in an effort to attract converts. And, also, data held in one kind of program can often be read and manipulated by another. For instance, SPSS PC+ can read and analyze data in Lotus 1-2-3.

In April 1989, the *Star Tribune* ran a six-day series by David Peterson that showed that "every year more than 40,000 Minnesotans enroll in vocational schools that claim a 90 percent job placement rate. This was the figure advertised in recruiting brochures and in reports to government overseers. But, in truth, only about half the students who completed training managed to find a lasting, full-time job in their field. And many of the 'successes' earned wages below the federal poverty line. The *Star Tribune* found pervasive patterns of deceit and statistical errors which enhance the exaggerations made by the schools. Meanwhile, Minnesota had spent millions in tax dollars on programs that, under state standards, should have been canceled."

Here's what you do with a relational or flat file database: You make a master form, a template, that has a separate line (or field) for each type of information you plan to collect. For example, say you are doing an arson investigation. Your master form might look like the Fire Form on page 75:

In November 1989, the *Dayton Daily News* ran a three-day series by John Dougherty and Dave Davis that showed "Though generations of families have grown up next door to the sprawling steel mills, paper plants and auto makers of Ohio's Miami Valley, few really knew what toxins came from their industrial neighbors. The series provided readers in a seven-county-area with a definitive account of what toxins are dumped in their community and what dangers those toxins posed. Some of the region's neighborhoods were found to be among the nation's dirtiest. Millions of pounds of toxins that cause cancer or wreck the ozone are released next door. For example, we found a steel company in Middletown, Ohio, releases a million pounds of cancer-causing benzene each year just across the fence from an elementary school. Many of the most dangerous neighborhoods are inhabited by workers and their families who have accepted pollution as necessary to their paychecks. Some companies have avoided reporting their toxic releases by playing a complicated game that hides their waste from public view."

Fire Form

Address of fire-damaged home

_____

Homeowner(s) name(s)

_____

Date of fire

_____

Name of fire captain on the scene

_____

Ruling on cause of fire

_____

Name of person making ruling

_____

Police report

_____

Name of public adjuster

_____

Insurer

_____

Cost of structure damage

_____

Cost of content damage

_____

Court challenge and result

_____

Land record search

_____

Homeowner interview

_____

And any other thing you think of, now or later.

The template or master form is what you use every time you want to make an entry. Each time you open a new fire record, you start with a copy of the basic form. Each individual line is called a "field" and you can ask the computer to sort according to those fields, arranging them to suit your needs.

After, say six months, you may have analyzed 1,000 fires, each a record in your database, and each record with 35 or so fields.

By asking the computer to sort on individual fields, you may find, hypothetically, that

- A half-dozen or so addresses have suffered three or more fires over a 25-year period.
- Most homeowners who used a public adjuster used the same person.
- Virtually all of the fire repairs were done by the same firm.
- The fire chief himself has suffered fires on various properties he owns or has a financial interest in—very bad luck.
- Seven of the chief's close business associates have suffered dozens of fires on properties they own or have a financial interest in—phenomenal bad luck.
- By comparing the dates of the building repair permits to the actual dates of the fires, you find that on two occasions the building permits issued for fire damage repairs were taken out days or weeks before the actual fires—stupendous foresight.

And on and on.

> In November 1990, WRC-TV in Washington, D.C., aired a four-day series by Lea Thompson, Chris Szechenyi, Sandra Thomas and Rudy Scott that found that "more than 3,300 deaths and 52,000 injuries associated with malfunctioning medical equipment designed to save lives. The series focused attention for the first time on the failure of heart-starting machines called defibrillators. During the previous six years more people died from defibrillator malfunctions and misuse than from any other medical device regulated by the Food and Drug Administration (FDA). Some of the 512 deaths were the fault of paramedics who failed to use or maintain their equipment properly. But in at least 128 cases, the FDA blamed the deaths on design defects, broken components or other flaws with the machines themselves . . ."

Now let's make our inquiry more complicated.

Suppose we decide to analyze the quality of justice administered by the five criminal court judges in our town.

We download the computer tapes of every single decision over the last five years. Then we break down the defendants by crime, race, sex, income.[3]

We load the name of every lawyer representing the defendants. What might we find?

- Judge B is more than twice as likely to sentence women to jail than men for the same crime and similar criminal record, as compared to the other four judges.
- The lawyers defending the accused win only about 20 percent of the time in front of these judges. That is, 80 percent of the time their clients fail to walk out of the courtroom free of some kind of penalty. But three lawyers, all from the same firm, average twice that success ratio when their defendants are in Judge E's court. Why?
- Moreover, lawyers are no longer allowed to shop for judges as a result of judicial reform six years ago. But our three super lawyers get 80 percent of their cases before Judge E. Why?
- On average, these five judges are very hard on first-time heroin dealers. During our five-year study, 95 percent of the convicted dealers get jail time. Astonishingly, however, repeat offenders are much more likely to be kept out of jail, spending their time instead in court-ordered alternative rehabilitation programs.
- Persons convicted of all classes of felonies get widely disparate sentences, despite mandatory sentencing guidelines, and the most significant pattern is that those defendants living in wealthier neighborhoods get significantly more lenient treatment from the five judges.

In December 1990, the *Sacramento Bee* ran a two-day series by Faize Alim, Michael G. Wagner and Jim Mayer analyzing the war on drugs in Sacramento County in 1989 and found that "the drug war was a costly failure that had targeted blacks, the poor and addicts. While whites comprise a majority of the drug users in Sacramento County and make up a majority of the population, blacks comprise a majority of those arrested on felony drug charges. The strategy is primarily a war on drug users, rather than traffickers and major dealers. The most frequently charged drug crime was possession, and 88 percent of those arrested admitted using drugs. Of those convicted of the three most frequently charged drug crimes, nearly 80 percent were unemployed and nearly all of those with jobs were working for minimum wage. Fewer than half had a high school diploma. Most of those arrested for drugs had been arrested for drugs before, and about half were on probation or parole at the time of the most recent arrest. The cycle was found to be increasing. The average felony drug arrest and conviction cost the county $11,500, more than twice the amount spent to educate a child for one year in Sacramento County."

Can it really be that easy to pull information together using CAR? Yes and no.

The PC software can come up with the answers amazingly fast, no matter how many cases you load into it. How fast? Faster than it took for you to read this far.

Overcoming Roadblocks

But there are a number of roadblocks that must be overcome, including,

- the need for a fairly fast computer set up;
- the need to perservere when trying to get the government agency to give up the data;
- the need to badger the government to lower its fees to a reasonable amount once the custodians finally give up the data;
- the ever-present need to clean-up the data, checking it for errors and internal inconsistencies;
- the need the first time you use your software to climb a long, slow learning curve to make the thing work (excepting the flat file programs);
- the need to enlist help from persons experienced in analyzing data.

Each of these issues is discussed below.

In December 1991, the (Akron) *Beacon Journal* ran a three-day series by Jolene Limbacher and Bob Paynter that showed that "in Ohio the 'system' is unwilling or unable to stop repeat drunk drivers from getting back on the road. The series found Ohio lags far behind other states in actually getting tough on repeat drunken drivers; judges continue to reduce or dismiss thousands of drunken-driving and related charges every year; convicted drivers rarely get anything close to the maximum sentence, no matter how many offenses they've committed; because some Ohio judges are so lax in making good on threats, the Ohio Highway Patrol has intervened and is sending reminders to judges urging them to get tough on repeat offenders who have openly defied their orders; and tough laws that have been on the books are going unenforced by judges."

Here's how Scott Clark, business editor at the *Houston Chronicle,* described his initial rocky voyages on the CAR boat ride:[4]

The use of computer records has brought with it a whole new set of problems for us. A lot of them revolve around cost and accessibility.

One ongoing project is typical.

We began by seeking certain employment data from a state regulatory agency through an open records request, the Texas equivalent of an

FOIA inquiry. Before making her request, the reporter discussed with contacts at the agency what information was available in the agency's computers.

The response we first received was that the information was not compiled in a way that would suit our needs. When we told them we wanted it anyway, they said they weren't sure that their "computer" records were open to us, suggesting we only had access to their paper files. After we convinced them that the Open Records Act didn't discriminate on the basis of how the records were stored, they quoted us a price of $4,000, which would include about 80 hours of programming time. We next spent a couple of conference calls going around in circles with their public information officer.

The bottom line was that we didn't have enough information to ask the right questions about their data storage, and the public information officer did not have enough information to answer them. We finally arranged for our programming analyst to talk directly to the agency's analyst.

Armed with a strong understanding of what we were trying to do, our analyst was able to provide a good picture of what was available in the agency's records and how it could most efficiently be retrieved. We ended up making a request that would give us most of what we were seeking for about $200, with our own programmers doing the work that the agency had proposed doing for us.

Before they sent us the entire files, we requested a printout of one random record from each database so that we could make sure they had what we thought they had. (On an earlier request for credit union data, we spent $150 for files that we later found out did not contain a key piece of information the agency official had assured us would be there.)

In addition, once we were able to get a good description of how the employment agency processed its data, it became apparent that it forwarded a large portion of the information to the Department of Labor. We since have contacted people there who are much more accustomed to dealing with requests for computer data and whose data is in a form much more suited to what we're working on.

The end result is that after almost four weeks it appears we will be getting our hands on almost everything we were seeking.

We made a lot of mistakes, but we learned some lessons.

1. Some agencies are much more protective of computer records than their other files; they somehow feel that once you get into their computer, you will be able to get into everything. And, even though there is a lot of

computer-aided reporting now, a request for computer records, particularly on the state level, is likely to be the first. As with any request for information, it helps to connect with the people who actually maintain the records.

2. Even for the computer literate, a discussion of the manner in which records are stored can be daunting. As soon as it becomes apparent that your request will be complicated, get your own computer systems people involved. They appreciate the break from their other work and there's a good chance they'll be of more help later.

3. Don't be intimidated by cost. Look at it as a starting point for negotiations. As with everything, there's almost always a cheaper way to do it. Agencies may throw out a big figure to start with to try to make you go away.

4. Raw data is almost always cheaper than processed data. Consider getting raw data files and tailoring them to your needs. The more voluminous the data, the cheaper it may be because of the agency's cost—passed on to you—for paring down their data files to contain exactly what you want. Get more than you need. You can always discard the surplus.

5. Once you settle on a group of records you want, get a printout of one record to see that it has everything you need before getting the entire file.

6. Agencies often share data. Follow the data to other agencies or even private companies who may be more cooperative or who may already be using the data in a way more compatible with your goals.[5]

In January through November 1991, the *San Antonio Light* ran a series of articles by Dan Kelly that reported that "ticket fixing, once a way of life in San Antonio's municipal courts, was found to be costing the city more than $1 million in revenue. Bribery and fraud by lawyers, judges and police officers, as well as a deterioration of faith in the court system, were some of the effects of ticket fixing. Beginning in 1990, reporter Dan Kelly uncovered the scams, and his 47 installments during 1991 finally resulted in the city instituting reforms and launching criminal investigations. Nine judges were eventually fired, 12 police officers suspended, and the Bar Association and State Commission on Judicial Conduct conducted administrative ethics inquiries."

What about cleaning up the data? Know first that it's always dirty and always must be cleaned. Here's how Rob Daves, assistant managing editor for news research at the *Star Tribune,* explains the problem and what to do about it:

After wrangling with the agency's lawyers and bureaucrats, the tape finally came.

You wrestled it into the mainframe or PC and now you're on the road to high adventure and excitement, since all that's left to do is tab the numbers and write the story, right?

Not quite. If you have one of these projects under your belt, you know there's a lot more to it than that—including cleaning the data.

As a survey researcher and database reporter, I've spent a lot of time with the database equivalent of a scrubbing pad and soapy ammonia making sure that there were no basic problems with the data before tabulations, queries and analyses actually began.

What is dirty data? Really, it's any data that doesn't conform to the specifications of your documentation. But that's a pretty stuffy definition.

Let's do a quick review. Most databases are composed of records— horizontal lines of data. These lines of data can be text (what computer mavens call "alpha"), numbers or both. The lines of data are broken up into meaningful chunks called "fields."

Each field—date of birth, the badge number for a cop, the amount of a contribution to a politician—has a format. If it's dollars and cents, there's a currency format to show that 121145 really means $1,211.45 and not 0.121145.

When you get somebody else's tape or disk or download a database through a modem, you're depending on their data collection methods, data entry operators and programmers.

Dirty data can come from many of those sources, including thick-fingered data entry operators, clerks who didn't fill in the original document correctly or programmers who wrote a line of code that computed a field of values incorrectly.

Dirty data could be the result of a bad tape or even the gremlins of line noise when your data were being transmitted from one computer to your PC.

But whatever the cause, dirty data mean one thing: getting out the scrubbing pad and soapy ammonia. Before you begin your tabulation, queries or analyses, you need to check for dirty data. For survey researchers, cleaning data just means making sure that what the respondent indicated on a questionnaire got translated into the correct numbers and text on data file.

But for database researchers, it's a little more complicated.

There are two ways to find dirty data: trolling through the data file visually (dull, but sometimes necessary) or examining summary tabulations to see what doesn't add up.

If you troll through the file and see several lines of gibberish, it's likely that you've gotten hold of a bad tape or there was line noise when the data were being shipped via modem. With more modern telecommunications hardware and software, that's not as prevalent as it was a decade ago. But there's not much you can do about that.

If the problem is extensive enough, you might have to have the data dumped to a new tape (likely enough, your source used a worn-out "scratch" tape that had been written over many times) or transmitted again. If there are only a few records, you must make the decision whether to disregard them or to go back to the paper documents to key in the correct data yourself.

Make sure formats look right at some point during the cleaning process. This means that currency fields have dollar amounts and not decimals; numeric fields have the right number of decimal places; expected alpha fields actually have text, and not numeric values.

If there is a formatting problem, many software packages will just let you reformat the field.

Next, check for out-of-field punches. Survey researchers—your counterparts who do media polling—have known this trick for a long time. In a field where you are expecting only a *2, 3* or *4* and you find a *0,* you know there's a problem with the record in which you find the zero.

In these cases, you have to decide whether to ignore the field for that record, go back to the paper document (if there is one) to get the correction, or compensate for it in the analyses and reporting.

Sometimes you have a field in which there should be data and there are not, or vice versa. This requires another judgment call you have to make.

Did a field indicate there was at least one PAC contribution to a politician but the total PAC contributions come up zero? You need to decide if there is information missing (and is it important to your effort) or if there was just a mistake made in the PAC field and there really should be a zero in the contribution field?

Most of these problems are easily fixed if you have access to the paper documents and the time to correct the data. Many times you don't have either. In those cases, you have to make a decision on how to actually use the data.

Do you ignore the record totally? Do you take all the other data in the record and ignore that particular field for that record? Or do you get creative? Those are decisions you have to make, and only you can make them since you know how you want to use the data.

Good luck with the scrubbing—and may you always have sparkling clean data, no bad sectors on your hard drive and a boss who appreciates how long it takes to do a good job.[6]

In February and December 1991, *New York Newsday* ran several articles by Walter Fee that reported that "in 1991, New York City's vital services cracked under the weight of its severe fiscal problems. Amid cutbacks and protestations that there was no money for vital services, a city-run program was rewarding some of New York's richest and most influential citizens with hundreds of millions of dollars in automatic tax giveaways. Fee reported that the fast-growing Industrial and Commercial Incentive Program had gone awry, granting automatic tax breaks based solely on geography and construction rather than on need. More than $100 million in property taxes had gone uncollected in 1991, and hundreds of millions more were in the pipeline."

And here is Daves's tipsheet for avoiding many of these problems, or at least making them easier to solve:

When you request data:

1. Try to get your sources to modem their data to your machine. This gets away from compatibility problems.
2. Get all the documentation. That could be any of several things.
   A. An example of the form from which the data were keypunched;
   B. Instructions to clerks so you'll know the rules by which they entered the data;
   C. The record layout. This should tell you the names of the fields in each record, their lengths and their formats;
   D. The labels or values for special codes in each of the fields.
3. Make sure the tape or diskette can be read by your computer system— hardware and software. Know each of the following, or have your computer expert talk to your source's expert:
   A. Tape density. Density is how much data are stored on a given amount of tape. It is measured in bytes per inch, or BPI. A current standard is 6250 BPI. Your computer must be able to read the tape density in which the data was written. (The same is true for diskettes. For instance if you use an old IBM XT, like your newsletter editor does, you won't be able to read a high-density disk.)
   B. Block size. Block size is the size of a chunk of information on the tape. Computers read tapes more efficiently if records are grouped into blocks. Block sizes can be fixed—all blocks are the same size—or variable. Know the tape's block size and make sure your

computer can handle it. If it can't, get your source to block the data the way you computer can best read it.

C. Know if it's in ASCII (American Standard Code for Information Interchange) or EBCDIC (Extended Binary Coded Decimal Interchange Code, usually the language IBM mainframes recognize). It doesn't matter which it is in, only that your computer can read the language.

D. Labeling, or "tape structure." Is it IBM standard or nonlabeled? This doesn't mean the flashy self-sticking labels on the outside of the tape; it means the way the files on the tape are organized. If it's nonlabeled, only the data file should be present. If it's IBM-standard labeled, other information will be on the tape. You simply need to tell your computer if the tape is labeled or not.

Many of these concerns should be prompted by the PC computer software—but perhaps not by mainframe software—before you load the data. It's enormously helpful, however, if you've gotten the answers in advance and made the adjustments before that time.[7]

In March 1991, the *St. Petersburg Times* ran a series over seven days by David Barstow, Susan Taylor Martin, Chuck Murphy, Bob Port and Richard Bockman that reported that "courts were abusing a state statute that allowed people charged with crimes to have their records sealed. The statute, originally created to give first-time marijuana offenders a second chance, was being used to hide convictions of murder and fraud. A follow-up story showed how four judges in Tampa sealed records as a favor for friends."

Selecting Hardware and Software

What are the minimal hardware needs for CAR? Your PC should be a 486 or faster. These systems, including monitors, run for under $2,000. A 486 souped up with a math coprocessor and other speed-enhancing devises sells for under $2,500, with monitor. Faster is better.

Moreover, you need a lot of hard disk memory to contain all of the data you want analyzed and to be able to run the software. Think in terms of 16 megabytes (MB) of RAM and 300 MB on the hard disk, or more. At this writing, MB in RAM and on disks is very inexpensive—perhaps an additional $200 to $500 over what the computer makers offer in their initial setups.

In April 1991, the *Columbus Dispatch* ran a three-day series by Alan D. Miller that showed that "a handful of landlords own some of the worst housing in Columbus. The landlords found holes in the housing safety; laws that allowed them to rent substandard apartments and avoid fixing them up without penalties. Of 1,500 properties studied, 500 with the most violations were owned by nine landlords. Their tenants lived in unhealthy and sometimes life-threatening conditions for months, even years, while the landlords legally avoided making repairs. . . . One landlord balked for seven years. He got away with it until the series ran. His building that at times housed more than 80 tenants is now closed. . . ."

My first CAR project was in 1984 with reporter Eric Black, who wanted to examine the civil court system in Minnesota. In 1984 it was quite common for government record custodians to first respond to journalism requests for computer data with a resounding *"no,"* often claiming that records in computers were not governed by the same disclosure rules as their paper counterparts. Then they'd say that the information wasn't kept in such a way to answer the reporter's questions. It would require a special programmer to write a program. That, they'd say, would take 8 to 20 years and cost the journalist some $20 million dollars.

It was this resistance to disclosure, plus the outstanding teaching to hundreds of journalists by Elliot Jaspin, an accomplished reporter who bothered to learn how to do this kind of work and then set about teaching others, that has led to the diffusion in journalism of computer-assisted journalism.

If the government agency couldn't or wouldn't provide the answers, reporters would resort to taking the entire data off the government's computers and analyzing it themselves, which is a lot easier now because of data-analysis software.

Moreover, nearly all judicial jurisdictions have ruled that if data kept on paper is open to the public, it must also be released if kept on computer. Some judges have even ruled that the software developed by the government to access these records is also public and must be given when asked.

In December 1991, the *Kansas City Star* ran a seven-day series by Jeff Taylor, Mike McGraw, Michael Mansur and Gregory Reeves that "investigated the U.S. Department of Agriculture (USDA), dubbed by President Lincoln as 'the people's department' when he founded it. [The series] exposed a department usurped by the richest farmers, the giant food conglomerates and powerful lobbyists. The findings: thousands of farms soaking taxpayers, making a mockery of USDA payment limits—and with USDA help; a meat inspection system failing to protect Americans, putting them at deadly risk; black farmers on the verge of disappearing, in part because of discrimination in all white USDA offices; giant corporations taking in millions of dollars to help them advertise their food products at taxpayer expense; a dreadful environmental record that is continuing at the department; and a USDA office approving thousands of labels each year that are misleading and often dead wrong."

There are additional advances in PC software and hardware of great use to investigative reporters:

- Scanners and optical character recognition software that allow you to take printed material—paper records, articles, depositions, news stories and the like—and copy them into your computer automatically rather than typing them by hand.
- Sophisticated and relatively easily mastered software is available to organize this kind of data. The most promising are the hypertext programs—software that lets you organize the material in your computer the way you might organize it in folders. But the hypertext is better because it does it in the computer.
- CD-ROM technology has become very cheap and readily available. Chapter 4 details how CD-ROM—just like the CDs you use for listening to music—can help you search text or bibliographic databases at no cost. You can also load a CD-ROM reader into your computer for under $400 and, because they hold so much more information than floppy disks, this is technology you should explore.

We will examine all of these technologies below.

In May and December 1991, the *Times Union* ran six days of reports by Harvey Lipman that showed that "in New York, Blacks and Hispanics were found to be 65 percent more likely to be sent to jail than whites for first time felony offenses. And nearly 90 percent of all drug arrests in Albany were made in two primarily black neighborhoods. Even when police busted drug dealers outside those neighborhoods, they arrested blacks virtually exclusively; only one white man was charged with selling drugs outside a black neighborhood over the entire six months. A subsequent study by a criminologist hired by the state confirmed the *Times Union* findings that minorities who are first time offenders receive a harsher sentence."

Here's how David Armstrong at the *Boston Herald* has made use of scanners:

Not unlike dozens of other newspapers across the country, the *Boston Herald* has grappled with the problem of transferring reams of paper records into electronic databases. This is a particular problem for the *Herald* because one very valuable information source—state and city campaign records—are not stored electronically.

Initially, we contacted data entry firms to solicit prices for entering the records. This resulted in the newspaper contracting with an Ohio company to enter campaign records at 13 cents a record. This price was about half the quote from the next lowest bidder. Many of the quotes ranged from 26 to 33 cents a record, plus consulting fees and other costs.

We encountered several problems with the data entry. First, it became very expensive. During the gubernatorial campaign in 1990, we spent more than $10,000 to create electronic files of contributors to several candidates for statewide office. In addition, we experienced delays in getting the information and errors in the records we were receiving. Turnaround time was also a problem. At this point, we started to search for alternatives. Because many of the campaign records were typed or produced by laser printers, we investigated the possibility of scanning records in-house.

The data systems department at the *Herald* was already exploring the potential of scanners for another department at the newspaper. Together with our request for scanning information, the data systems department studied scanner options and eventually secured approval to purchase a unit. (Disclaimer: Ordinarily I am a zealous advocate for having the newsroom purchase and operate its own computer equipment, most particularly when it comes to equipment for investigative reporting and special projects. In this case, because of our part-time need for the scanner and the cost of the equipment we had no problem with having the data systems people take control.)

Here is a quick breakdown of our scanning system components:

- A Hewlett-Packard HP ScanJet-Plus scanner. The cost of the scanner was $1,455 and included all of the equipment necessary to connect to the PC. An auto–document feeder was included in the package as an extra, but extremely valuable, feature. The HP ScanJet has an optical resolution of 300 PPi.
- A Zeos 486, 33 MHz personal computer with 200 MB hard drive. The cost of this unit was $4,453. (Note: It is not necessary to buy a new PC to establish a scanning system.)
- The software we use is Wordscan by Microsoft. This operates only on Windows. The software retails for $795, but with our corporate discount we bought it for $595. The software can scan 300 words per minute. It also has a very valuable pop-up image verifier that flags possible errors. Once the information is scanned in, the data can be exported in 30 different word processing formats.

Our first—and only—experience with the scanning system was a limited success. We had 300 pages listing contributions to the governor that we needed entered. Using the auto–document feeder, we stacked the records on the scanner. The pages were read at a rate of one every 20 seconds. In all, more than 3,000 records were scanned within a couple of hours. The data was exported in an ASCII file to XyWrite. Most of the record cleaning occurred in XyWrite. We encountered one major problem. The scanner frequently confused lowercase *l* with lowercase *t* because of a slight dip at the bottom of the *l*. As a result, cities like "Lowell" often appeared as "Lowett." Most of the other words and letters, however, were read accurately.

Had the campaign data been shipped out for data entry, the cost would have been $389, plus mailing costs. In this case, the scanning and proofing of the data was accomplished in less than a day with minimal manpower. In addition, we successfully developed a XyWrite program to export this data in comma delimited form after it was cleaned up. Overall, the scanner proved to be a worthwhile investment.[8]

In July–December 1991, the *Albuquerque Tribune* ran a series of articles by Dan Vukelich that showed that the "New Mexico legislature was dominated by special interests; 72 percent of all campaign funds came from special interests; state campaign finance laws were a joke; fund-raising occurred simultaneously with law making; lobbyists failed to report properly; bills with money behind them would go further; appalling conflicts of interest were tolerated in the name of a 'citizen legislature.' The series took New Mexicans into the process and let them judge for themselves whether the flood of cash that descends on lawmakers during each year's 30- or 60-day session of the legislature influences them."

The actual flatbed scanner—a machine similar in appearance to a small photocopier—sells for just over $1,000. But pay attention to the software.

One kind just takes a picture of the page you are scanning and puts it into the computer as a picture. You can't do anything with it except what you'd do with a picture, such as change its size.

Scanner software with optical character recognition (OCR) capabilities allows you to scan in the pages and use the text the same way you would if you typed it in; you can edit these scanned documents. If the software doesn't say it has OCR capabilities, you don't want it. This software sells for around $100 to $500 or more.

In July and August 1991, the *Oakland Tribune* ran a three-day series by Michael Collier and Paul Grabowicz that showed how "special districts in California [were] a hidden layer of government [and] had proliferated in the past decade even as the state and most municipalities and counties in California were struggling under severe budget cuts and financial chaos. The first part of the series detailed how many of these obscure agencies existed, the money they were spending and how local elected officials were raking in extra income

serving on the boards of small districts that had long since outlived their usefulness. Part two examined one district, a sewer planning agency, that had
completed its last project years before, had no office or full-time staff, and yet
mysteriously had $13 million in a bank account and had tripled the pay for
politicians serving on its board of directors. . . ."

Hypertext software allows you to search across all of your files by word,
string of words or even parts of words. It can create indexes for you and make
sure that you don't forget anything you've collected over the many months of
your project.

For instance, you can't remember who told you about the guy with the
unusual relationship with three pigs and a donkey. You search on *donkey,* and
the software pulls up the sentences where that word is located, shows you that
sentence and gives you the slug. Then you remember that the source has
come up in a number of interviews. You can re-search your hundreds of files
on that source and you find him in your notes in five other files.

So then you place a special key on all of those files, after creating your
new index on this one issue, so that every time you are in there you can
automatically jump into these interview notes with the push of a button.

Here's how Kathy Hansen, a former news librarian at the *Star Tribune,*
explained a hypertext program to other librarians and journalists:

> For librarians or reporters willing to invest some time in document
> preparation, Folio VIEWS's search-and-retrieve capabilities offer quick
> access to cumbersome documents.
>
> Although there are many full-text search software products, those
> that can handle large amounts of text are generally too complex for
> everyday use. And easy-to-use text retrieval programs often can't handle
> large amounts of text, or they perform poorly when the database being
> searched grows larger than the available memory.
>
> Folio VIEWS, the first commercial product from the Folio Corp.,
> strikes a balance between these two extremes and brings sophisticated
> text retrieval to the PC.
>
> The program gets its name from its ability to create "views," virtual
> organizations of text blocks. VIEWS can be extracts or narrowed looks
> at a database or the entire database itself.
>
> The company believes that the $695 program is a boon to informa-
> tion services and publishers who want to create searchable electronic
> versions of their works.
>
> One of VIEWS's greatest strengths is the amount of data it can
> handle. A VIEWS database (called an infobase) can grow as large as

2 gigabytes, containing nearly four times as much information as a CD-ROM can accommodate.

I tested Folio VIEWS on an IMB PS/2 computer as well as on 386 clones. Search and retrieve performance was very good on either PC; however, I would recommend the power of a 386 or 486 for creating or authoring large-size infobases.

The product needs only 512K of RAM to run under DOS 3.0 or higher. In addition, performance was not affected by the differing sizes of infobases, ranging from 250K to 1M. In whichever infobase I worked, search-and-retrieve performance proved equally fast.

The various structural elements in Folio VIEWS—infobases, folios, groups and links—are designed for fast, easy, accurate information retrieval.

The package's first-rate search features allow search strings up to 256 characters—about 42 words. By searching on words like *to* and *or* you can find very specific expressions, such as "To be or not to be." Finding this expression would be time-consuming and difficult in a program that doesn't have complete indexing.

VIEWS provides users with standard search criteria. You can search using all logical operators, such as *and, not* and *or.* You can search for a single word or phrase. Nested searches, wildcard searches and proximity searches are supported as well.

As a user types in the search criterion, Folio's proprietary indexing scheme, called Underhead Technology, continually narrows the search in the index. In most cases, VIEWS located all occurrences by the time the last letter of the word was typed.

Folio VIEWS maintains a strong sense of order through these search techniques and through the structure it imposes on information. It provides excellent tools for linking information and grouping ideas. This flexibility is especially useful for building tables of contents, cross-referencing items and adding footnotes to lengthy investigative projects extending over many weeks or months—footnotes that allow reporters and editors to go to the original material when checking the final project for accuracy.

Hot links can be set up to launch external applications, graphics files, digitized sound files and animation programs. VIEWS maintains a 10K terminate-and-stay resident program that lets users move between an information base and another application.

VIEWS's comprehensive documentation includes an on-line tutorial, an on-line reference manual and a quick-reference guide. The on-line documentation is comprehensive, but the "hypertext manual" approach doesn't work well to train users. A written manual is preferable.

According to Folio Corp., several vendors, including Mead Data Central, which recently purchased Folio, and others are developing ready-made databases for VIEWS processing.

A catalog of offerings can be obtained from Folio and includes such items as the Federal Register, Matthew Lesko's books, Roger Ebert's Movie Home Companion, California and other state codes, the U.S. Code of Federal Regulations, the Great Books series, environment regulations, history books and different versions of the Bible.

At the *Star Tribune* we also have a CD-ROM product called Magazine Rack, which uses Folio VIEWS as a search engine.

Photo librarians may also be familiar with Photo VIEWS, the new electronic photo archive system recently announced by Lexis/Nexis. This product also uses Folio VIEWS as the search engine, linking photo captions to the digital photo.

Users send their data file through the create utility, which organizes the ASCII information into infobases. Information bases are created by using VIEWS's convert command to import files in 41 different formats, including WordPerfect and Microsoft Word, or by using VIEWS's built-in text editor.

Text is indexed and converted to the Folio proprietary file format at approximately 6M to 8M per hour. The resulting file contains both the index and original text, compressed to approximately half the size of the original text file.

You can create a menu that makes the infobase easier for others to use by typing a text file that includes the menu items.

Mark each menu item as a link, and simply tab among the links to select topics in the infobase.

Explanatory footnotes and cross-references can be included. Also, hypertext-like links to other sections of the infobase can be added.

For instance, links can be created between technical terms and a glossary, or between the index and the specific textual reference. If a user finds an interesting reference in the index, pressing one key automatically retrieves the information pertinent to the reference.

The links are not limited to text information. An infobase can create multimedia effects by linking to other programs that display photos, graphics, animation or even play music.

Ties to other programs are so smooth that the user is unlikely to notice the transitions from VIEWS and back again.

Here are ideas for news librarians and reporters:

■ Develop secondary products from published stories—major feature stories or a group of stories related to a subject could be electronically published to specialized markets. Because photos and graphics can be linked to text, the infobase still reads and "feels" like a newspaper. As an example, Buckmaster Publishing has created a product called "Front Page News," a compilation of articles from multiple wire services, using Folio VIEWS.

■ A newspaper could electronically publish feature stories to specialized markets. For example, a *Star Tribune* foster-care series would be useful to government social service departments, schools and public libraries. These secondary products could be marketed with full-text searching right on the floppy. An infobase of your newspaper's editorials can be created.

■ VIEWS can be used to manage personal information files. Librarians can upload important searches—especially those supporting investigative work—into a searchable infobase.

■ Topic research done for different reporters, all writing from a different angle, can be shared. For example, support campaign research by downloading an excellent series such as "The Bush Record," by Andrew Rosenthal and Joel Brinkley, which ran in *The New York Times* beginning June 25, 1992. Create an infobase for quick reference questions, such as "How many bills did Bush veto?" The librarian can now begin campaign research here before having to go on-line again.

You could build a mini-infobase on a major project extending over months or years, such as the Mall of America. I don't know how many times I typed Ghermezian Brothers into Nexis or DIALOG.[9]

Or, create an infobase on the World Series in anticipation of the Minnesota Twins (or your local team) winning the pennant (or other championship). For several weeks we had sports reporters asking us for the same information with just a slightly different spin. One librarian could have done a comprehensive search on the World Series, anticipating the questions from our previous experience. This could have been uploaded into an infobase and stored on our end-user search station for use by sports reporters—or put directly on PCs in the newsroom.

■ Rapid retrieval of unstructured information—the librarian or reporter can load all his or her on-line files into VIEWS. Once loaded, the information can be used and reused for everything from micro-research on cross linkages for investigative studies to legal protection in a court of law.

Any person who needs to manage dynamic information will find VIEWS valuable.[10]

In September 1991, *Newsday* ran a three-day series by Lou Dolinar, Alan Eysen, Celeste Hadrick and Michele Slatalla that showed that "the Nassau County Republican Party rigged the awarding of hundreds of competitive civil service jobs for the benefit of officials, contributors and friends of the party. Top scorers were passed over for political favorites and job qualifications changed for politically connected workers. Jobs were limited to Republicans by limited advertising of the positions. Party officials earned more than average in every category. More than 80 percent of the workers in the top pay category were party officials, or relatives or contributors."

Here's how Steve Doig, associate editor for news research at *The Miami Herald,* explains their experience using CD-ROM:

Basically, CD-ROM uses the same technology as the digital compact disks that have taken over the music business.

The advantage of CD-ROM over floppies is extremely high data density: one 4.5-inch CD-ROM disk can hold over 600 megabytes of data. That's the equivalent storage of about 1,800 of the old 5.25-inch 360K floppies.

An apparent disadvantage is that CD-ROM is, as the name says, read-only—you can't write data to a CD-ROM disk. But for newsroom uses that's a little problem. Typically, we want to use bulk data, not generate it.

(You can buy so-called write-once-read-many [WORM] drives, but they are expensive.)

Another disadvantage of CD-ROM is speed of access. It typically takes a good hard drive 15 to 20 milliseconds (ms) to find the piece of data for which the software is searching. By comparison, a good CD-ROM reader will take 350 ms, and some have access times as high as 500 ms. In other words, CD-ROM is 15 to 25 times slower than a hard drive.

However, for most newsroom applications the relatively slow speed shouldn't be a real problem.

If you're using CD-ROM to access individual pieces of information, such as a phone number from a national directory or a head count from a particular census tract, then the supposed delay is trivial.

And if you're using CD-ROM for large-scale database work, then the answer is to use a high-capacity hard drive for temporary storage. You simply copy the data you need from the CD-ROM to the hard drive, and then do your statistical work on the hard drive.

Let me give you an example: I wanted to create a map file of South Florida for our mapping software (Atlas GIS). So I bought the Florida TIGER files (a giant geographic database) CD-ROM from the Census Bureau. The files for Dade County (Miami) alone totaled more than 47 megabytes. Using DOS, I copied the Dade files onto my Doolittle to turn the TIGER line segments into the polygons necessary for Atlas. The conversion process took several hours; but doing it straight from the CD-ROM would have taken well over a day.

The uses of CD-ROM are limited only by the kinds of data you can get on CD-ROM:

■ There are already a lot of reference material—encyclopedias, indexes, directories—available on CD-ROM. (Some of it is junk though; a lot of the early CD-ROM disks were filled with out-of-copyright textbooks and such.)

■ Some of the large on-line database vendors are selling CD-ROM versions of their data. I'm most familiar with the offerings of Dialog, including its Standard & Poor's Corporations database and *The Miami Herald* on disk. If you need a few facts from such a database, it's cheaper to go on-line; but if you're looking for patterns in a large database, then having it on CD-ROM is the way to go.

■ More and more government data is being distributed on CD-ROM. The Census Bureau has led the way, selling much of its 1990 census data on CD-ROM at bargain prices. There's also a lot of international commerce and trade data on CD-ROM.

I can't tell you what kind of CD-ROM drive to buy; prices are dropping steadily, and new models are coming onto the market all the time.

But I'll describe the system I use. My computer is an IBM PS/2 Model 55SX with an internal 60 megabyte hard drive. The CD-ROM is a Toshiba 3201B external with a Small Computer System Interface (SCSI, pronounced "scuzzy") adapter.

We spent about $800 for the unit and adapter early this year, though I've seen other models advertised lately for less than $500. CD-ROM drives also are made by NEC, Chinon, Hitachi and others.

In addition, I have a CMS Lanstack external hard drive (204 megabytes) that daisy-chains off the back of the CD-ROM (the advantage of the SCSI adapter is that you can daisy-chain up to eight external devices off the single adapter card).

In sum, CD-ROM is a handy and relatively inexpensive way to handle a lot of data—if the data you want to use is available on CD-ROM.[11]

In November and December 1991, the *Dallas Morning News* ran articles by Ed Timms and Steve McGonigle that showed that "the U.S. military disregards its own laws to convict service members of crimes—and sends a disproportionate number of minorities to its toughest prison. The investigation uncovered cases in which commanders intimidated witnesses or stacked courts-martial panels with conviction-prone officers. Defendants are convicted with evidence that experts say would never stand up in a civilian court. And while minorities are disproportionately represented among military prisoners, military judges are typically white."

There are a great many inexpensive tools available now for people who work on PCs. Why not explore some of the available options?

And where can you get help?

The two most prominent help organizations are these:

- The Missouri Institute for Computer Assisted Reporting (MICAR) gives seminars and will help you analyze data. Its address is University of Missouri, P.O. Box 838, Columbia, Mo., 65205. It is now ably headed by Brandt Houston and MICAR is now part of IRE.
- The Indiana University National Institute for Advanced Reporting is best known for its annual three-day national conference on many aspects of computers and reporting. Write NIAR, ES 4106, 902 W. New York Street, Indianapolis, Ind., 46202.
- Finally, be sure to read the two sidebars to this chapter. One will show you how to get started on a CAR project that will lead to a series of articles and is easy to do; the other will show you how to get longer stories into your newspaper.

In December 1991, the *Sacramento Bee* ran a four-day series by Mike Wagner and Marcos Breton showed "the extent of exploitation of migrant farm workers in California and reveal[ed] how federal and state regulators have failed to carry out their duties to ensure humane working and living conditions. The state only conducted 28 minimum-wage investigations in six years involving farm workers. More than 20,000 farm workers suffer disabling injuries in California each year, but few receive workers' compensation benefits. Only 2 to 6 percent of the workforce lives in regulated housing. There was not a single revocation of pesticide licenses over three years, even though thousands of workers suffer from pesticide poisoning."

NOTES

1. This exceptionally helpful booklet, edited by Jonathan Schmid and Andrew Scott (a former IRE executive director), contains examples from IRE's contest entry forms where reporters explain what they did and how they did it.

Each page of the 73-page booklet contains a summary of the reporters' findings, along with brief explanations of how the story got started, the actual database used or created with descriptions of the data, sources for the data, results and follow-up where appropriate, advice to others who might want to do the same thing, a discussion of difficulties or other special circumstances and the amount of time the project took.

I've reproduced (with permission) the edited summaries of a small portion of the booklet's contents. If you are looking for excellent ideas, along with the names of good reporters to call for advice, you will find no better source.

The booklet sells for $17, including postage and handling. Write IRE, PO Box 838, Columbia, Mo. 65205.

2. Software prices are very fluid. Since the start of this decade, they've been flowing one way—down. The prices quoted here are used only to show the relative costs between the various types. There are many legal ways to save money on software. Instead of buying the most current version, buy a previous version. One of my students bought an earlier version of Works for $10. Even the latest versions often have huge discounts. Paradox, described in this chapter, was selling for under $150 as the publisher was lowering prices to gain market share. Moreover, many of these programs are very cheap if you upgrade by switching brands. For instance, Microsoft was selling its spreadsheet software, FoxPro, at a fraction of the retail cost if you upgraded from a competitor. Finally, most software stores—especially those advertising in national magazines—offer substantial reductions in the prices advertised by the publishers. Check out the ads.

3. Of course, the court doesn't keep information about income. But here we can use a surrogate to make at least a rough cut that's probably usable. It's the zip code of each defendant's residence.

4. There are many other problems in addition to those detailed by Clark. The biggest is that government workers at all levels can easily erase information on disks, as some in the Bush administration were caught doing just before the transition to the Clinton administration. Moreover, many crucial decisions are made through messages sent back and forth on connected computer systems, and these messages are rarely saved and often not susceptible to access laws. That means that a lot of what goes on in government is no longer available to historians or their counterparts, journalists.

5. Reprinted from the *The Newsletter,* June 1991, 1–4. I publish this newsletter for people involved in computer-assisted reporting. We share our successes and failures. Subscription is $35; publication is episodic—roughly six to eight times per calendar year. Write *The Newsletter,* 5622 Wood Lane, St. Louis Park, Minn., 55436, for a sample issue.

6. Reprinted from *The Newsletter,* November 1991, 1–4.

7. Ibid., 4.

8. *The Newsletter,* May 1992, 1–3.

9. The Mall of America is this country's largest shopping mall and virtually every station and newspaper of any size sent reporters up to Bloomington, Minn., to check it out for their readers and viewers. The mall was instigated by the Ghermezian brothers of Canada, who previously built the world's largest mall in Edmonton.

10. This article is a slightly edited version on Ms. Hansen's review in *The Database Files,* another newsletter I publish. ("Folio VIEWS is a great way to handle your hordes of data and a [relatively] inexpensive way to jump into hypertext," by Kathy L. Hansen, *The Database Files/ The Newsletter of News Research,* January 1993, 1–3.) Subscription price for this six-times-per-year newsletter is $100. Write 5622 Wood Lane, St. Louis Park, Minn. 55436.

11. *The Newsletter,* February 1992, 1–3.

Computer-Assisted Reporting

by Anne Saul, Gannett, Inc.[1]

Starting with Nothing

You have just returned from a National Conference on Computer-Assisted Journalism (you paid your own way) and are all fired up about using computers to help you report on stories.

Unfortunately, your newspaper's only computer is in the controller's office and the only software on it is the Lotus 1-2-3 spreadsheet program he uses to crunch numbers.

But you've got your act together; you've done the research and crunched some numbers of your own. Armed with your proposal, you march into the editor's office and tell her that for only $20,000 you can win a Pulitzer Prize for the newspaper.

Get Real

The problem is obvious:

- Your newspaper, like many others these days, is short on cash.
- Your editor thinks a byte is something you take out of a hamburger—only spelled wrong.
- You let all those great Indianapolis presentations about how newspapers are doing huge six-month investigative projects go to your head. (They are great projects, but too big for you or your newspaper's budget at this point.)

Get Started

Journalists by nature and training are skeptics. What makes you think your editor is any different? Before you even think about requesting additional resources, you have to prove to her that a computer can help you do a better job as a reporter.

First, you have to have an idea for a story. As you probably heard in Indianapolis or read in one of the industry magazines, computer-assisted reporting projects don't start with the computer; they start with a story idea. The computer only helps with the reporting.

Second, computer-assisted reporting projects don't have to be big block-busters. Computers can help reporters with even small, rather routine stories.

Because of your almost nonexistent resources, that's where you need to start.

Get an Idea

Because it's an election year, most newspapers will do stories on voter registration trends. Depending on the type of information (race, sex, political party) required for registration in your state, voter registration rolls can help you determine whether there are shifts in party affiliation, increasing registration among minorities in certain precincts or simply changes in overall registration.

To do this story without a computer, you have to manually sift through huge printouts of registration roles to spot these trends.

If these numbers were in a computer, you could quickly sort them by any of the criteria (race, gender, party) available.

If the registration rolls are available on a 9-track tape and you have no 9-track drive at your newspaper, you might be able to get a local university to crunch the numbers for you.

But let's assume the worst—that the only way you can get the registration rolls is on paper.

Get a Loan

Ask the controller if you can use his computer when he's not there. If you can't afford the $500 for Paradox or another relational database program, you can always start with the Lotus 1-2-3 program already on his computer. Lotus will perform the simple sorts you need for this story, and when you can afford Paradox, you can import the Lotus files into that program for future voter registration stories.

If you don't know how to use Lotus, you might check into the availability of a class at the local community college (usually inexpensive) or the controller might be willing to help you get started.

Get Going

Start with the current voter registration list. If you have time, you can enter the figures for prior years and, when the registration books close for the November elections, you can enter those, too. You can also enter the number of people who actually voted in prior elections and create a cell formula to compute percentages of voter turnout. This can provide a nice little story on precincts with the highest/lowest turnouts in prior years—based on actual numbers rather than on information provided by the registrar's office or a candidate's campaign headquarters (the latter is often suspect).

After you've entered the information, start performing some simple sort operations. Remember to save your basic list and perform the sort operations on a copy.

Now you can instantly analyze voter registration turnout and voting patterns. And you've created a database that you can build on for several years.

While this won't produce a Pulitzer Prize–winning story for your newspaper, it will produce some worthwhile stories now and in the future. And it will help convince your editor that computers can help reporters do a better job.

Get Reasonable

Even if you've convinced your editor the computer helped you do a better job on some simple stories, now is no the time to hit her with the $20,000 question.

Take the list and put the items in priority order. Start with the small items that can be expenses—like a database software program. Make sure these are items you can use right away so that the editor will see results from each of her expenditures.

As you probably heard at the various workshops you attended in Indianapolis or read in the various computer-assisted reporting newsletters, even the big guys now doing huge projects with help or computers started small.

The important thing is that they started.

(Anne Saul is news systems editor for Gannett newspapers and assists reporters in that organization in computer-assisted reporting.)

And Here's an Even Easier Way

by John Ullmann

Buy a copy of Microsoft Works for around $100. Next, create your template like this: Column one has the slug of your stories. Column two has the date. Column three has the length of the story as you sent it to your assistant city editor (ACE). Column four has the length of the story the ACE sent to the copy desk. (ACEs show you what they sent, right? If not, arrange to know.) Column five has the name of the copyeditor who worked over your story. (Call at night to see who has it in case there's a question.) Column six has the length of the story once published.

Do this for, say, six months.

Now you've built your first relational database. Congratulations.[2]

Here's what you do with the data. By sorting on several fields, you can determine which copyeditor is trimming you most often and at greatest length. Take that copyeditor to dinner and find out what the hell the problem is, anyway. (And turn in the dinner expense as a sourcing meal.)

Now you are a relational database expert.[3]

NOTES

1. *The Newsletter,* May 1992, 3–7.

2. Okay, okay, it's a flat file. But even flat files have some relational capabilities. For you, I'll overlook the distinction.

3. *The Newsletter,* May 1992, 8.

4

Making the Most of Databases

Although many journalists have now enjoyed the fruits of electronic libraries, most librarians only use a small fraction of the 5,000 available. This chapter tells you how to make better use of the databases you frequent and, in the sidebar, how to expand your use.

You already know that electronic databases are outstanding tools for backgrounding just about any topic. How do I know that? Because you are reading an advanced investigative reporting book and database searching is now routine in investigative reporting, just as it is for hundreds of print and broadcast reporters just trying to get out the next day's story.

Maybe you use databases routinely to find sources. A search librarian is someone you see regularly now, maybe even frequently. But did you know what a fine investigatory tool databases can be when manipulated by a sophisticated searcher?

Here's an example of a search by a librarian at the *Philadelphia Inquirer* for Don Barlett and James Steele on a project that earned the team its second Pulitzer Prize, this one about all the breaks Congress gives to selected individuals or corporations. The facts were especially difficult to track down because complete identifying information was often missing from the public record. (The anecdote is recounted by Barlett.)

> The transition rule in the tax bill provided only the following information about the identity of the beneficiary of the special-interest tax legislation:
>
> A Delaware corporation incorporated on Aug. 10, 1928, which had the following indebtedness on May 28, 1986:
>
> - $975,000,000 face amount of variable rate bank loan due May 31, 1994;
> - $400,000,000 face amount 12½ percent subordinated debentures due June 1, 2001; and
> - $225,000,000 face amount 12¼ percent senior subordinated debentures due June 1, 1998.
>
> I called Jennifer Ewing, a young librarian we have worked with for a number of years. The conversation went something like this:
>
> Barlett: "We need some information on a company."
>
> Ewing: "What's the name?"
>
> Barlett: "We don't know."
>
> (There is a long pause here during which Jennifer, who is accustomed to our bizarre requests, clearly is choosing her words carefully, as well as privately questioning our ancestry. Finally, she replies.)
>
> Ewing: "Give me a hint."
>
> Barlett: "We have a couple of numbers."
>
> I gave her the dollar amounts of the indebtedness and the dates of the debt. Five minutes later she called back with the name of the company.

In *The Wall Street Journal* (housed in the Dow Jones News Retrieval database) she found a story about the FMC Corp. offering $225 million of 12¼ percent senior subordinated debentures due June 1, 1998, and $400 million of 12½ percent subordinated debentures due June 1, 2001.

A check of Standard & Poor's showed that the present-day FMC Corp. was incorporated in Delaware on August 10, 1928, as the John Bean Manufacturing Co. That was the other piece of identifying information.

For those of us relegated to life here on earth, that anecdote seems like a spectacular piece of detective work, right? For Jennifer Ewing, the *Inquirer* librarian who did the on-line search, it was not a particularly difficult task. The hardest part was selecting which database was best, from among the many databases she has available. And, Ewing says, the request was almost routine. In fact, the anecdote represents the good and the bad, without the ugly, about database searching.

The Good

Databases continue to constitute one of the greatest, fastest, most up-to-date sources of information for a reporter—any reporter, working anywhere. In addition, they are tremendously cost-effective. Database searching is no longer just a frill for the wealthiest newspapers, although database diffusion throughout U.S. newsrooms remains relatively nascent. Moreover, there are many databases from which to choose, and several hundred more continue to become available every year.

For example, the *Cuadra Directory of Databases,* now published by Gale Research Inc., reports that in 1979–80 there were 400 databases available from 221 producers. In the July 1991 issue, *Cuadra* listed 5,026 databases from 2,158 producers.

Information in databases keeps you from having to reinvent the wheel, or, as is most often the case for reporters, let's us in on the fact that the wheel is already invented and is being used quite often.

The Bad

For nearly all reporters, a database search remains a two-step process, one that removes the reporter an important step away from finding information for himself or herself.

A reporter has the idea. A librarian translates the question into a search, selects the database(s), does the search, hands the results to the reporter, then waits to see if it fits the bill.

Until recently, I thought that this was how it would always be. Why? Because librarians put the information in there and it takes a librarian to get it out.

For example, I've taken graduate courses in database searching as part of my Ph.D. program at the University of Missouri, Columbia; I've taken vendor search classes; I've written articles and conducted newspaper surveys on the topic; and I've been doing my own searching off and on for more than a decade. On a scale of 1 to 10, with 10 being the best, I'm a 3 in a few familiar databases, a near zero in all the others, and even a negative number in some databases.

All trained librarians—those with a masters degree in library science (MLS) are 9s and 10s in any database. What are you?

Why is this so? Because successful database searching takes training and continual practice. Understanding the classification schemes used for databases requires the rigor, time and expense of formal library course work, as much of it is not intuitive, sometimes not even to trained librarians.

Here's an example. Suppose your city is about to accept bids from private companies for garbage removal, having decided it could save money by using private firms instead of full-time public employees. You learn from a possible variety of sources—tips, sources, reading—that the Mob has infiltrated this business and you decide to see what's printed by doing your own search.

You know that one of the great strengths of databases is that they can take disparate concepts, combine them and not chafe from the chaff because the computer eliminates all but the relevant data. For one part of the equation, you select such terms as "organized crime," "the mob," and "Cosa Nostra." For the other part, you select "garbage," "waste hauling" and "refuse."

You somehow get into the right database, but your search produces about a million hits—article citations containing your concepts. Why? Because "refuse" also means "decline" and "won't" and "turn down," and you've now dredged up all the articles where someone refused to run in a political campaign, get married, sign on the dotted line and thousands of other permutations. Instead of capitalizing on one of the great strengths of databases— saving research time—you've perverted it. This is especially true if you are searching in a full-text database and haven't limited your search to, say, titles or abstracts.

And, throughout your search, as you struggle to redefine and delimit, the clock is running and costs are mounting.

On the flip side is another common problem.

You select search terms for information not catalogued under the terms you favor, even if they are the most common terms used by you and the rest of the (nonlibrarian) literate public. Librarians catalog differently from the way you and I would do it, which is why they can find things when we cannot.

You may conclude from your misguided search that the information isn't there, but you may be tragically wrong. I once wasted countless hours searching information for a "Frontline" documentary on the collapse or imminent collapse of commercial fishing around the world. It wasn't until I turned to the professional searchers—trained librarians one and all—that I quickly got to the useful information lodged infrequently at best in the specialized press. Had I been less familiar with the process and less knowledgeable about my own weaknesses, I may have concluded that useful information simply wasn't there.

A development in the technology, however, has made your mastery much more possible, more likely, less expensive and much quicker.

CD-ROM

CD-ROM for data are similar to the CDs you've been buying for music.[1] For storage, CD-ROM is much better than floppy disks. For instance, a CD-ROM holds as much as 600 MB of data, or some 300,000 pages of text. By comparison, the old 5¼ inch floppy disk that I still use for back-up holds about 270 typed pages and the IBM XT, which was used for writing this book, has only a 10 MB hard disk.

Many on-line database vendors have recently been offering several years or more of their data on CD-ROM and public, university and even news libraries have begun to subscribe to them. The *Star Tribune* library subscribes to three—Newspaper Abstracts on Disc and Periodical Abstracts on Disk, both from University Microfilm Inc. (UMI), and *The New York Times* on CD-ROM.[2]

Bob Jansen, chief librarian at the *Star Tribune,* says he gets CD-ROM because, "Reporters themselves are able to come into the library to find what they need and if we have a subscription they can go right to it. If not, we save time and money going on-line to get exactly what they need.

"Reporters do use them and they like the fact that it's available right when they come into our library. Popularity has grown so that we will need another CD-ROM reader very soon."[3]

Public libraries and university libraries have many more titles. The Minneapolis Public Library makes available to its patrons more than half a dozen; the University of Minnesota more than three dozen.

Why does this help you? Let me count the ways.

But for You, It's Free

It was a great title for an article: "The Unconscious Fraud of Journalism Education." The drop heads were almost as good: "Computer database skills are essential for serious journalism. Why are J-schools failing us?"

The author, a journalism professor, was lamenting in a June 1992 *Quill* article that schools of journalism weren't doing nearly enough, when they did anything at all, to prepare their students to enter the new electronic age of computer-assisted journalism, both for number crunching, data analysis and, especially, for access to electronic databases. Two articles that followed were wee primers on on-line services.[4]

The September issue drew one response, a letter that said database skills weren't being taught by this particular college teacher because there wasn't any money to cover the search costs.

Well, how does "free" sound, to them and to you?

It's becoming harder and harder to walk into an academic or public library that doesn't have some kind of CD-ROM reader set up for its patrons.

You sit down at the computer and answer its questions. This is not only user-friendly, it is journalist-friendly. You basically need only know what you wish to know.

And many have printers attached to them. You don't even have to take a note.

And, did I mention, it's free?

It neither costs you nor your organization a dime.[5]

Learning Search Strategies Off-Line

Although the search strategy capabilities of most CD-ROM products are few compared to their online counterparts, doing a lot of searching—as you should—gives you a feel for classification systems and the way they are maintained.

That in itself doesn't lead to an expert's rating as a database searcher. Far from it. What it does lead to, however, is a more expert database "queriest" —someone who can sharpen an on-line search conducted by the librarian in significant ways: 1) You get better at thinking in terms of concepts and key words; 2) you get better at knowing how to interact with librarians who, after all, don't themselves want any of this stuff. You do, and the better you get at talking to them, the better they get at searching for you.

And, significantly, your journalism takes a quantum leap in usefulness, completeness and sophistication that pays off for you and the reader and/or viewer.

A Search Strategy

Now that there are so many CD-ROM databases available to me in the Twin Cities, here's the way I do my searches, and a way you may want to do yours.

■ First, I troll through the CD-ROM databases to flesh out any ideas I may have become attracted to. (See the first section of Chapter 6 for suggestions on coming up with project ideas.)

In this way, I am able to capture much of what's been printed in the popular press about my topic. This educates me about the possibilities for my project and alerts me to what's already out there. When I read the articles, I also underline some key concepts and key authors and sources who seem to be especially knowledgeable and thoughtful.

I return to the CD-ROM database and search on the new terms, as well as on the names of the authors or sources, or any titles of books and articles I picked up from my reading.

■ Second, I now consider whether I need to pay someone to go on-line at all. Usually the answer is yes, and for two reasons. 1) The CD-ROM is only as up to date as when the disk was printed. That is, you will need to go on-line to get the most current information. 2) The CD-ROM databases most readily available to me rarely include the specialized or technical press—those publications in which the experts talk to each other, of which there are thousands. I usually need these articles as well, both for the knowledge and opinions about the topic that they contain as well as the introduction to the top sources.[6]

■ Third, I present the printout of my searches to the on-line searcher (or describe them over the phone), so that the searcher can design a specifically targeted (read cheaper) search of great utility.

■ Then, after assimilating all of this, I write award-winning memos that convince supervisors to let me do the project.

Tracking Topics

A vendor is a company that takes a lot of databases from disparate sources and packages them together so you (or your searcher) don't have to learn a new set of search commands every time you switch databases.

The best and the biggest is DIALOG Information Services, now owned by Knight-Ridder, the newspaper publisher, which has some 400 databases.

I use it all the time when I request searches. Here's how and why:

DIALOG has a feature that lets a searcher run the same search across all or selected databases at the same time; then it tells you how many hits are in each before you get into them. This feature is usually called global searching.

When backgrounding individuals, I usually include some or all of the following DIALOG databases. (You can usually tell why by their titles, but I've added some tips where appropriate.)

- AP News, which is the Associated Press filings back to 1984.
- Arts and Humanities Search, which monitors "1,300 of the world's leading arts and humanities journals, plus relevant material from 5,000 social and natural science journals."
- Book Review Index, which goes back to 1969 and has more than 2 million records.
- Books in Print, which lists books currently in-print and has more than 1.3 million records.
- Congressional Record Abstracts, which goes back to 1981 and contains about a half million records. Committee and subcommittee reports, along with hearings, cover all aspects of life and are terrific for finding sources and understanding all aspects of a problem, including its political dimensions, though not limited to that in any way.
- Legal Resource Index, which goes back to 1980 and contains a half million records by culling from 750 "key" law journals and other legal sources. The articles in law journals are often a gold mine of information because in the United States, we litigate all of our problems. The journals' authors examine the state of law and its judicial interpretations, usually outline what is good about a law though they devote most of their attention to what is wrong, why and what needs to be corrected. Often, this database is among the most useful.
- Magazine Index, which goes back to 1973 (some to 1959) and contains more than 2.5 million records. How helpful would you think a database full of articles by magazine writers—who have more time, more space, quote more experts and often are more up to date on a project idea— would be to you? Say, critical?
- Papers, which, depending on the newspaper, goes back many years and has more than 5 million records is an important resource. In addition to the several dozen U.S. daily newspapers in the file up until January 1993, from that point on it also includes virtually all of the Knight-Ridder files from VuText, one of two major newspaper databases. (The other, of course, is DataTimes, which has dozens of newspapers you will want to search as well and is not on DIALOG.)
- Social Scisearch, which goes back to 1972 and has well over 2 million records from culling 1,500 of the "most important" social science journals, plus 3,000 additional journals for social science articles in the "natural, physical and biomedical" journals.

Depending only on the money available, this core of databases could be expanded for two reasons.

1. Money. When I can pass the search charges on, I often include:
   - PTS Newsletter Database, which goes back to 1988 and has a half million records culled from some 400 newsletters related to business or trade interests. Newsletters make their money on providing information you can't get elsewhere, or at least not as fast, and newsletter editors are great sources for other journalists.
   - Scisearch, which goes back to 1974 and has more than 10 million records culled from 2,600 "major" scientific and technical journals.
   - U.S. Political Science Documents, which goes back to 1975, and has about 60,000 records culled from 150 of the "major" U.S. political science journals.
2. Topic specialization. Of course, if my interest is in any of dozens of specialized topics—such as science, business, environment—I'll include databases from DIALOG specializing in these topics.

Now, the engaged reader will have noticed that the database directory I cited earlier lists more than 5,000 databases and that DIALOG has "only" 400 or so. What about all the others?

For one thing, the numbers are a little misleading. The directory lists, for example, each newspaper offering its own holdings electronically as a separate database, which it is. However, many of these newspapers can be found captured in one DIALOG database, Papers.

Nevertheless, the general premise is true. There are many databases out there unfamiliar to most librarians at newspapers and public or university libraries, because searchers everywhere tend to use the offerings of only a handful of vendors.

For an idea of what databases might be of particular use to reporters that are not available from major vendors (and a shamelessly self-serving methodology for learning about them), see the sidebar that accompanies this chapter.

Government Databases

The federal government is still the greatest producer of information in the world. In a sense, information is its only product. However, since the early 1980s, the federal government has been diluting, suspending and privatizing its only product in numerous ways and instances, all boding ill for people making a living off information's availability and integrity.

The irony is that this occurs at precisely the moment when the long-heralded information age is really upon us and the federal government, at least with its increasing use of the computer, has joined it.

The issues are important and complex. However, there is a great deal of literature on the topic in the library science and legal fields. (Alas, little in journalism.)

The good news is that the federal government is so vast that numerous of its arms make data available electronically. A key to finding which data is available on the electronic circuit is the Federal Database Finder.

Moreover, in 1993 legislation was introduced in both houses of Congress to make access to federal electronic information even easier. This occurred in the waning days of the Bush administration. It is unclear what will happen under the Clinton administration.

At the state and local government levels, electronic access is increasing greatly. For instance, the state of Minnesota has operated a database with demographic and natural resource information for nine years. Hennepin County, Minn., allows electronic searching of district court records, county recorder records and some property tax information.

(A good project for a student Society of Professional Journalists chapter would be to canvass state and local government to find out what records are available this way. The findings can be published in a little booklet, and students can earn bylines and some money from the professionals in the state who would buy the booklet each year, and professionals can keep up to date. This is much better for them, and you, than selling T-shirts.)

NOTES

1. CD-ROM is an acronym for compact disk—read only memory.

2. *The New York Times* offers three years of full-text for about $2,250 per year. Newspaper Abstracts contains eight newspapers: *Atlanta Constitution* (and some *Journal* articles), *Boston Globe, Chicago Tribune, Christian Science Monitor, Los Angeles Times, New York Times, Wall Street Journal* and *Washington Post.* Most newspapers go back to 1985. The disks costs about $2,950 per year, with monthly updates. Periodical Abstracts has 450 periodicals, and one year with monthly updates costs $1,175. Call 800-521-0600 for further information.

3. In fact, the *Star Tribune* has just begun marketing its own newspaper on CD-ROM through NewsBank.

4. The cited article was written by J. T. Johnson, the other two by Lawrence Krumenaker. See *Quill,* June 1992, 31–38.

5. Of course, these are bibliographic databases. That is, they contain citations of the articles and brief abstracts from which you can judge if the articles might be applicable to your needs. You must still track the articles down in the rest of the

library. This is pretty easy because the library has a list of all the publications it subscribes to and where to locate back copies. Moreover, it has a list of all the other publications available at all the other cooperating libraries in town.

But if you can't find the publication in town, don't despair. Look up the address in any number of publications directory and call the publication directly. They usually respond to journalists' requests for back copies promptly. If you don't want to take the time each week to run down the articles, see if you can set up a system where the copy aides will do it for you. And some libraries will do it for you, at a fee.

6. Make no mistake about it, you have a lot better chance of having a meaningful conversation with an expert once you've read some key articles he or she has written than you would by calling them cold. In addition, when I find a particularly insightful or provocative article, I also hunt down the next three issues of the magazine that ran the article to see if anyone has written a letter to the editor that might change my mind about the value of what I've written. And, of course, you could go on-line and ask the searcher to find articles in which this author was mentioned or footnoted. And, if it's a book, I often hunt down a handful of reviews to see what the experts thought of it and what I should know about any criticisms.

Databases Not Available in Your Librarian's Arsenal

by John Ullmann

Most news librarians depend on a handful of vendors for the databases they use: DataTimes, Dialog, Lexis and Nexis (from Mead Data Central), VuText and one or two others. However, there are many databases out there that aren't carried by the favored vendors. Here's a sampling that includes a partial description of the database holdings that might be of particular value to investigative reporters:

- Duns Legal Search contains information culled from public records on businesses in all 50 states, including UCC filings, suits, liens and judgments. (Offered on Dun & Bradstreet)
- Facilities Index System contains information on nearly a half million business and sites tracked by the Environmental Protection Agency (EPA) because of hazardous materials located there. (Chemical Information Systems)
- Family Tree contains information on the "family trees" of 200,000 corporations and their subsidies. (Dun & Bradstreet)
- FDA Electronic Bulletin Board contains a variety of information released by the Food and Drug Administration, including its weekly enforcement report about drugs under recall orders. (BT Tymnet Dialcom Service)
- GAO Reports and Testimony contains the full text of reports from the Government Accounting Office reports, the investigatory arm of Congress. (NewsNet)
- Government Activity Report contains information on businesses, foundations and educational institutions receiving money from the U.S. government. (Dun & Bradstreet)
- Long-term Forecast Database contains more than 3,000 yearly time series on U.S. economic data. (The WEFA Group)
- National Referral Center Database contains the names, addresses and phone numbers of 14,000 organizations willing to offer expert opinions. (LOCIS, the Library of Congress)
- People Finder contains the names, addresses and phone numbers (and sometimes date of birth, names of family members and neighbors and other information) of more than 100 million persons. (Information America)

- Prentice-Hall On-line contains credit information on 60 million people and business in nine states: California, Delaware, Florida, Illinois, Massachusetts, Missouri, New York, Pennsylvania and Texas. (Prentice-Hall On-line)
- Public Record Information contains 85 million public records covering such things as courts, Uniform Commercial Codes, liens, corporation filings, in 19 states. (Prentice-Hall On-line)
- Regional contains monthly and yearly time series of economic indicators for 19 states and 40 cities, MSAs and PMSAs. (General Electric Information Services)
- State Macro contains 47,000 monthly, quarterly and yearly economic data for each state. (WEFA Group)
- State UCC and Lien Filings contains the Uniform Commercial Code statements filed in 12 states: California, Colorado, Florida, Illinois, Iowa, Maryland, Massachusetts, Missouri, Nebraska, North Carolina, Pennsylvania and Texas.
- Tax Information Service contains information from the county tax assessor rolls in seven states: Arizona, California, Colorado, Indiana, Missouri, Ohio and Texas. (TRW Title Information Services)
- Title Information Service contains records from county clerks and recorders and bankruptcy courts for property in seven states: Arizona, California, Colorado, Indiana, Missouri, Ohio and Texas.
- Westlaw Federal Legislative History Database contains the public laws and, especially useful to reporters, the histories of the laws and any reports. (West Publishing Co.)
- Westlaw Federal Tax Database contains, among other tax information, all the Tax Court cases since 1954. (West Publishing Co.)
- Westlaw Government Contracts contains the text and headnotes on federal court decisions, including hearings by the Small Business Administration office and other courts. (Westlaw)

5

Using Social Science
Methods

Some of the tools of social science—including unob-
trusive measures, the census and survey—can be used
to elevate a project using more traditional reporting
tools. And sometimes, you can challenge the conven-
tionally held professional views of a situation by chal-
lenging their assumptions while producing outstanding
journalism.

To err is human but to really foul things up you need a computer.
—1978 Farmers' Almanac[1]

In November 1991, the *Star Tribune* cast a revealing, groundbreaking light on the way Minnesota punishes rapists. Reporters Allen Short and Donna Halvorsen, with the research help of Rob Daves, assistant managing editor/research, examined the records of 767 rapists and child molesters convicted of first-degree charges during the previous decade. Their findings included:

- The convicted rapists and child molesters accounted for nearly 3,000 rapes, an average of almost four apiece.
- Rapists who got psychological treatment in prison were rearrested more often than those who didn't.
- During most of the 1980s, Minnesota sentencing guidelines called for first-degree sex offenders to serve 43 months in prison. But 27 percent of them spent no time in prison, and those who did served an average of only 24 months.
- In 1989 the state legislature doubled the sentencing guideline to call for 86 months in prison. But in Hennepin County (Minneapolis) the following year, nearly half the first-degree sex criminals were given probation, combined with treatment and perhaps jail time. Some of them are already back on the street.

Here's the lead from the main story on the second day of the series:

> Minnesota is dispensing a gentle brand of justice that gives breaks to rapists and child molesters.
>
> It clings to the hope of rehabilitating sex criminals, but doesn't test to see if its psychological treatment programs keep them from attacking again. They don't.
>
> Its progressive programs have won Minnesota praise, but they have not made the state safer for its women and children.

It is worth taking a little more time to study how Short and Halvorsen came up with the findings for this series. Their approach shows that once you engage in primary research yourself (rather than merely accepting and quoting from research already done), you may find that things are not as they are accepted.

The three-day series contained a number of case studies detailing horrible stories about rapists, but the heart of the study was some good old-fashioned social science research. Here's how the newspaper explained the study to its readers:

The crime patterns of rapists and child molesters reported today are shocking, perhaps even frightening.

The reality is worse—far worse.

All studies of sex criminals, including this one, underestimate how many crimes they commit. This kind of research can only count recorded events such as arrests or convictions, a sex criminal's brush with the law. But the majority of rapes and other sexual attacks are never reported or, if reported, never solved.

Two years ago, a team of Oregon researchers reviewed dozens of major studies of sex criminals' careers. They concluded that because of design flaws and other errors, no study had produced a reliable measure of how often rapists repeat their crimes, or whether treatment had any effect in stopping them.

The newspaper's study was designed to avoid those flaws, and Dr. Lita Furby—a research psychologist who headed the Oregon team—served as a consultant in a final review of the findings.

"I don't recall a study that's done as good a job as this," said Furby. "There are very few that looked at recidivism rates year after year after year. The way the rates were calculated here is one of the few studies where it was done right."

There are many ways to not do it right. Some common research flaws include:

- Short follow-up periods. Many studies followed sex criminals for only a year or two after their release, not enough time to draw meaningful conclusions.
- Faulty study groups. Much of the research has focused on only a handful of sex criminals—too few to draw conclusions. Others have lumped all types of sex criminals together—rapists with incest offenders, for example—even though their patterns are as different as apples and oranges.
- Poor counting techniques. Many studies noted only subsequent convictions or returns to prison, failing to count such reliable indicators as arrests.
- Erroneous time calculations. Many studies were sloppy in calculating the time frames in which sex criminals committed later offenses; for example, many didn't deduct the time a rapist was in prison and therefore unable to commit another rape.

For the *Star Tribune* study, avoiding these problems was largely an investment of time. The work took nine months to complete.

Using records from several state agencies, the newspaper gathered the criminal and confinement histories for 932 first-degree sex criminals convicted between October 1980 and November 1989. Under Minnesota law, a first-degree conviction requires sexual penetration; many of these crimes also involved the use of a weapon, death threats, abduction or physical injury to the victim.

The information was assembled in a computer database for analysis, and the sex criminals were divided into three groups: rapists, child molesters and incest offenders. A total of 392 rapists and 375 molesters were examined, together and separately. (A group of 165 incest offenders, whose patterns are very different, was studied by itself.)

Arrest dates were isolated for two groups of crime: sex crimes and "serious" crimes (including not only sex offenses but also assault, burglary, domestic violence, robbery and murder). Entry and exit dates for prison and treatment were also recorded. Events after March 31, 1991— the end of the study period—were excluded.

Each sex criminal was tracked from the date of his release from custody on his first-degree charge. If he was arrested for a later sex crime, he became a repeat offender. The time between release and arrest was calculated in each case, and actuarial methods were used to compute arrest rates for groups of repeat offenders.

For some purposes, the study also looked at offenses prior to the first-degree charge to compare patterns of one-time offenders with two-, three- and four-time offenders.

The newspaper's research avoided many stumbling blocks of previous studies: the study group was large; rapists were separated from child molesters; the maximum follow-up period was nine years; arrests were counted; and confinement time was considered.

As a result, the statistics are more accurate than those found in other sex criminal studies. They are also more horrifying. For example, a quarter of the rapists were arrested for new sex crimes after just six years of freedom. And rapists and child molesters who completed treatment were more like to be arrested again than those who did not.

"I was really surprised they were as high as this, because I know what a small percentage of them get into the record," said Furby, referring to the rearrest rates. "We keep finding more offenses as we follow more years." [2]

Where were the records found?
As the newspaper told its readers, three state agencies provided the data:

- From the Sentencing Guidelines Commission (SGC) the newspaper got the names of 767 rapists and child molesters convicted of first-degree charges between 1980 and 1989. Information included all felony convictions during the 1980s; some convictions prior to 1980; actual sentences in 1980s; and the criminal history scores used in applying sentencing guidelines.
- From the Bureau of Criminal Apprehension (BCA) the newspaper got complete computerized criminal histories assembled by BCA from police agencies and other sources around the state, including such information as arrests, charges filed, some details of crimes, and court actions for most of the 767 criminals identified in SGC records.
- From the Department of Corrections the newspaper got the following information about those sex criminals who actually went to state prisons: prison admissions (locations and dates); prison discharge dates; treatment admissions (locations and dates); treatment discharges; treatment outcomes (whether the criminal completed the program, was rejected during treatment, dropped out or was still in the program).

Why has this project been singled out? It illustrates how some of the best journalism ties itself firmly to social science methods and how, sometimes, existing social science can be supplanted by doing it better.

Committing Social Science

Elsewhere in this book are several brief discussions about what investigative reporting and the social sciences have in common. This chapter explores four ways reporters can elevate their projects by using methods traditionally left to researchers in the social sciences: 1) unobtrusive measures; 2) a census; 3) a survey; 4) making it up.

Unobtrusive Measures

Suppose you wanted to know which painting is the most popular at the local art museum. How would you find out?

You could ask people—that is, survey patrons—as they left the museum over a period of days or weeks. But surveys are not without their problems. They demand a certain kind of rigor and specific methodologies—the very act of your asking may influence and distort the responses. Surveying is one of the more expensive ways to get answers, not to mention time-consuming; it's more work than our editors want to commit to for answering the question.

You could go into the museum yourself and try to watch, but that, too, involves many problems. First, you've never been there before and it may take you days to get over the novelty. Second, what's going on in the rooms you aren't observing, since you're stationed in but one at a time?

You could ask people you might expect to know, such as the guards or the museum management, but anecdotal information is rarely that persuasive.

You could measure the wear in the tiles in front of each picture to see which tiles have deteriorated the most from footsteps. That's a good way and one we all might accept as the answer.[3]

That's an unobtrusive measure. On reflection, unobtrusive measures are a mainstay of investigative reporters. Afterall, following the paper trail is exactly that—an unobtrusive measure. It's unobtrusive because the reporter had nothing to do with the creation of the paper, and the person or business backgrounded is unaffected by you looking at the documents. The documents have already been created. They are the daily detritus left by us all as we walk this earth.

A Project Predicated on Unobtrusive Measures

> Like a latent fingerprint found at a crime scene, a clear pattern has appeared in the vast sprawl of destruction left by Hurricane Andrew.
>
> The storm's deadly imprint emerged from a three-month *Miami Herald* investigation that used computers to analyze 60,000 damage inspection reports.
>
> A computer created a color-coded map showing how 420 neighborhoods weathered the storm. When a map of estimated wind zones was superimposed over the damage, the pattern became unmistakable: Many of the worst-hit neighborhoods were far from the worst winds. . . . Newer houses did worse than older ones.
>
> A lot worse, in fact. Houses built since 1980 were 68 percent more likely to be uninhabitable after the hurricane than homes built earlier.

Thus began a 16-page special report on December 20, 1992, by Jeff Leen, Stephen K. Doig and Lisa Getter. It is an outstanding example of how unobtrusive measures can be used to produce a terrific project.

Among the *Herald*'s findings in their report, which contributed to winning a Pulitzer Prize in 1993, were these:

There was ample evidence of breakdowns in the construction and inspection safeguards meant to protect the public from exactly the sort of devastation dealt out by Andrew.

A close examination of eight storm-damaged subdivisions built by some of Dade's largest developers revealed houses shot through with so many construction and design flaws they became easy targets for the hurricane.

Building inspectors, faced with a boom in construction, were pressured to perform up to four times the number of inspections that should properly be done in a day.

Here's the newspaper's explanation to its readers of how the project was conducted:

Many of the conclusions in this special report come from computer analyses conducted by *The Miami Herald* on information derived from several large databases. These databases include:

■ A special database of more than 50,000 storm-damage inspections done by Dade County in the area south of Kendal Drive through early December.

■ The 1992 Dade County property tax roll, which contains detailed information about the location, type (single-family, apartment, condo, etc.), value year of construction, size of home and lot, and ownership status of the more than 100,000 residential parcels south of Kendal Drive.

■ The county's Building Master File, which contains information about type of construction and materials used for each building in Dade.

■ The county's Building and Zoning database, with more than 7 million records on all building permits issued in the past decade and all inspections done since 1987. This database identifies the contractors, architects, engineers and building inspectors who worked on each house, and gives the results of each inspection.

The county damage inspections database varied considerably in the amount of damage recorded. Many reports lacked specific details on damage; however, every inspection included an overall assessment of the home's condition in one of three categories: "habitable," "uninhabitable but repairable" or "destroyed."

The available damage inspections cover two-thirds of the housing units in the storm area. About 25 percent of the inspection addresses either weren't residential or didn't match addresses in the property tax roll. However, several statistical tests were performed to ensure that the inspected addresses represented a valid sample.

The damage maps in this section are based on reports through mid-November. Other statistics include data updated from the latest batch of reports, which were received less than a week ago and after the deadline for printing the graphics.

The four databases—totaling more than 45 reels of magnetic tape—were merged and analyzed on the *Herald*'s mainframe computer.

The analysis compared the damage categories against such variables as distance from the center of the storm, value, square footage, lot size, type of home, building materials, direction facing and year of construction.

Also, to examine the influence of the building industry on the Metro Commission, the *Herald* acquired paper copies of all the required campaign contributions reports for every major commission candidate since 1980.

The *Herald* hired Data Entry Professional Services of Miami to create a computer record for each contribution of $100 or more, including the contributor's name, address, stated occupation, date of contribution and the candidate who got it.

The result was a custom database of more than 17,200 contribution records totaling more than $8.3 million. This data was analyzed on the *Herald*'s computer to produce the total amounts given by those connected to the building industry.

The computer analyses of storm damage and campaign contributions were done using SAS, a major mainframe statistical program. Supplementary analysis also was done using Atlas-GIS, a microcomputer-based geographical information system mapping program, and Statistica, a statistical graphing program. The analyses were done by Stephen K. Doig, the *Herald*'s associate editor/research.[4]

The Census

In 1984, *Star Tribune* reporters Tom Hamburger and Joe Rigert began to look at how minority contracts were given out and administered in Minnesota. It was a project I supervised.

The way it was supposed to work is that 10 percent of government contracts were to be awarded to qualified minority- or woman-owned construction companies.[5] (This was an effort to overcome the problem of white males having a stranglehold on the industry.)

What Rigert and Hamburger found was massive abuse. Millions of dollars each year went to "front" companies—companies owned by minorities or women in name only—that would take their 10 percent of multimillion dollar contracts, and then subcontract back most of the money to white, male-owned construction companies; minority firms got none of the work.

One of the questions we wanted to answer was whether the legitimate minority contractors thought fronting was a big problem.

To find out, we and the news research arm of the newspaper designed a questionnaire. The researchers then contacted virtually all of the 400 minority contractors certified by the city of Minneapolis. Among the questions were those related to how the contractors would rank their biggest problems— fronting, government paperwork, capitalization, knowledge of the business, size. In addition, we asked minority contractors if they had been recently approached to act as a front, and if any of them had acted as fronts. The interviewers promised the contractors anonymity.

The research office was tremendously aggressive, getting to all but two or three of the contractors. One contractor, who was Vietnamese, decided about halfway through the telephone interview he didn't know English. A Vietnamese speaker was found, but halfway through the new interview, the contractor decided he no longer knew Vietnamese and hung up.

When the results first came in, the researcher told us that the contractors ranked the problem of fronting dead last. We were devastated. Here we just spent several thousand dollars on a survey to find out that minority contractors themselves were downplaying the problem. Of course, we'd have to report the findings. I began to compose paragraphs in my head that started like this: "Even though Minneapolis minority contractors themselves don't think fronting is a major problem compared to other hurdles they face, nevertheless . . ."

A few hours later, the research director on this project came back to our office and told us they had mistakenly reversed the finding, and that the contractors actually thought fronting was their number-one problem. Moreover, dozens had been asked to be fronts and about half had agreed at least once.

These were powerful findings and added measurably to the strength of our conclusions.

Survey

In 1986, *Star Tribune* reporters Mary Jane Smetanka, the newspaper's education reporter, and Paul McEnroe, a national reporter who frequently does investigations for the newspaper, began to probe the Twin Cities teens for a series on drug use, a project I also supervised.[6]

It turns out that a lot of teens in the Twin Cities were using drugs. Of course, we were stunned. "Wow, kids are using drugs. I wonder if anyone else knows. Maybe we should tell them." Which we did, in six incredibly compelling days.

Perhaps the most powerful conclusions in this series were the insights gained through a survey of more than 5,000 teenagers conducted in the suburban schools around the Twin Cities.[7] Again, working with the newspaper's research team, we designed a survey to administer to the students.

It was patterned after a survey administered nationally by researchers at University of Michigan and had numerous filter questions to be sure the students weren't scamming us. (If anything, drug use was under-reported.)

I was particularly interested in why kids who used drugs did so and why those that didn't use them didn't.

What we found was that strong parents and strong religious beliefs were the best predictors of students who would stay away from drugs. Moreover, it turns out that "Reefer Madness" was right. That is, alcohol abuse was a gateway drug to marijuana abuse, which was a gateway to cocaine abuse, which was a gateway to worse drugs.

There were strong prescriptions for teen drug abuse in our findings and in our case studies. In many ways, the survey overwhelmed the more traditional reporting efforts by the insight gained and the power of those insights when based upon more than 5,000 surveys.

The survey was on page one for several days, including the first and last, and mentioned throughout the series. It was invaluable, even though it cost tens of thousands of dollars.

So what's the difference between a census and a survey? A census asks questions of virtually everyone in the targeted population. A survey does a random sampling of a small part of the population and claims that its results are representative of the whole population of people even though the entire population is not actually asked.

As these two projects show, a census or a survey can add measureably to the power of your projects and both should be made a part of your arsenal, when appropriate.

Some Warnings About Surveys

It doesn't take much math nor too much experience to conduct and analyze a census. Surveys are a much different matter, however.

When news organizations have professionals conduct a random survey for them, they usually tell their readers and viewers that it was a "scientific" survey or poll. It's true that the mathematics used to analyze the survey is scientific—that is, there is a science related to the math itself, and how it is used.

The rest of what the term describes is really just plain, old hogwash. There is no science related to selecting the population, writing the questionnaire or interpreting the results. As the old saw goes, any discipline that puts "science" in its name isn't.

That's not to imply that a competently done survey isn't "accurate" or "right." Political polling will show you the power of accurately predicting, once it's done close to an election and those surveyed are only people who will vote.

There are many rules that need to be followed when constructing a questionnaire, administering it and evaluating the responses. But after you avoid breaking the rules, finding the meaning is art, not science; experience, not mere training; craft, not rote.

The best book about the rules is *The Newsroom Guide to Polls and Surveys,* by Indiana University professors G. Cleveland Wilhoit and David H. Weaver. This little booklet was published in 1980 by the American Newspaper Publishers Association, which now calls itself the National Newspaper Association (NNA). (You can obtain a copy by contacting the NNA in Reston, Va.) The book takes the approach of telling you how not to be taken in by the innumerable survey and poll results flooding every newsroom every day.

This is a much better approach than trying to teach you how to conduct surveys, as many journalism schools try to do. The idea of a journalist conducting a survey is akin to asking a journalist who has taken a media law course to defend you in a libel suit. Sheer suicide.

However, making sense of all this stuff is what daily and project reporters are confronted with frequently by the so-called news releases that flood in. To get good at this, I think you should go back to school and take a course in social science research methods. However, I think you should make a deal with the instructor on the conditions:

- You want to spend the bulk of the time on interpreting, not conducting.
- You want the language of instruction to be English, not Statistics.
- You want a reading list of the best books on interpretation and weekly one-on-one sessions with the instructor on what the books mean.
- If you have to have a grade in the class, let's just agree at the beginning it will be an A.

Making It Up

Making it up is harder than it sounds.

The reason: I'm not referring to fiction.

Sometimes the way to measure something, the way to evaluate something, has yet to articulated.

So what's a poor journalist to do.

In the first sidebar to this chapter, Tom Hamburger tells you how he, Joe Rigert, Dan Sullivan and I devised a way to evaluate the performance of Minnesota's Public Utilities Commission related to whether or not they had been fair to the people paying the bills—the public—or overly generous to the huge companies they regulate—the telephone companies and energy providers.

We had invaluable help from Dan Sullivan, who still spends most of his time at the *Star Tribune* on important issues such as market reach and company performance issues. For us, he made better use of his Ph.D. in economics from Yale University and his former editorship of the *Northern California Review of Business and Economics* by devising a method to answer the main questions.

Hamburger's sidebar gives you all the details.

Emphasized here is the constant need in projects to settle on a method, or series of methods, that evaluates performance and allows you to come to conclusions about your findings.

Remember, it's the conclusions we are after. The facts are not enough. And social science methods are often the only way you can write with explanatory power about what is going on.

Paradigm Shift: Part One

For many years, the dominant form of research in the social sciences has been the survey, augmented by a dizzying and difficult set of mathematical tools.

But there are other methods.

One of them is spelled out by Jack D. Douglas in his 1976 book, *Investigative Social Research.*[8]

The investigative paradigm is based on the assumption that profound conflicts of interest, values, feelings and actions pervade social life. It is taken for granted that many of the people one deals with, perhaps all people to some extent, have good reason to hide from others what they are doing and even to lie to them. Instead of trusting people and expecting trust in return, one suspects others and expects others to suspect him (or her). Conflict is the reality of life; suspicion is the guiding principle. As those involved in using the paradigm love to put it, "Life is a jungle and all the animals in it are predators." It's a war of all against all and no one gives anyone anything for nothing, especially truth. The "do-gooders" who trust others and expect them to tell the truth are looked at as kooks, "do-do birds" destined for extinction. Sure, people tell the truth most of the time in their everyday lives, at least as they see it. How often do people bother to lie about the weather or where the salt is? But the outsider trying to find out what the truth is about the things that count most to people, such as money and sex, must look upon all their accounts of those things as suspicious until proven otherwise.

Spies, counterspies, police, detectives, prosecutors, judges, psychiatrists, tax collectors, probation officers, child protective service workers, FCC staff, FDA staff, NLRB staff, investigative journalists and all others involved in the vast array of investigative occupations in modern society are the most obvious practitioners of the investigative paradigm. They share the paradigm in its most extreme and pure form. But business people of all kinds, especially business people who must deal with strangers, also share it to varying degrees. Indeed, wherever there exist important conflicts which members of society recognize, individuals use some form of the investigative paradigm in ferreting out the truth about others' intentions, thoughts, feelings and actions. Any suspicious lover can suddenly turn into a dedicated investigator, showing how available the basic ideas of the investigative paradigm are to all members of society." [9]

And what is the major ingredient to the investigative paradigm? Well, it seems that what you do is: You go out there and look for yourself, not just ask a bunch of people you never met through a survey. And God knows, you don't just believe it because they told you. You've got to find some corroborating evidence, or conflicting evidence.

You and I call that reporting.

Later chapters of his book describe how to do this type of social science work, including sections titled, "Understanding and Reporting on the Research Setting," "Infiltrating the Setting," "Building Friendly Trust and Opening Them Up," "Setting Them Up" and "Adversary and Discombobulation Tactics," among others. In fact, if you explore the methodology books of many social sciences, you'll find chapters on how to find, train and deal with "informants," as well as many painful chapters on related ethical issues.

Paradigm Shift: Part Two

More recently, really just in the 1980s, you will find that many researchers in the social sciences have rebeled against what you and I were taught as the scientific method, and against the survey and most mathematical models of any kind.

The movement has a number of names, like naturalistic inquiry or, in journalism research circles, qualitative (as opposed to quantitative) studies.

The main component of this kind of research is that after reading everything about the area of study, the researcher then spends a great deal of time with just one or two members of the specific population and generalizes from them to the larger population unaided by statistics, relying instead on thinking about what you've heard and what you've seen.

There are dozens of qualitative studies from numerous disciplines examining the news media. In fact, one is discussed in Appendix Three of this book.

If you lay two research reports side by side, one based on statistical sampling and the other based on a few in-depth interviews, you usually will find that the later report is written better, comes to stronger conclusions, is more useful and certainly more interesting.

Qualitative researchers people are thinkers and this wave of research will become the norm.

Conclusion

Four suggestions:

1. Don't ask your editors for permission to commit social science research. Ask instead if you may involve a researcher to find answers to some particular thorny question.
2. Go out to the local university, college or even school district, and find one or two researchers doing the most interesting stuff and attach yourself to them to learn, borrow or steal their way of thinking about things.
3. Go back to night school for one class on social science research. Better yet, go to day school and get the time off with pay and the company to pay the enrollment fees.

4. Do look for ways that social science methods can elevate your projects, then do something about it.

NOTES

1. Quoted in The Oxford Dictionary of Quotations, (Oxford: Oxford University Press, 1992), 19.

2. The data was loaded into Paradox on stand-alone PCaz and into a PC network; the initial data was provided to the newspaper on floppy disks and was copied into Paradox. Other data from hard copy and disk were also entered into Paradox and, after cleaning, uploaded onto an IBM mainframe to use SAS (Statistical Analysis System) because Paradox couldn't do the statistical analysis that was needed.

3. This example—measuring the tiles—is purloined from a truly outstanding book: "Unobtrusive Measures: Nonreactive Research in the Social Sciences," by Eugene J. Webb, Donald T. Campbell, Richard D. Schwartz and Lee Sechrest (Chicago: Rand McNally College Publishing Co., 1966).

4. "What Went Wrong," *Miami Herald,* December 20, 1992, 15SR.

5. "Women and Minority Contracts/Blueprint for Abuse," by Tom Hamburger and Joe Rigert, supervised by John Ullmann, *Star Tribune,* September 30 and October 1, 1984.

6. "Teens and Drugs," *Star Tribune,* December 14–19, 1986, 1 ff. Tom Hamburger later joined us as assistant city editor working directly with the reporters on a day-to-day basis.

7. It would have been better had we been allowed into the Minneapolis schools, but we weren't. So we oversampled for the characteristics of the Minneapolis school population.

8. "Investigative Social Research/Individual and Team Research," Jack D. Douglas (Beverly Hills: Sage Publications, 1976.)

9. Ibid., 55–56. The seven major problems to overcome are misinformation, evasions, lies, fronts, taken-for-granted meanings, problematic meanings and self deception (see page 57).

How Social Science Techniques Can Elevate an Investigation

by Tom Hamburger, *Star Tribune*

The nervous voice held promise of great scandal, which in Minnesota was hard to come by. So in the fading light of a December afternoon, I stayed on the line, encouraging and cajoling, ignoring my aching ear and a promise to cook dinner.

It involved, she said after much prompting, the state Public Utilities Commission, the obscure but important body that approves rates charged by gas, electric and telephone companies.

"Sport tickets."

Utility executives, our source alleged, had provided commissioners with occasional tickets to ball games. Big deal.

The story received good play on page one, only because it was a slow news day. I never dreamed it would lead to a broad-scale consumer story that would make its way to the United States Supreme Court—and change forever the character of Minnesota's regulatory politics.

The day after the story appeared brought another anonymous caller. Then I received another and then another. Projects boss John Ullmann assigned veteran investigative reporter Papa Joe Rigert to help field the calls.

From across the newsroom we smiled, gave thumbs up and nodded in agreement. There was too much here. The sports ticket caper was clearly part of a broader pattern.

Our callers alleged that some commissioners received not only sports tickets, but partially subsidized vacations, below-cost automobiles, travel, theater invitations and other gratuities.

Some were promised jobs at high salaries when they left their relatively low-paying commission jobs. These job offers were sometimes made while high-stakes rate cases were being considered by the quasijudicial panel.

The most serious accusation was that one member of the commission had received a handsome consulting fee from Northwestern Bell Telephone and had never disclosed it, all the while voting on Bell rate cases.

Since the commission had recently approved a $53 million rate increase for the phone company, we decided to follow the "consulting fee" allegation first.

If such payments were made, they should have been disclosed in the commissioner's ethics disclosure forms. A check at the state capitol showed no such disclosure.

Following the Money

Our source was willing to talk with us, meet with us and guide us, providing we guaranteed anonymity. We did—and on the following Friday afternoon we met our Deep Throat in a downtown St. Paul bar called Smugglers Inn.

The Inn was a dark watering hole with a central fireplace surrounded by red leather swivel chairs. This story, that once seemed so prim and dull, now had at least one scene from a cheap detective novel.

Our source told us that Bell paid a large fee to a St. Paul law firm, which then passed the money to the commissioner. Our source knew the name of the firm.

To flush out the truth, we decided to make simultaneous calls to all key parties.

Feverish activity paid off. At the end of the afternoon, the principal targets were calling back. We honed in on a single member of the law firm, who finally confirmed that he had made pay-outs to "a fellow-lobbyist working on behalf of phone interests." We then decided to confront phone company executives and utility commission officials with the evidence we had accumulated.

During a hastily arranged interview, a Bell executive then confirmed that his company had paid $30,000 in stages to the firm, with the last payment arriving after the date the commissioner had joined the commission. Bell did not confirm paying the commissioner the money, so we went directly to the source.

The commissioner dodged us at first. We staked out his apartment in downtown St. Paul.

After we had left dozens of messages he finally called saying only that he would be getting in touch with us over the weekend.

On Saturday afternoon, the commissioner confirmed that, yes, he had received one payment while on the commission—for lobbying work he had done on behalf of Northwestern Bell conducted before he joined the rate-setting panel.

The amount was so small, he said, he neglected to include it on his financial disclosure report.

The small amount, he confirmed, was $30,000.

Before we could ask further questions about his relationship with the company he regulated, he told us he was resigning from the commission, effective immediately.

Our copyrighted story headed the *Star Tribune*'s Sunday edition. It ran also across the front page of the rival *St. Paul Pioneer Press*—attributed to us.

A Bigger Picture

The following week, Rigert, Ullmann and I received more calls about more favors that had allegedly been offered to commissioners. Nearly all utility companies were implicated in some way, but most of the callers and the most disturbing examples involved Northwestern Bell. Some of the allegations could be confirmed quickly, others would take weeks.

As we sorted through the growing list of favors and alleged favors the bigger question occurred to us: Was there a way to show what impact these favors had on ratepayers of Minnesota? Perhaps we could show how Minnesota phone rates compared with other states and whether relationships changed as favors occurred.

We almost gave up. The complex and arcane world of utility regulation was difficult to understand. Our utility contacts told us that the state-to-state differences made it impossible to really compare one commission to another. No way, they said.

Through fortunate coincidence we learned that there was a way.

Developing a Hypothesis and Way to Test It

Ullmann, a master of getting others to loan expertise to projects, went to the director of research to borrow a statistician for a "few days." You don't need a statistician, you need an economist he was told. You got one? Yes.

That's how we met Dan Sullivan.

Sullivan, like so many geniuses and parents of five, lets his appearance go. The effect can be rather unnerving. His hair was perpetually disheveled. His tie, if it was on, would be thrown over his shoulder as if he had just walked through a wind tunnel.

Eyes always gravitated to Dan's shoes, which bore a dozen white lines where salt and snow had left their mark the previous season. He always came late. But while Dan dressed sloppy, he thought clearly.

His training—Ph.D. in Economics from Yale, several years as an analyst with the U.S. Justice Department, teaching experience in the University of California system—was perfect for this assignment.

Sullivan was clear about what we could and could not do. Social science, he told us, could not help us make a normative judgment about what the PUC did.

"Data is simply a form of evidence about things that happen. Whether those things are good or bad depends on the readers' values.

"We can't claim that the way the PUC voted was wrong. For all I know their decisions were right. All you can test is whether the panel has been more favorable to Northwestern Bell than were other PUCs to the companies they regulated," Sullivan said.

Before beginning work assembling data on the relative performance of Minnesota's PUC, Sullivan told us he believed "data should reach a conclusion. If you gather data to say 'on the one hand it means this and, on the other hand, that,' you haven't added much."

Given what we had seen, we developed a reasonable hypothesis and we wanted to test it. That's what social science is all about: testing a hypothesis empirically.

And what was the hypothesis we wished to test? Danny suggested this: "Did the pattern of intense lobbying from Northwestern Bell influence the commission to the detriment of Minnesota's ratepayers?"

After agreeing to the question, we brainstormed over how to test it. Again, social science dictated. To determine whether Minnesota ratepayers were "worse off" we needed a group to compare them to.

Sullivan suggested that we find comparable sets and the first choice was obvious: Northwestern Bell (NWB) operates in several states and the company's relationship with regulators should be roughly similar.

When we showed a rough study draft comparing Minnesota to the four other NWB states, Bell and PUC officials objected that the sample was too small to draw conclusions from.

So, we broadened the comparison, adding 18 additional states.

Although circumstances varied in each state, regulatory experts confirmed that the task facing utility regulators in all states is basically the same: to balance the interests of ratepayers with those of the utilities.

Ultimately we developed three different groupings for comparison.

- The five states served by Northwestern Bell because they were nearby and regulated the same company;
- The 14 states served by U.S. West. Since all were served by the same parent company we believed that large differences could generally be attributed to differences in regulatory behavior;
- The eight other Midwest states that regulated other companies. This group was intended to serve as a check of the first two.

Look for a Pattern of Outcomes

"Don't focus on any single measure, but on the overall pattern of outcomes," Sullivan cautions. "One test isn't convincing; you need many of them because no single test tells you much."

That's why we developed 14 measures of rates, profits and regulatory climate to compare between Minnesota and the 26 other states. The 14 measures in the study included a comparison of the quality of each state's regulatory environment as rated by Wall Street investment houses; basic residential rates authorized in each state; the percentage of utility requests granted by each commission; and authorized profit levels for each state's Bell company.

Compiling the information for each category took from March until midsummer.

But it was worth it. We found that Minnesota was the only state in which the telephone company came out above average on every measure. In other words, it showed that the Minnesota commission was consistently more receptive to Bell requests than the commissions in 21 other states between 1980 and 1985.

Most significant to consumers, we found that Minnesota's telephone rates were through the roof compared with rates in most other states. As of 1985, Minnesota had the highest urban residential phone rates in the five states served by Northwestern Bell. And the rate differences were sometimes dramatic. In metropolitan Denver, which is roughly comparable to the Twin Cities in population and toll-free calling area, residential customers paid $8.80 a month for telephone service in 1985, roughly half of the $16.76 average rate in the Twin Cities.

As the evidence rolled in, we were hooting and hollering. "This proves they were out to soak the Minnesota ratepayer," we said. Sullivan cautioned us harshly.

Don't Overinterpret

His study, Sullivan pointed out, did *not* conclude that Bell was out to screw ratepayers. It did not deal with intent at all.

"It's entirely possible that the process by which they influenced the decision occurred in a way that they were unaware of the possible outcome. In fact, they may have been pro-ratepayer at heart. This study doesn't address their intent."

In the absence of inside sources telling us the company's motivation, we could not speculate. We were obliged to use the company's official position to explain why they repeatedly requested higher rates in Minnesota.

Prepare for Challenges

The first major objection will be data quality, Sullivan predicted. But he was ready for that.

"I knew that we couldn't defend all of our data as 100 percent correct," Sullivan said.

But thanks to the multiplicity of states and factors that were considered, a series of systematic errors would have had to occur to change our conclusion.

"Social scientists don't assume their data is error free. They assume errors are random."

To anticipate challenges, we decided to send our study drafts to the utilities and the commissioners for a critique before publication.

(The PUC told us that they were taking the position that our study could be released to competing news organizations, just like any other document they had in their files. This caused us quite a bit of concern until Ullmann pointed out the obvious. If anybody ran it, they'd had to say "a *Star Tribune* study has shown . . ." And we'd marked every page with a red stamp exclaiming "not ready for publication," a motto that fits the projects office. He was right. No other news organization used it before we published the finished version.)

With each organization—the commission, NWB, the attorney general's office and another utility companies—we went over each page of the report and its conclusions. When they said we erred, we went back and checked. We tried to look at it as critically as they did, adopting their suggestions wherever and whenever we could.

When telephone officials suggested that we had used the wrong data set for cross-state comparisons, we tried using other data to see if the outcome changed. It did not. Time and again we found that Bell was treated better in Minnesota than comparable phone companies were in other states.

After three weeks of responding to criticisms and suggestions from Bell, the attorney general's office and the commission staff, we felt we had answered primary and technical objections. In essence, the company and the state agencies had proofed our story for us.

From the ferocity of the response to our initial comparison drafts, we still anticipated strong efforts to attack our credibility after the articles appeared.

The Comfort of Consulting National Experts

To further test the soundness of our study we decided to hire a top regulatory expert to review it and help respond to questions and comments lodged by critics.

Indeed, many of the waves of highly technical questions or complaints about our methodology from Bell economists and state regulators could not have been answered without access to experts.

Among our experts was David Chessler, Ph.D., a private consultant who had just left a senior faculty post at Ohio State's National Regulatory Research Institute, the academic center of utility research.

When Chessler pronounced our study sound, fair and accurate, we felt confident—and slept well the night before publication. The project ran August 10, 1986.

The Articles

The project was published under an umbrella headline that said, "PUC's Generosity Helped Bell" and an underline that said, "Study finds PUC gave company high rates and profits." We reported the above information, but tied it back to the investigative stories we had run earlier with paragraphs such as these:

> The high rates were approved in Minnesota during an era when Bell greatly increased its lobbying effort and several commissioners became involved in conflicts of interest.
>
> Between 1982 and 1985 Bell took three commissioners and a key staff member to lunch hundreds of times and discussed matters that would later come before the PUC. In addition, the company offered jobs to two sitting commissioners, one of whom voted on a Bell case after discussing a possible consulting job.

In addition to citing the criticisms lodged by Bell and the PUC high in the main story, we also wrote a separate article highlighting their disagreements. Under a headline that said, "Bell, PUC Criticize Methods, Results in Paper's Study," the article started this way: "Northwestern Bell and the PUC disputed the methodology, accuracy, fairness and conclusions of the *Star* and *Tribune* comparative study and urged the newspaper not to publish it."

The Reaction

As predicted, Bell came down hard on the study. With Sullivan and Chessler on our team we felt confident discussing the toughest complaints.

The paper's work on the PUC cases drew a strong response from the PUC and the community.

About six months after the story appeared, the PUC voted to reopen a Northwestern Bell rate case that had been decided at a time commissioners were being excessively wined, dined and provided job offers.

Ultimately, the commission ordered Bell to refund about $40 million to its customers.

From the private sector came a civil suit seeking class-action damages from Bell for violating the RICO act by engaging in a "pattern of racketeering activity" in illegally influencing the commissioners. Bell sought to throw the case out and succeeded until 1989, when the case went to the Supreme Court.

The principal question before the Court was whether Bell's activities constituted a criminal pattern as defined in the law. Our articles revealed a pattern of aggressive lobbying by Bell officials offering meals, job offers and other amenities to PUC members as they were about to vote on rate cases. Lawyers arguing the RICO case cited our findings as proof of "a pattern of improper, criminal behavior." The court ruled that Bell could be tried under RICO.

The most gratifying development, however, has been visible only recently. In the years since the newspaper's stories appeared, the pattern of high-powered lunching and lobbying commissioners ceased. And after several years of being a pro-utility commission, Minnesota's PUC returned to its place as a utility regulator that considers the consumer's interests.

(Tom Hamburger is the Washington bureau chief for the *Star Tribune* in Minneapolis-St. Paul and is a longtime project reporter.)

Ullmann's Ten Rules for Understanding Science, Social and Antisocial

by John Ullmann

Rule One

Did you hear about the statistician who didn't believe what he read in the morning newspaper so he bought 1,000 more copies to increase the sample size?[1]

If the sample isn't random, it doesn't make any difference how big the sample size is. The results cannot be used to describe the population in general. The results only describe the people who responded.

Rule Two

The same statistician was afraid of flying, fearing that a terrorist had planted a bomb on board. But because he was a professional in dealing with numbers, he called the government and got the statistics for the number of planes that actually do crash because of a bomb detonating. It's a small number. He thought about it for awhile, and called back for the number of airplanes with two bombs on them. That's a really, really small number. Satisfied, the statistician now carries a bomb on all flights.

Sometimes true numbers have no real meaning. Remember, correlation is not cause. That's the chief potential problem in all the campaign finance reports juxtaposed with voting records. The numbers cannot tell us whether Politician A voted the way he did on Issue A because he got $50,000 from Political Group A, which also favors Politician A's position as expressed in votes. Did he get the money because he already shared the position or did he get the money and then change his position to reflect the will of the moneygivers? (Or, are other options more logical?)

That's not to say that these stories have no value. Out here in the real world, things sometimes appear to be so logically correlated that it is worth reporting. You must, however, not rely on just the numbers. Number correlation by itself does not establish cause.

Rule Three

Three statisticians are on patrol in Vietnam when a sniper pins them down. The first statistician fires off a round, but misses 10 feet to the right. The second statistician fires, but is 10 feet to the left. They wait in vain for the third to shoot. Exasperated, they yell at him to fire. "No need," he responds haughtily, "he's already dead. If you'll just bother to compute the average, you'll see that I'm right."

No figure is more poorly used by scientists or journalists than the "average." If right now you calculated the averages of all the pieces of furniture in the room where you're reading this book, you'd come up with three numbers— the height average, the width average and the depth average. None of these averages, however arranged, either separately or together, adequately describes a single item in the room. Never forget the value of asking for the range and mode, and for an adequate explanation of what the averages are calculated from.

Rule Four

Way back when, a fellow living in a desert kept hearing from returning travelers about how delicious apples are. He was so moved by the glowing reports, he decided to travel north to the land where apples grew. Upon arrival, he was directed to the nearest orchard. There he found hundreds of apple trees in bloom. In truth, these "apples" smelled great. He tasted many petals, sampling more than 100. However, they were either tasteless or bitter. He concluded from his firsthand experiment that apples are greatly overrated and henceforth "refuted" all claims to the contrary, based on his personal, extensive investigation.

Even science that is published in journals is not always on point to what it claims to be showing. Generally, journalists too frequently give up their professional skepticism when covering scientists and the findings of their work. Be skeptical.

Rule Five

A mathematician, an engineer and an accountant were chatting when a kid came by looking for the answer to a homework problem: What is the square root of four?

"Are we talking integers here, or natural numbers?" asked the mathematician. The kid looked blank. "Okay, never mind. It's plus two or minus two."

"I can make that considerably more precise," said the engineer, whipping out a calculator. "It's 1.99762, correct to four decimal places."

"You two are forgetting the most important thing," said the accountant, giving the kid a penetrating look. "Tell me—what do you want the square root of four to be?"

Elsewhere in this book I suggest that you hire outside experts as consultants—hire, because you want their full attention during the time it takes to evaluate your work. I try always to choose from the most esteemed and politically removed experts available, and I always charge them with the task of rebutting or refuting our work. I hope it isn't possible for them to do that, but if it is, I want to know before publication, not afterward.

I always inform readers that the expert quoted was hired and the expert is only used to offer opinions as to the methodology of the study and conclusions drawn by the journalist. And, of course, that the expert we hired is not the only expert whose opinions we sought.

A tangential point is to find out who funded any studies you plan to quote or write about, whether on a project or daily story. If you've ever covered a meeting where risk assessment experts on both sides of an issue testified, you will realize that who is paying for the assessment often preordains the results.

Remember the old saw: There are two kinds of scientific fact—those that support a proponent's view 100 percent and those that are very difficult to interpret. Or, sawed another way, In God We Trust, but all others must share their data.

Rule Six

Newsperson's addendum: Where can you publish a statement that you can't prove, that you don't understand, that isn't true and that has been published before by someone else? In any newspaper.

Of course, that's the stuff of daily journalism. But in projects, you have been given the time to really understand something. That was your assignment. Be sure that you do.

Rule Seven

Human curiosity is a funny thing. How else to explain the fact that reporters always want to know what clergymen think about sex and what biologists think about God?

The distinguished British geneticist J. B. S. Haldane (1892–1964) was asked a somewhat fancier version of the usual question. "You've spent a lifetime gazing into the face of Nature," legend quotes his interviewer. "Can you tell us what you have learned about the mind of God?"

Haldane puzzled over this for a minute. "I'm really not sure," he said, "except that He must have an inordinate fondness for beetles."

It's simply not true that there is no such thing as a dumb question. We ask them all the time. Included in this category are questions that terminate promising interviews; questions that elicit responses and not answers; questions that are so imprecise that they allow the person interviewed to evade the heart of the issue; questions that are just not on point and therefore fail to produce a valuable answer.

It's always a good practice to go over questions in advance, anticipating answers and considering the order in which the questions should be asked.

Rule Eight

Here's the difference between a demographer and a mathematical demographer: A demographer makes wild guesses about the future of populations. A mathematical demographer uses computers and statistics to make wild guesses about the future of populations.

Don't let the use of computers, elaborate statistics, large budgets, large staffs, huge numbers of subjects or a lengthy study time influence you. The difference between good and bad science, or so-so science and great science, is the mind behind it.

Rule Nine

How many economists does it take to change a light bulb? Two. One to assume the ladder, the other to assume the light bulb.

And then we all stay in the dark. Just like the economists. Remember, "all things being equal" is an oxymoron. That's the real reason economics is called the dismal science.

Rule Ten

On the East Coast especially, it's possible to travel to work by just taking a long commuter train or subway ride. One editor, after making his daily trip, came home looking unusually ashen and distraught.

"What happened?" asked his significant other.

"I had to ride the whole trip in a backward-facing seat. You know how that always distresses my liver.

"Well, Mr. Bigshot Editor, we've talked about this before. Why didn't you just ask the person in the seat facing you to swap?"

"Alas," said the editor. "On this trip I could not ask. There was no one sitting in the opposite seat."

Never, ever tell your editors that you want to commit social science. It never works because it always scares them. For one thing, they've all heard the saw that anything with the name science in it isn't. Second, they'll never understand the gain from the pain.

You learned a long time ago never to call someone up and ask for an "interview." Instead, you say, "May I come over and talk to you." That's because to many people, "interview" is a bad word.

Same with social science. Instead, always tell your editors that you've discovered a really nifty, inexpensive, fast way to elevate your project to the top of the pyramid. Your success ratio will improve dramatically.

Bonus Rule

How many journalists conversant in social science does it take to screw in a light bulb? Two. One to assure the editors that everything is under control and another to screw the bulb into a water faucet.

It may be that you need more of a primer about using and understanding numbers than provided in this book. Just possibly.

There are a number of books available on social science methods. Browse in any library.

To make sure you aren't victimized or, worse, perpetrate your own crimes in this arena, I suggest two books:

- *News and Numbers,* by Victor Cohn, the long-time reporter at *The Washington Post* (Ames: Iowa State University Press, 1989).
- *Newsroom Guide to Polls and Surveys,* by G. Cleveland Wilhoit and David H. Weaver, two professors at Indiana University (Reston, Va.: American Newspaper Publishers Assoc., 1980.)

Both volumes are slim and both are terrific. They should not only be on everyone's desk—everyone should actually read them, underline the text, make notes in the margins and return to the books often.

NOTES

1. The anecdotes recounted here are from one of three places: "The Anatomy of Judgment," by Philip J. Regal (Minneapolis: University of Minnesota Press, 1990); "Qualitative Evaluation Methods," by Michael Quinn Patton (Newbury Park, Calif.: Sage Publications, Inc., 1980); or "Absolute Zero Gravity," by Betsy Devine and Joel E. Cohen (New York: Simon & Schuster, 1992.)

   In many cases these jokes do not appear to have been written by the authors. Therefore, using the best social science methods available, I only repeated jokes found in two of the three books, unless they were in only one or three.

   In some instances, I have edited or substantially altered the joke.

   In all circumstances, these books are well worth buying and reading.

6

From Ideas
Through Reporting

Techniques that increase the odds of producing an outstanding project are detailed in this chapter, including tips on how to get ideas that are better, how to sell them to management and strategies that will help make the reporting better. These ideas will work whether you are a beat reporter, general assignment or even a full-time project reporter.

Great project ideas come from one of two places.

Sometimes, clever editors who read widely, listen to the talk of those around them, who venture into the community to hear from readers and who are otherwise questers after what's new or important, dream up good ideas and present them to reporters.

The success ratio here is 1 in 100, both for clever editors and clever projects dreamed up by editors.

The other 99 come from reporters.

To be sure, reporters may come up with the idea only because their sources embarrass them into doing a better job, because information in the form of unsolicited documents shows up at the reporter's doorstep, or other reasons unrelated to reporter brilliance and more tied to the belief of a citizen that approaching a reporter was the least of all other evils.[1]

And sometimes reporters, fearful they will be forever tied to producing daily bulletins of small, incremental value to readers or viewers, propose excellent project ideas as a way of getting a change of venue.

Still other reporters *are* clever and brilliant and want to know why something doesn't work like it's supposed to, and it turns out that editors too, once asked, also want to know the answers. These reporters mine their beats expertly, using strip or tunnel methods as appropriate, see the patterns and develop the needed sources.

Having spent years as an editor plumbing my sources—other reporters and editors—I've developed a number of techniques that help increase the possibility of coming up with a good project idea. I force myself to do all of them regularly.

Generating Ideas

■ Periodically I leave my office and go talk to actual reporters—those not engaged in a project, which, at any one time, is the vast majority of reporters.[2]

This can be very alarming to reporters who are unused to an editor walking up to them just to chat. Eventually however, they can be convinced you don't intend to ask for anything that requires additional work, or worse, the same amount of work, but done earlier.

I never ask if they have a project idea. Reporters who don't do projects rarely have a "project idea" although they have plenty of ideas about the projects we publish, most of them negative. (For instance, "You took three months for that?" or "I knew that. Everybody but you knew that.")

Instead, I just ask what's going on, what's amusing or what's shocking. Often, it turns out, reporters who don't do projects have lots of information about things that could or should be projects. Then I may ask the reporter if I can pass the information on as a possible project and would he or she like to be involved if it's approved.

If the reporter would like to be involved, I ask the reporter to write me an electronic note (I've learned not to say "memo") containing the relevant information and then I start working through the chain of command. If the reporter is not interested, I talk to other editors about the idea and maybe it evolves into a project. If it does, I or the reporters assigned to the project go back to the original reporter to tell them we're doing it and ask for advice.

(Sometimes I have failed to do this and it's always led to interpersonal disasters that easily could have been avoided by this common courtesy. In addition, at least for a time, the original reporter knows more about the topic than anyone else and can save us a lot of time.)

■ I always use the resources of Investigative Reporters and Editors (IRE).

I regularly read their quarterly publication, *The IRE Journal,* and their annual publication describing IRE's selection of the 100 best projects. It's great for ideas. And, when I have even the hint of a project possibility, I call IRE and ask for all the related projects they have in their vast storehouse. IRE is a wonderful resource.

To make it work to its maximum potential, you should call the reporters or editors who did those projects you especially like and ask them how they were done, what problems they encountered and how they solved them, if they did. Then you explain what you are doing and ask for more advice, after quickly acknowledging that your effort will be a pale shadow of theirs.[3]

■ Many of the 200 or so newspapers that do any kind of ambitious reporting project in any given year reprint them as a special section and send them to their colleagues at other newspapers.

Scores of reprints pour into your newspaper every year. Get them. I went around to all the editors in the building who get these reprints and asked them to route the reprints my way after they'd read them. Then each year a graduate student intern abstracted them into a formatted queue I'd created and—presto—I had my own electronic database that included around 300 of the best projects I came across during my six years at the newspaper.

■ As explained in Chapter 3, I use databases for trolling as well, especially now that CD-ROM databases are so common.

Just one reminder: It saves a lot of time and embarrassment to remember to troll one's own newspaper clips before flying off to sell a project idea. Best to be sure your newspaper hasn't already done it. Doing something "better but second" may sometimes be a good project, but doing something "first and best" is always superior.

■ This suggestion is not only useful, it's very fun to do. It's called, going to the library.

The awful truth of the matter is, most of us in journalism fall out of the habit of reading. For instance, it's a rare reporter or, for that matter, editor, who even reads the entire newspaper where they work. Most of us read what we need for the next story we're assigned or enough of today's newspaper to evaluate our colleagues' efforts. Some of us even manage a little recreational reading, but usually nothing we can bring up in a conversation any more advanced than, say, how the Celtics are doing.

That's why most people, except our significant others whom we chose with great care (much more care than they exercised), find us so interminably boring. And even our significant others no longer will go to journalism parties with us.

So start going to the library for some eclectic reading and all kinds of good things will happen to you.

When you get there, head for the various periodical racks and start down through the tables of contents from art magazines to those covering zygote cloning. Pick a half-dozen articles covering things you know nothing about. (This, of course, is no problem for most of us. The problem will be getting out of the A's and B's to near the middle of the alphabet before we become eligible for Social Security.) Pick one or two that may challenge what you think you already know. Read them, copy them and start some file folders back at the office.

The library I frequented even had a copying center where I could arrange to directly bill the newspaper for all my copying.

Next, walk over to the specialized, technical periodical literature, like those covering, say, public management or, for a real treat, those where sociologists talk to each other. This allows you to see what the professionals think are the most pressing issues facing them and us. You will often find great story ideas, sometimes great project ideas.

For instance, if you had been browsing the many magazines about libraries and librarianship over the past ten years or so, you'd come across a great project idea that librarians shorthand among themselves as "fee or free."

Because library budgets have remained mostly static or fallen at a time when the cost of information has skyrocketed, many libraries now charge fees for services you used to expect to receive free. This has caused great debate among librarians, many of whom believe that libraries should be the last refuge where the poor can receive free as much information as the wealthy can buy.

Your readers and viewers would benefit a great deal by being waltzed through the debate in a thoughtful series.

Even if you don't get any good project ideas right away, you suddenly will be much more interesting to talk to—no meager boon.

■ Sometimes the best decision is to admit a project idea is not a very good one and to kill it.

Every once in a while a reporter or editor will come to me with an idea and by the time we are done talking we agree it's not worth devoting weeks or months of our life to it.

I always try to get reporters to answer two questions. 1) Would they read this story if their bylines weren't on it? 2) If everything went exactly right for them, what would the most powerful lead say?

These two questions are very good focusing devices and often lead to the conclusion of, "Just say no."[4]

Getting Started

A constant theme of this book is that there are more barriers to good project reporting inside the building where you work than outside.

Outside, you need only struggle with reticent sources, threats of lawsuits or death by dismemberment, legally or illegally closed-off information sources or your appalling initial ignorance about the topic you've chosen.

Inside, the very first hurdle—getting approval to tackle a project—is more than many reporters can get over or around, especially if they aren't one of the lucky few assigned to do projects.

Here's a method that almost always works. It's called the Red Meat Theory and I learned it from Bob Greene at *Newsday,* a journalist who's studied this craft more than any other modern-day practitioner and to whom all of us owe a great deal.

The details of how to work the technique are explained in Sidebar 6.1. Here are the generalities.

Never, ever talk in generalities to your supervising editor about a possible project. When you talk to an editor about the possibility of sniffing around for, say, some kind of city hall project, the editor's only thoughts are these: "If I let you off to go snooping around for a project, who will cover the meetings? What will I put on the budget every day you are gone? What will I say to the hordes of other reporters who will want to do a project because you are?"

However, all editors are interested in good stories. They salivate over offering a dynamite budget item and basking in the success good journalism usually brings, at least outside the building.

That means you have to expend a bunch of your own time, as Sidebar 6.1 details, on getting the story to a good minimum. In other words, you nail down a certain set of facts, which are not going away, and which by themselves will be a damned fine front-page article. It would still take you four or five days to finish it up—interviews with the key people as well as writing—but it's a very good story.

However, you say, if you were given several weeks to work on it, an even larger pattern of abuse might be uncovered.

Then you tell your editor your speculation or thesis that is tightly based on your initial sniff—what people have said that you just haven't had a chance to check out, what reporters working similar types of stories have found elsewhere (remember that call to IRE?) and so forth.

Now we are dealing in the area of specifics and the editor knows there is a great budget item just around the corner. The editor will gladly, often even eagerly, seek to get you the time—because no matter what happens, you've got the minimum, the "red meat."

Here are an additional eight ideas that might work for you and ought to be considered and talked about between the reporter and supervising editor up front.

■ You need to set thresholds and goals at the beginning.

They help you know if you are on course and when you are done. Set them, review your progress against them, revise them, follow them or kill them.

Here are some examples of thresholds. Is the abuse you are investigating illegal with real jail time for the miscreants a possibility, or does it just involve violations of regulations, or contrary to codes of conduct or is it merely contrary to common decency and fairness? It makes a big difference in how you'll spend your time, not to mention in how you'll write the article. For example, is it a conflict of interest as defined by law or as defined by common sense?

Will a circumstantial case suffice, or will you need to make it as legally rigorous as any courtroom prosecutor's?

These kinds of considerations should be identified and talked out at the beginning and throughout the life of the project.

■ The reporter and supervising editor must become partners, as never before.

For the editor, that means meeting with the reporter every day and reading everything in the queue as it arrives, or soon thereafter. It means the editor should actively help identify and solve problems the reporter faces, inside the building and outside. If the editor cannot offer that kind of time and help, he or she shouldn't accept the assignment. Projects are a team sport. No other reporting effort needs or benefits more from this kind of cooperation.

For the reporter, that means sharing everything with the editor in a timely fashion so the reporter can benefit from the partnership. It means religiously

typing everything into the system so that your partner (including other reporters you are teamed with) can benefit from your work and so that your
editor can help you keep things on track. It also ensures that you don't forget,
or worse, overlook something.

■ Once a story is given project status, a reporter should not have to work
on anything else.

It's too hard to keep focused when moving back and forth on different
topics or working for different editors. And it is a lot less efficient. Time is
the great enemy of projects and the more you can do to get done quicker (and
the sooner everyone can return to their normal assignments) the better everyone will like it.

I've never met a reporter who liked working on a project in his or her
spare time. Nor have I ever read a part-time project that appeared to be more
than just that—a part-time project.

Having said that, reporters removed from their beats to do projects often
can work on special one- or two-day efforts for the editors they have tempo-
rarily left. Sometimes it only makes sense for the person who knows the most
about a topic or source to come off a project to help out on a breaking story.

I always said "yes" to other editors when they asked to borrow their
reporters back for a day or two, unless we were barreling toward a publication
deadline ourselves. This cooperation was always appreciated by the harried
editors from whom I stole reporters, and never remembered when I'd return
to steal some more for other projects.[5]

■ It's a law of physics[6] that two-person teams are better than one-person or
many-person teams.

Most projects are too tough for one person to slug through, if it takes any
length of time or has any degree of difficulty.

Two people can share things, back each other up, cover for each other's
weaknesses, be sounding boards and grounding boards.

Some things they will do together, like early or important interviews, but
many things they will do separately, including handling different parts of
complicated projects, and there can be a real savings in time.

In a team of three or more people meshing together is difficult and such
large teams should be avoided unless really needed.

■ When possible, it's a good idea to see if a project can run on two
tracks—the main, complete project and articles that can be broken out early
and run as complete stories by themselves, if a need arises.

The need can be dictated by events, such as the discovery of other news
media working on the story, new activity by government agencies or impend-
ing action by the persons you are writing about.

You can never, of course, break out stories until they are rock solid and ready, and sometimes it is just inappropriate to break out a part, no matter what the concern.

But you usually can't break out a part unless you prepared early on to do so. Therefore, you should periodically try to identify what parts could be broken out and what it would take from that moment on to get them done. Then, try to get them done before you move on to other parts.

If you don't end up running them out early, you still benefit from having some parts finished early.

■ One of the great organizing/managing tools for reporters and editors alike is the "T" chart.

On one side you write down the things you know,[7] which are relatively few at the beginning. On the other side you write down the critical things you don't know but will need to find out. The chart might look like this:

We know	We don't know
H. Kevorkian works there	Get copy of contract
Kevorkian's address	All land, $$ papertrails
Secondary witness says he did it	Primary sources—as in eyewitnesses
	Motive
	Opportunity
	Motives of others?
	Opportunity of others?
	Court records
	Kevorkian backgrounding
	Comp time for reporters

All of the items on the right need to move to the left, except the last one. If, after a suitable length of time, some haven't, why not? And how important is the item, given subsequent information?

You can make a very good action list in this fashion and it helps keep track of progress or lack of progress.

I've noticed that when reporters make "T" charts, or lists of what to do, they don't date them. Editors should date theirs. That way you'll be reminded of the enormous numbers of days that have gone by since the project was approved, and this clever little tool can help identify and solve the major hang-ups.[8]

■ Have at least one overall chronology.

Next to certain functions of relational databases, the chronology is the most useful single tool for finding patterns and associations that otherwise wouldn't be apparent.

Set up one slug in the system where a copy of every sentence with a date in it gets sent to be inserted in the appropriate place. You can reduce a version of it later to one that contains only the most important items, but in the beginning you don't know what will be important later so put everything in there.

■ Then, there is the occasional memo.

Every two or three weeks, reporters should sit down and write a memo about what they've found out so far.

This works best if the memo is written in story form for these reasons:

1. Actually writing a memo as a trial draft lets you practice on the story line—is the project a good read and is this the best way to tell it? This lets you show it to your bosses or someone else you trust to get an early reaction to the project as a story. That way, if it doesn't fly you can get the reaction early, before you have invested a draft with so much creativity and energy that suggested (or ordered) changes become like pulling teeth or killing baby seals.

2. Reporters often know more than they think they know and writing it down can convince them that a section is done, or needs only a few extra details to get it done. Paradoxically, there's also nothing like putting words to paper to illustrate beyond doubt what you don't know as you try to write around, say, a response that isn't an answer. Both sides of this coin are enormously helpful, especially if the currency is gotten early.

3. In all projects, hours, even days, are wasted as reporters or reporters and editors argue about how to write a story. Keep these initial discussions very brief and let the reporters tell it like they want to. Then everyone has something concrete to argue about, rather than something that is just an idea in someone's head. If the approach doesn't work, other people you show it to will be only too happy to tell you. Believe me.

Of course, none of these drafts you are writing throughout the life of the project have any value after they are discussed and all copies should be rounded up and thrown away, their electronic versions spiked.

Reporting

The previous chapters and sidebars contain numerous tips on reporting and will not be repeated or summarized here. In addition, this book is designed to complement IRE's "The Reporter's Handbook," originated, coauthored and co-edited by one of America's great project editors. That book has many additional tips on how to go about investigating numerous topics.[9]

One overall suggestion, however, is worth emphasizing here.

It's unusual to get the really big story by stumbling into it. Don't count on luck. Think big and cast a wide net at the very beginning. You can narrow later. If you don't try for the best story possible, at least at the beginning, chances are you won't end up with it, either.

Serendipity is for the state lottery and we all know the colossal odds against any one of us winning it.

NOTES

1. According to unnamed sources (unnamed because I can't remember where I heard this), the phrase "to be sure" is an invention and staple of the long thumb-suckers produced regularly by the *Wall Street Journal.* A careful and scientific analysis conducted by me over many years of encountering that phrase has deciphered why it is used now throughout the land. It means that fairness and the fear of a libel suit compels us to acknowledge that our hard-hitting thesis could be devastated by some well-known facts that would seem on their surface to obliterate our argument. Therefore, we pooh-pooh these facts early on in the piece and at the same time signal the reader that we aren't so dumb as to be ignorant of these things. This device is of no value whatsoever in an investigative project, but has outstanding use in public policy projects, *Wall Street Journal thumbsuckers and their clones* in other news media, and chapters in journalism books.

2. It is a myth, perhaps the biggest in journalism, that all reporters want to do projects. In fact, most do not. They want to be considered, then they want to say, no, thank you. The reasons are many and most of them are good and sufficient. There are a couple of corollaries that are true, however. There is a great hunger among daily reporters to learn how to do their job better, to learn the techniques that investigative reporters, for the most part, pioneered. And no reporter wants to be overlooked when considerations are on-going about who to put on the project.

3. Journalists are outstanding sources for other journalists. Journalists really like to tell other journalists how brilliant they are. In fact, once you ask the first question, you can just put the phone down and go about other important work if you tape the call, remembering to return to the phone every half hour or so and mumble, "Uh huh." Then, if you have even more time, ask the journalist what they are working on next.

4. This technique is not fail-safe nor should it be.

Consider: Minnesota is a high tax state. Depending on how you measure it, we are in the highest three, four or five.

My executive editor got interested in where all the money goes. He passed the question to the managing editor who passed it to my boss, the deputy managing editor. Guess where he passed it?

I went directly to the executive editor and said, Why don't we spend just a little time on this and then call the two people in the state who actually would care to read this project and just tell them the information and save all the time and energy, not to mention dead trees, it will take to do this project. And since one of those two people is in this room, it might not be too difficult to find the other one.

Then I explained that it is not anti-intuitive to find out that the state spends a lot of our money on things, because they take a lot of money and we are all of us reminded of this every time we get our greatly reduced paycheck.

I went on: Unless he thought people were actually stealing the money—and who knows how long an *investigative* project would take—I seriously doubted we'd have any "findings" or any riveting stories.

He smiled through all of this, I think actually laughed out loud once, then asked me who I'd need on the project.

So, of course, we did it. And it turned out to be a pretty interesting two-day package with some real findings.

The reporters and I agreed we had only two story-telling devices to rely on— pace and color. Therefore, no story was more than 25 inches and we had some spectacular, full-color graphics.

And, I even got a lot of requests for reprints of this project from editors around the country.

I've got to remember to tell the executive editor, who is now publisher, that it wasn't such a bad idea after all.

One of these days.

5. Alas, a project editor's life is a lonely one.

6. You can look it up. Isaac Asimov himself probably wrote at least two books about it.

7. Remember, the rumor or tip that got you started usually is not something you "know." It is something you will check. It starts out in the right column.

8. Believe me, your bosses are aware of all the days that have gone by and this method allows you to tell them what the hang-up is before they decide the hang-up is curiously spelled the same way you spell your name.

9. "The Reporter's Handbook: An Investigator's Guide to Documents and Records," 2nd ed., edited by John Ullmann and Jan Colbert (New York: St. Martin's Press, 1991). To order, call IRE at (314) 882–2042. The book is available in hardcover or paperback. And that book is designed to complement the first edition, a limited number of which are still available from IRE.

The Red Meat Theory in Practice

by John Ullmann

Let's make up an example of how to make the Red Meat Theory work for you.

In this hypothetical situation, you are a city hall reporter who gets a tip that one of the city's largest contractors has an improper relationship with the city's purchasing agent.

We'll call the purchasing agent Ullmann and the contractor Kevorkian.

You know you can't get time off to check out this tip, so you open up the precursor of relational databases—a manila envelope—and put in a typed version of the tip. Now, over the next few weeks or so, we'll gather some specific information to see if it leads anywhere.

Here's how.

The next time you're over at city hall on some other errand of journalism, stop down at the finance department and request a list of the top 10 contracts let each of the last 10 years. You want dollar amount and contractor. This way, no one will be tipped that you are looking at Kevorkian Contractors (KC), and you can see if anything leaps out.

Some days later, you stop by and pick it up, or maybe they mail it to you.

The list shows that KC got 10 contracts during this period totaling $10 million. Is that a lot? Does it mean anything? No way to know.

So you call back to city hall and request the bids on all 10 KC contracts, plus 10 others just for smoke. A few days later you get the information and it shows this: KC was the high bidder on three, low bidder on three and in the middle on four.

What does this tell us? You don't know; it's not much of a pattern.

You call down to one of the several hundred state assistant attorney generals who are usually idle at any given moment and ask if your municipality must take the low bidder. The answer is no.

The next time you're over at city hall, you pull the history on Ullmann's property and, surprise, he bought his house from Kevorkian Construction. Not illegal, maybe not anything, but it sure is interesting.

Now you call down to IRE to see if they've got any projects on contracts and bids, and then go over to the business desk and ask a colleague who you can talk to in the public construction business who's straight. Or maybe you read the city hall chapter in "The Reporter's Handbook."

At any rate, you learn about change orders.

A change order is written after a contract is let. Let's say KC gets a contract to pave a mile of city streets for $9.2 million. Then KC starts the work and finds bad dirt. Or running water. Or an Indian burial ground. Or any of a dozen or so other legitimate reasons why the job will cost more money.

KC goes back to the city with a change order and, if it's approved, gets more money.

Guess who approves the change orders? Ullmann. No public hearing, no public notice, no nothing. Just Ullmann. Or, at least Ullmann's office. Remember, you haven't seen the paper yet.

You go back to the city hall and ask for a list of the total dollar amounts paid to each of the top 10 contractors each of the past 10 years.

When you get it you do a simple set of calculations that shows: KC's change orders amounted to 43 percent over and above the original contract. The average of the other 90 construction jobs was 13 percent. You haven't seen the paperwork, but you're ready to bet that Ullmann's signature is on every KC change order.

Then you call the state agency that lets construction contracts and ask for the average (and median) percentage they paid on change orders for each of the last 10 years. It's right around 15 percent. Using the "Encyclopedia of Associations," you talk to various national organizations who suggest to you that change orders on public projects run in a range of 10 to 20 percent.

Remember Kevorkian Construction's average? It's two to four times that number.

Now you have some "red meat" to hang in front of your editor's nose: You got a tip that says the city's purchasing agent has an improper relationship with one of the city's largest contractors. So you did some checking and here's what you found out. Ullmann bought his house from KC. Also, Ullmann's office, at least, approved change orders totaling millions of dollars for KC during the past 10 years, at a rate way over the city, state and national averages.

You tell your editor it'd take you the rest of the week anyway to finish this story—interviews with KC and Ullmann and other contractors, city engineers to see if there can be any possible reason KC has been so unlucky at their construction sites, other public officials, checking out that property deal and so forth—but if the editor can give you more time, you might find an even bigger pattern.

You could do all the paper trails on Ullmann and KC, looking for relationships. You could talk to other contractors who might tell about other relationships. It might be a much bigger story. But no matter what happens, you've got this story for sure.

Everything above was made up, but it shows exactly how a little invest-ment of your time can convince your editor to give you more to do an investigation. How much time have you got invested? Everything I mentioned above could have been done in four to five hours total, even though it was spaced out over several weeks or so.

This is how you make Bob Greene's Red Meat Theory work for you.

Managing Data

by Joe Rigert, *Star Tribune*

The details of the death were horrifying. An elderly woman in a Minnesota nursing home was found hanging in a jackknife position over the side of her bed. It happened quickly. When she fell out of bed, her restraint jacket caught around her chest, causing asphyxiation. No one was there to catch her or save her.

The report of her death was found in the files of the Minnesota Department of Health. It was a coldly clinical report, lacking even the name of the victim or anything about her life and times.

Many other patients in nursing homes had died this way. Reporter Maura Lerner and I had to learn who they were. But how? The answer was in the death certificates. To find them, in the same state agency, we used the date and location of each fatality to search the death files, which were arranged chronologically for each country.

We found them all and much more.

The findings were dramatic—and tragic. Hundreds of people in the U.S. nursing homes and hospitals strangling and suffocating in devices meant to protect them. The federal government and the leading manufacturer of the safety devices were doing little to prevent the deaths. It had long been one of the darkest secrets in health care.

We spent eight months gathering evidence on this disaster, probably the worst in the history of modern medical devices. By the time we finished, we'd collected eight boxes of documents, reviewed five sets of government data on computer tapes and talked with scores of people in health care, government and industry.

Without a system to manage our data, we would have been lost in our own information long before we were finished. With such a system, we had literally compiled a book of indexed material, enabling us to know what we had in the boxes of files and on the reels of computer tapes.

Managing data assembled churned out by computer or from old-fashioned reporting methods is critically important in any major investigative project. Memories alone aren't good enough to keep track of the masses of information collected. Important facts and relationships are missed. Names are forgotten. Gaps in knowledge remain unfilled.

Or worse, you can't find information you know you've collected. I once saw a reporter break down in tears when he could not find the one document that would pin blame on a corporation for a major health hazard. Another veteran reporter, as he was writing, frantically searched for facts in documents scattered on his desk and all over the floor. Both suffered from information overload and organization underuse.

The nursing-home project provides a case study on how reporters can deal with tens of thousands of facts, and still maintain their sanity.

I started the project, planning to do a quick and easy story on how old people were being over-drugged in nursing homes. All it would take was an analysis of data collected in Minnesota state government surveys, all nicely etched onto computer tapes and available for the asking.

But another story got in the way. A government source told of another serious problem, and this problem, unlike drugging the elderly, had received little attention. Many residents of Minnesota nursing homes, the source said, were being strangled in the vests, belts and other devices that were used to tie them to their beds and wheelchairs in an effort to keep the elderly from falling and injuring themselves.

Evidence of the deaths was available in the reports of state investigations of complaints against nursing homes. I went through more than 1,000 of these reports in the Department of Health, becoming a familiar figure in the department—so familiar that one staff member, who had become aware of my mission, slipped me a confidential report giving the name and gruesome details of the suffering of a restrained patient. It helped us produce a gripping story on how people are forced to wear restraints against their will, and how they suffer for it.

As the project grew, Maura was brought in as a full-time partner. Later on, Monte Hanson joined the team as a researcher. With the help of news librarians, we obtained practically everything that had ever been written about protective restraints, including research reports in medical journals to articles in newspapers. With the cooperation of families of victims, we got copies of confidential hospital and nursing home records. We went through the private files of attorneys in major lawsuits, obtained police investigative files and reports of medical examiners.

In the Minnesota cases, we didn't just take the word of physicians or coroners on the causes of death; we investigated and found additional strangulations that had been passed off as deaths by natural causes.

Midway in the project, it became apparent that this was not just a problem in one state. So we also began to collect evidence of restraint deaths across the United States and Canada from such places as government reports, lawsuits, state surveys or nursing homes and articles in medical journals.

To help in evaluating the cases, we retained a medical consultant, Dr. Steven H. Miles, an expert in treating the elderly. I had seen his name as a panelist at a national conference and found he was on the medical staff of a hospital two blocks from our newspaper.

He was just the person we were looking for—intensely interested in the subject and eager to help us. But first we did what any project reporters must do when they rely heavily on an expert. We checked him out.

We searched our library for stories about him, reviewed his resume and publications, talked with his colleagues and looked for court cases, malpractice suits and disciplinary actions. Then we had three other experts review his work. He passed without a question. (And, of course, we informed our readers that we had hired him for his review.)

In his work for us, Dr. Miles examined more than 100 reports of restraint deaths, becoming the foremost authority in the country by the time he was finished.

At the same time, we were using the computer to deal with what we were gathering. With the assistance of a colleague, Lou Kilzer, we entered the details of more than 100 restraint deaths and injuries into our own specially constructed database. From this data we were able to sort out patterns in the cases; whether the restraints were properly or improperly applied, causes of death or injury, rule violations.

More importantly, we obtained major findings from four sets of computer tapes containing information from state and federal surveys of nursing homes. I had learned about them by an old reportorial method: asking. I merely asked the agencies what kinds of surveys they did and whether the data was entered in their computers. I also asked for copies of the survey forms and instructions to the surveyors—so I knew exactly what was in the data.

There was plenty.

One tape contained data on drugs being given to patients at the time they were admitted to nursing homes. Another gave information on use of drugs, personal dependencies and health problems of each patient. A third gave details on per capita spending for nursing services in the homes. The fourth tape included the percentage of restraint use and health characteristics of patients in each nursing home.

Assisting in the analysis of the data were Rob Daves, assistant managing editor for research, and Glenn Trygstad, programming consultant. Together, we determined levels of restraint use for each nursing home, percentage of homes with abnormal restraining rates, health characteristics of restrained patients, use of "chemical restraints," relationships between use of physical and chemical restraints and relationships between restraint use and nursing costs.

We worked closely with the computer experts from the beginning.

I determined what information was available on the tapes, not only from the questionnaires and instructions for the surveys, but also from the people who conducted them. Then, on the basis of my reporting and other research, I devised a set of questions for the computer analysts: Did nursing homes use restraints to save staff costs? Were drugs being used in place of restraints? Did "bad" nursing homes restrain patients more than "good" ones? What types of patients were being restrained the most?

The results of the computer analyses then were carefully integrated into the stories, so they were part of the big picture, not isolated into a separate article.

The same combination of reporting and computer analysis helped the team develop an estimate of restraint deaths nationally. It took painstaking work to collect evidence of 33 restraint deaths in Minnesota and more than 200 nationally over a period of a dozen years.

It also took careful analysis by experts—and yet another set of computer tapes—to project the state totals to a national annual estimate. The additional tapes provided data on all suffocations in U.S. hospitals and nursing homes. A careful review of that data helped support the estimate developed by the newspaper's expert, with back-up from three other experts in other parts of the country.

The result of all this work: A conclusion that more than 200 people were strangling each year—a medical device catastrophe, far worse than a much-publicized heart-valve problem.

Along the way, we and our editor, Ron Meador, regularly discussed our findings and plans. Maura and I met each morning over coffee to talk about problems, what we had discovered the previous day and what we would do the next day. More than that, we performed as cheerleaders for each other, one inspiring the other when depression set in. Then, periodically, we wrote memos to keep the editors informed of what we were doing and whether we were making good progress. (A chance meeting in the hall is just as appropriate for this essential reporter-editor communication.)

Most important of all, however, was the system we used to keep track of the piles of data—the research articles, death reports, computer findings, interviews with families, nursing-home staff members and experts.

Each document was placed in a subject-matter file folder (one for each victim, another for enforcement, still another for hazards). Each piece of paper was given a number. Each fact in each document was entered into the computer, beginning with a key word, and ending with the file source. Each fact or opinion in each interview also was entered. Some facts would be cross-indexed two or three times.

By a simple alphabet command in the computer, the key words were sorted together, so we would know exactly what we had at any time on any subject.

We would have more than 100 printout pages in this index when the project was concluded. We even kept a discard file for notes we might wish later that we hadn't thrown away.

The indexes on any project are exceedingly helpful in preparing for interviews and save much time in writing the stories. We would write from the indexes, not from notebooks or file folders. Later we would fact-check each line of our stories, using footnotes in the body of the copy to find the documents and interview that would support what we wrote.

This fact-checking process, developed by former project editor John Ullmann, would assure that we made absolutely no mistakes.

Chronologies also were an important part of the data-management system. We compiled four date-by-date lists of the actions, failures, deaths and other events involving the main manufacturer of restraints, the federal government and Canadian authorities (who had done far more about the problem than had the U.S. regulators).

At the same time, we produced a list of each of the more than 200 documented deaths, by date, with every detail available. From that list, using search words in our computer program, we could find patterns in the deaths. And, of course, we maintained a growing list of sources, with identifying information and home as well as office telephone numbers.

By keeping track of our information, we also were able to keep our reporting in focus. We used our indexes to maintain—and regularly update— our task list, or questions we needed to answer, or additional data we needed to obtain. At times, in fact, we felt that we needed an index to know what we had in our indexes and lists. One list would lead to another—or to a sublist.

From our information on each of the restraint-related deaths in Minnesota, we developed a checklist of failures by local authorities in determining the causes of the deaths. Some nursing homes, for example, failed to notify the medical examiner in time for him to see the body of a victim, while some coroners ignored strong evidence of strangulation. From this list, and with the help of our expert, we made our finding that many deaths were improperly attributed to natural causes, when instead they were strangulations or suffocations caused by restraints.

None of this record-keeping or record-managing was any substitute for basic reporting. A New York coroner, for instance, told me in a chance phone call that state health agencies counted suffocation deaths in hospitals and nursing homes. Upon inquiring about these statistics, after three more phone calls, I learned of a study in the agency that found an additional 11 restraint strangulations. Further, a Canadian researcher told Maura about an obscure U.S. government data category, which produced more than 40 additional restraint deaths suffered in wheelchairs.

When it came time to write, we had already summarized our findings in a series of bullets—developed from the indexes. By then we and our editor also had determined the number and makeup of the articles for our series. This meant we could rearrange the information in our indexes by article, to assist in the writing.

The writing was not easy; it never is. But it was many times easier than it would have been if we had been confronted with the results of eight months of research, piled on our desks or stuffed in file drawers, without roadmaps on how to get where we wanted to go. Our record-keeping system took lots of time to maintain, but it saved much more time at the conclusion. It also left us with the feeling that we had left no fact unnoticed or unused—if it was fit to print.

(Joe Rigert is a long-time investigative reporter for the *Star Tribune* and a former president of IRE.)

7

From Writing
Through Publication

*Techniques that will help you produce an outstanding
project are detailed in this chapter.*

When the world was young and green and I was middle-aged, project reporters had it easy.

They picked their own project ideas, decided when they would do them and how, and all by themselves. Then off they'd go, no one knew where, and there they stayed until they were good and ready to return.

Once done, the reporters would stroll back to the cave at a leisurely and dignified pace, gather everyone around a roaring fire and take their own sweet time telling the story exactly the way they wanted to tell it. Back then there were no restrictions on length—the story went on as long as the readily available firewood held out.

When they were finished, everyone stood up and cheered. No one said, "You took three months for that?" or "I already knew that." There were no acrimonious recriminations, such as "I had to hunt extra mastodons while you were gone, so now you have to get my share of the firewood for the next three winters." People just shook the reporters' hands and asked, respectfully, when the next project might be coming—this Ice Age or the next.

Media sociologists disagree on when and why things changed. However, by placing all the relevant dates into a master chronology, as espoused in the previous chapter, the reasons become crystal clear.

First came civilization and then its decline, along with lawyers, television, newspapers and management by objectives, or its relatively recent news media surrogate, management by objection. All of these things are related.

It's now been determined that project reporters actually need a lot more help than they thought.

Consider: Now project reporters have project editors. This, of course, is an honest-to-god actual improvement.

But they also got lawyers, designers, artists, photographers, copyeditors, other department heads and senior editors of various ilk. The jury is still out on whether all of these layers are an honest-to-god actual improvement. (Unless, of course, you are reading one of their books.)

For instance, newspaper project reporters used to design their own projects.

Reproduced below from the Official Journalism Archives are the four developmental phases of reporter-designed projects.

Newspaper reporters loved these designs because they accommodated every word they cared to type, including bursts of brilliance that occurred to them between editions on the days the projects were published.

To be sure, only in the *Wall Street Journal* can we find pages like these any more because of all the aforementioned "help" we've given project reporters.

Read this story, it's very important

This is the earliest reporter-produced project page and remains to this day the most popular among reporters. It may appear that the project ends here, but actually it goes on. And on and on. And, when in the *Los Angeles Times,* on and on some more, even today. However, a page designer passing by the projects office one day suggested the following, "Hey, I haven't read that but I think it's a little gray. You need more entry points for readers."

Read this story, it's very important

Ged efiit anbes lashit hout elayt hiseat indivi ualta ut. Pnaoe onaul obeve shednes ayst artof heenten perio dofpena. Cesmud ging sheson foreads of astul ad urg igelor te wordor.

Socia listan cois itter ranin a releco nid latay. Akes ifab atapo litica cormack yannoun isampa infoac outf fice. Esi tres residoin entum pragmanoria it ielori nome stabovum. Minumu bolus tret domin eagan ueils a progrˈae ottra ivementu. Tad rectec onomi oc aidor touble aribea baideclar ihat ewil ovatev.

Ris prudena decesario esure ece deur atap nechil lio ronjur. Isios obre ad liebia kailure pleped leris senly inue yars hahec. Urent reion wipung itos ometi nar ore. Woiec oers he invent tsengsa totemin on rnsow deot muc ohistim troiden. Tifyt hoyinte resie eaga an amini strato ofial talto ugabou heckina lege.

Wil resie eaga an amini stratio ofial talto ugabou heckina lege abanac ked insur ences. Entra lenca. The nited ates sofah ashra nished malmil itarsti. Reabud ged efiit anbes lashit hout elayt hiseat.

Socia listan cois itter ranin a releco nid latay, akes ifab atapo litica co-mack yannoun isampa infoac outf fice Omnes galo est tres residoin en-tum pragmanoria it ielori nome sta-bovum gallo.

Quant minimu bolus tret domin ea-gan ueils a progrˈae. Avum otra de, ivementu etad rectec onomi oc ai-dor touble aribea. Baideclar ihat ewil ovatev ris prudena decesario esure ece deur ere.

More important stuff starts here

Pake yars hahec urent reion wipung itos ometi nar ore. Woiec aruze iseki ouni feommuni tary, oes he invent taloitee etig siceim posio omaria la, a eting egare a significa itepa rss torega in onolhe ovement. Ofluo riend estrog wistren gen he riteb ones-iro.

Moprop oler womest ad osthe fra tures tatare a omona flictio olage. astp dybvox. Ibues rearef oburia, as ouon ebuide wie odfabo aout earol. Sice telor ercoro nerin vestiga torem-mun on rnsow deot muc ohistim troi-den tifyt hoyinte box.

Wil resie eaga an amini stratio ofial talto ugabou heckina lege ubanac. Ked insur ences entra lenca. the nited ates sofah ashra nished malmil itarsti. Reabud ged efiit anbes lashit hout elayt hiseat indivi ualta ut.

Poe onaul obeve shednes ayst. Cartof heenten perio dofpena ncevmud ging sheson foreads of astul ad urg igelor te wordor. Socia listan cois itter ranin a releco nid latay, akes ifab atapo litica co-mack yannoun isampa infoac outf fice Omnes galo est tres residoin en-tum pragmanoria it ielori nome sta-bovum gallo.

More important stuff starts here

Galo est tres residoin entum pragman-oria it ielori nome stabovum gallo. Quant minimu bolus tret domin ea-gan ueils a progrˈae. Avum otra de, ivementu etad rectec onomi oc ai-dor touble aribea. Baideclar ihat ewil ovatev ris prudena decesario esure ece deur ere. sofah ashra nished malmil itarsti.

Resie eaga an amini stratio ofial talto ugabou heckina lege ubanac ked insur ences entra lenca. the nited ates sofah ashra nished malmil...

Reaga an amini stratio ofial talto ugabou. Heckina lege ubanac ked insur ences entra lenca. Aethe nited ates sofah ashra nished malmil itarsti. Ged efiit anbes lashit hout elayt hiseat indivi ualta ut. Pnaoe onaul obeve shednes ayst artof heenten perio dofpena. Cesmud ging sheson foreads of astul ad urg igelor te wordor.

Esi tres residoin entum pragmanoria it ielori nome stabovum. Minumu bolus tret domin eagan ueils a progrˈae otra ivementu. Tad rectec onomi oc aidor touble aribea baideclar ihat ewil ovatev.

Decesario esure ece deur atap nechil liwo ronjur. Isios obre ad liebia kailure pleped leris senly inue yars hahec. Urent reion wipung itos ometi nar ore. Woiec oers he invent taloitee etig siceim posio omaria a eting egare.

Ris torega in onolhe ofluo riend estrog wistren. Gen he riteb ones-iro moprop oler womest ad osthe fra tures tatare. Omona flictio olage aout rearef as ouon ebuide wie odfabo aout earol. Tefor ercoro nerin vestiga toremin on rnsow deot muc ohistim troiden. Tifyt hoyinte resie eaga an amini stratio ofial talto ugabou heckina lege.

Wil resie eaga an amini stratio ofial talto ugabou heckina lege ubanac ked insur ences. Entra lenca. the nited ates sofah ashra nished malmil itarsti. Reabud ged efiit anbes lashit hout elayt hiseat.

Poe onaul obeve shednes ayst. Cartof heenten perio dofpena ncevmud ging sheson for-eads of astul ad urg igelor te wordor.

Socia listan cois itter ranin a releco nid latay, akes ifab atapo litica co-mack yannoun isampa infoac outf fice Omnes galo est tres residoin en-tum pragmanoria it ielori nome sta-bovum gallo, e riteb ones-iro.

Moprop oler womest ad osthe fra tures tatare a omona flictio olage, astp dybvox. Ibues rearef oburia, as ouon ebuide wie odfabo aout earol. Sice telor ercoro nerin vestiga torem-mun on rnsow deot muc ohistim troi-den tifyt hoyinte box.

More important stuff starts here

Divi ualta ut. Poe onaul obeve shednes ayst. Cartof heenten perio dofpena ncevmud ging sheson for-eads of astul ad urg igelor te wordor. Socia listan cois itter ranin a releco nid latay, akes ifab atapo litica co-mack yannoun isampa infoac outf fice Omnes galo est tres residoin en-tum pragmanoria it ielori nome sta-bovum gallo.

Quant minimu bolus tret domin ea-gan ueils a progrˈae. Avum otra de, ivementu etad rectec onomi oc ai-dor touble aribea. Baideclar ihat ewil ovatev ris prudena dec

Desio atap nechil liwo ronjur isios obre ad lieba kailure pleped

---

'An important famous expert-type person embarrasses himself here'

–Important expert-type person

---

leris senly inue aga.

Pake yars hahec urent reion wipung itos ometi nar ore. Woiec aruze iseki ouni feommuni tary, oes he invent taloitee etig siceim posio omaria la, a eting egare a significa itepa rss torega in onolhe ovement. Ofluo riend estrog wistren gen he riteb ones-iro.

Wil resie eaga an amini stratio ofial talto ugabou heckina lege ubanac. Ked insur ences entra lenca. the nited ates sofah ashra nished malmil itarsti. Reabud ged efiit anbes lashit hout elayt hiseat indivi ualta ut.

Poe onaul obeve shednes ayst artof heenten perio dofpena ncevmud ging sheson foreads of astul ad urg igelor te wordor. Socia listan cois itter ranin a releco nid latay, akes ifab atapo litica co-mack yannoun isampa yannarhea.

Ibues rearef oburia, as ouon ebuide wie odfabo aout earol. Sice telor ercoro nerin vestiga tore-mun on rnsow deot muc ohistim troi-den tifyt hoyinte box.

Retysip eaga an amini stratio ofial talto ugabou heckina lege ubanac. Ked insur ences entra lenca. the nited ates sofah ashra nished malmil itarsti. Reabud ged efiit anbes lashit hout elayt hiseat indivi ualta ut.

Gnaul obeve shednes ayst artof heenten perio dofpena ncevmud ging sheson foreads of astul ad urg igelor te wordor. Socia listan cois itter ranin a releco nid latay, akes ifab atapo litica co-mack yannoun.

Omnes galo est tres residoin entum pragmanoria it ielori nome stabovum gallo. Quant minimu bolus tret domin eagan ueils a progrˈae. Avum otra de, ivementu etad rectec onomi oc aidor touble aribea.

Wevviuy lar ihat ewil ovatev ris pru-dena decesario esure ece deur ere. Desio atap nechil liwo ronjur isios obre ad lieba kailure pleped leris senly inue aga. Pake yars hahec urent reion wipung itos ometi nar ore.

Resie eaga an amini stratio ofial talto ugabou heckina lege ubanac ked insur ences entra lenca. the ni-ted ates sofah ashra nished malmil itarsti.

More important stuff starts here

Galo est tres residoin entum pragman-oria it ielori nome stabovum gallo. Quant minimu bolus tret domin ea-gan ueils a progrˈae. Avum otra de, ivementu etad rectec onomi oc ai-dor touble aribea. Baideclar ihat ewil ovatev ris prudena decesario esure ece deur ere.

Red efiit antes lashit hout elayt hi-seat indivi ualta ut. Poe onaul obeve shednes ayst artof heenten perio dof-pena ncevmud ging sheson foreads of astul ad urg igelor te wordor. So-cia listan cois itter ranin a releco nid latay, akes ifab atapo litica co-mack yannoun isampa infoac outf fice.

Atspi nechil liwo ronjur isios obre ad lieba kailure pleped leris

---

Ad lieba kailure pleped leris senly inue yars hahec. Urent reion wipung itos ometi nar aruze iseki ouni feommuni tary. Oes he invent taloitee etig siceim posio omaria a eting egare.

A significa itepa rss torega in onolhe ofluo riend estrog wistren. Gen he riteb ones rss moprop oler womest ad osthe fra tures tatare. Omona flictio olage astu rearef as ouon ebuide wie odfabo aout earol. Tefor ercoro nerin vestiga toremin on rnsow deot muc ohistim troiden. Tifyt hoyinte resie eaga an amini stratio ofial talto ugabou heckina lege.

Decesario esure ece deur atap nechil liwo ronjur. Isios obre ad lieba kailure pleped leris senly inue yars hahec. Urent reion wipung itos ometi nar aruze iseki ouni feommuni tary. Oes he invent taloitee etig siceim posio omaria a eting egare.

Socia listan cois itter ranin a releco nid latay, akes ifab atapo litica co-mack yannoun isampa infoac outf fice Omnes galo est tres residoin en-tum pragmanoria it ielori nome sta-bovum gallo. Tifyt hoyinte resie eaga an amini stratio ofial talto ugabou heckina lege.

Quant minimu bolus tret domin ea-gan ueils a progrˈae. Avum otra de, ivementu etad rectec onomi oc ai-dor touble aribea. Baideclar ihat ewil ovatev ris prudena decesario esure ece deur ere.

Desio atap nechil liwo ronjur isios obre ad lieba kailure pleped leris senly inue aga.

Pake yars hahec urent reion wipung itos ometi nar ore. Woiec aruze iseki ouni feommuni tary, oes he invent taloitee etig siceim posio omaria la, a eting egare a significa itepa rss torega in onolhe ovement.

Moprop oler womest ad osthe fra tures tatare a omona flictio olage, astp dybvox. Ibues rearef oburia, as ouon ebuide wie odfabo aout earol. Sice telor ercoro nerin vestiga tore-mun on rnsow deot muc ohistim troi-den tifyt hoyinte box.

Ehout elayt hiseat indivi ualta ut. Pnaoe onaul obeve shednes ayst artof heenten perio dofpena. Cesmud ging sheson foreads of astul ad urg igelor te wordor.

Divi ualta ut. Poe onaul obeve shednes ayst. Cartof heenten perio dofpena ncevmud ging sheson for-eads of astul ad urg igelor te wordor.

Socia listan cois itter ranin a releco nid latay, akes ifab atapo litica co-mack yannoun isampa infoac outf fice Omnes galo est tres residoin en-tum pragmanoria it ielori nome sta-bovum gallo.

Moprop oler womest ad osthe fra tures tatare a omona flictio olage, astu dybvox. Ibues rearef oburia, as ouon ebuide wie odfabo aout earol. Sice telor ercoro nerin vestiga tore-mun on rnsow deot muc ohistim troi-den tifyt hoyinte box.

More important stuff starts here

Werti an amini stratio ofial talto ugabou heckina lege ubanac ked insur ences entra lenca. the ni-ted ates sofah ashra nished malmil itarsti.

Red efiit anbes lashit hout elayt hi-seat indivi ualta ut. Poe onaul obeve shednes ayst artof heenten perio dof-pena ncevmud ging sheson foreads of astul ad urg igelor te wordor. So-cia listan cois itter ranin a releco nid latay, akes ifab atapo litica co-mack yannoun isampa infoac outf fice.

Red efiit anbes lashit hout elayt hi-seat indivi ualta ut. Poe onaul obeve shednes ayst artof heenten perio dof-pena ncevmud ging sheson foreads of astul ad urg igelor te wordor. So-cia listan cois itter ranin a releco nid latay, akes ifab atapo litica co-mack yannoun isampa infoac outf fice.

Akes ifab atapo litica comack yannoun isampa infoac outf Est tres residoin entum pragmanoria it ielori nome stabovum. Minumu bolus tret domin eagan ueils a progrˈae otra ivementu. Tad rectec onomi oc aidor touble aribea baideclar ihat ewil ovatev.

Ris prudena decesario esure ece deur atap nechil liwo ronjur. Isios obre ad liebia kailure pleped leris senly inue yars hahec. Urent reion wipung itos ometi nar ore. oun feommuni tary. Oes he invent taloitee etig siceim posio omaria a eting egare.

A significa itepa rss torega in onolhe ofluo riend estrog wistren. Gen he riteb ones rss domin ea-gan ueils a progrˈae otra de, ivementu etad rectec onomi oc ai-dor touble aribea. Baideclar ihat ewil ovatev ris prudena decesario esure ece deur ere.

Desio atap nechil liwo ronjur isios obre ad lieba kailure pleped leris senly inue aga.

Pake yars hahec urent reion wipung itos ometi nar ore. Woiec aruze iseki ouni feommuni tary, oes he invent taloitee etig siceim posio omaria la, a eting egare a significa itepa rss torega in onolhe ovement. Ofluo riend estrog wistren gen he riteb ones-iro.

More important stuff starts here

Isampa infoac outof fice.Omnes galo est tres residoin entum pragmanoria it ielori nome stabovum gallo. Quant minimu bolus tret domin eagan ueils a progrˈae. Avum otra de, ivementu etad rectec onomi oc aidor touble aribea.

Cutyfra tures tatare a omona flictio olage. astu dybvox. Ibues rearef oburia, as ouon ebuide wie odfabo aout earol. Sice telor ercoro nerin vestiga tore-mun on rnsow deot muc ohistim troi-den tifyt hoyinte box.

Wil resie eaga an amini stratio ofial talto ugabou heckina lege ubanac ked insur ences entra lenca. the nited ates sofah ashra nished malmil itarsti. Reabud ged efiit anbes lashit hout elayt hiseat indivi ualta ut.

Cesmud ging sheson foreads of astul ad urg igelor te wordor.

Wil resie eaga an amini stratio ofial talto ugabou heckina lege ubanac ked insur ences. Entra lenca. the nited ates sofah ashra nished malmil itarsti. Reabud ged efiit anbes lashit hout elayt hiseat.

Divi ualta ut. Poe onaul obeve shednes ayst. Cartof heenten perio dofpena ncevmud ging sheson for-eads of astul ad urg igelor te wordor.

Socia listan cois itter ranin a releco nid latay, akes ifab atapo litica co-mack yannoun isampa infoac outf fice Omnes galo est tres residoin en-tum pragmanoria it ielori nome sta-bovum gallo.

Quant minimu bolus tret domin ea-gan ueils a progrˈae. Avum otra de, ivementu etad rectec onomi oc ai-dor touble aribea. Baideclar ihat ewil ovatev ris prudena decesario esure ece deur ere.

Desio atap nechil liwo ronjur isios obre ad lieba kailure pleped leris senly inue aga.

Pake yars hahec urent reion wipung itos ometi nar ore. Woiec aruze iseki ouni feommuni tary, oes he invent taloitee etig siceim posio omaria la, a eting egare a significa itepa rss torega in onolhe ovement. Ofluo riend estrog wistren gen he riteb ones-iro.

Ropnum atspi nechil liwo ronjur isios obre ad lieba kailure pleped leris senly inue aga. Pake yars hahec urent reion wipung itos ometi nar ore.

Wil resie eaga an amini stratio ofial talto ugabou heckina lege ubanac ked insur ences entra lenca. the ni-ted ates sofah ashra nished malmil itarsti.

Cuifres lashit hout elayt hiseat indivi ualta ut. Poe onaul obeve shednes ayst artof heenten perio dof-pena ncevmud ging sheson foreads of astul ad urg igelor te wordor. So-cia listan cois itter ranin a releco nid latay, akes ifab atapo litica co-mack yannoun isampa infoac outf fice.

Galo est tres residoin entum pragman-oria it ielori nome stabovum gallo. Quant minimu bolus tret domin eagan ueils a progrˈae. Avum otra de, ivementu etad rectec onomi oc ai-dor touble aribea. Baideclar ihat ewil ovatev ris prudena decesario esure ece deur ere.

More important stuff starts here

An eting egare a significa itepa rss torega in onolhe ovement. ofluo riend estrog wistren gen he riteb ones-rss moprop oler womest ad osthe fra tures tatare a omona flictio olage, astu dybvox.

Oburia, as ouon ebuide wie odfabo aout earol. Sice telor ercoro nerin vestiga toremun on rnsow deot muc ohistim troiden tifyt hoyinte box. Wil resie eaga an amini stratio ofial talto ugabou heckina lege ubanac ked in-sur.

Ences entra lenca. the nited ates sofah ashra nished malmil itarsti. Reabud ged efiit anbes lashit hout elayt hiseat indivi ualta ut. Poe on-

---

Important Person Sr.

Important Person Jr.

Important Person III

Important Person IV

Important Person V

Important Person VI

Here's a page with more "entry points." Perhaps only a reporter would think to lighten up a page by adding more type, in this case darker and larger type called a subhead. A second addition is a blurb or readout that is a quote from the actual story, which reporters like because it allows them to say things twice. Finally, photographs were added because reporters find them to have occasional value if they aren't too big. These photos are called thumbnails because they can be covered by your thumbnail and, in this instance, were used over the objections of the subject portrayed.

But all of these changes and all of this help created a new set of problems and the rest of this chapter is devoted to techniques that reduce them while increasing the possibility of producing stellar projects.

Writing

The first thing you must remember when working on a project is that, in the end, someone other than you is supposed to read it.[1]

At many newspapers, this is forgotten until three days before publication when the project team finally shows it to the managing editor, who says, "Can someone please just tell me in a single declarative sentence what the hell this is supposed to be about?"[2]

How can this be avoided?

■ The story conference: At some stage during the project, earlier and often being better than later and never, the project editor and reporters should brainstorm on the best way to tell the story.

This should be done without the aid of notes and memos,[3] and should be done in a nonthreatening environment, say in a canoe or while waiting in a movie line, and on company time. I remain convinced that the best way to tell a story is usually the way we orally tell it to one another, as opposed to the way we are likely to write it, especially the first time.

As a result of the story conference, we often settle on a way that requires more reporting, because we don't often think to do reporting for storytelling purposes, erroneously supposing that technique is only for feature stories. That's another reason the conference should be done early.[4]

■ Settling on tone. The traditional way of telling an investigative story—a prosecutor's brief to a jury—is not the only way and, sometimes, it's the worst way.

Here are some examples of wrestling with tone.

Some years ago, the *Washington Post* produced a two-day package of stories about the head of Mobil Oil, who appeared to have helped his son advance in the shipping business through some very advantageous rentals of Mobil oil tankers.

The *Post* chose to tell the stories in the tone of a "gotcha," whereby the newspaper appeared to be writing about something of great moment that was somehow very, very wrong.

Unfortunately, there was nothing very, very wrong, at least nothing illegal. What followed was a protracted lawsuit in which various people differed on when, exactly, the Fat Lady sang.

I think there never would have been a lawsuit if the *Post* had written the fascinating story in this tone: Gee, look what life can be like if your father is the head of a major corporation.

I think this would have been the most appropriate approach for their findings.

A 1990 project by writer Paul McEnroe and photographer Stormi Greener at the *Star Tribune* on parents who abuse their children used a number of approaches for different parts of the series.

The first two parts, published weeks apart, were closer to the traditional approach—summaries of major findings with lengthy sidebars that illustrated the main points through the lives of various people.

But the last two parts took an entirely different approach, with the sidebars—photo and word essays showing how parents lose control and the awful consequences—started on page one and overshadowed the more traditional articles.

For instance, Greener and McEnroe spent months with a woman who teetered along the edge of physically abusing her two children. Greener's photographs were some of the most moving ever published by any newspaper and by themselves equal all the words printed on the topic.[5]

This approach was much more likely to give the reader a sense of the problem and its consequences than a typical project treatment.

Here are six more tips related to writing and presenting the final project:

■ Graphics and photographs make the difference.

Here's how most reporters introduce the photographer working on the project to sources: "Oh, and here's my photographer . . ."

That is as close to death as most reporters ever come, although few ever know it.

Photographers are not the reporters' photographer, any more than the reporters belong to the photographers.

For nearly all types of projects, the photographer should be a full-time partner.

In addition, someone from the graphics department who will either work on the project or supervise those working on it should be involved from the very beginning. I give them copies of all memos and drafts and ask them to come to our meetings and participate, as they see fit.

For most subscribers, how a project looks is the key determinant as to whether it will be read.

One of the things an aggressive, contributing graphics artist can do is find sections of a story that lend themselves to graphic presentation, thus livening up the presentation and, often, shortening the story.

■ The memo revisited.

As the project nears completion, one of the great fears is whether the top editors will also think the project has been completed and done well.[6] Remember those memos we wrote in story form throughout the life of the project. Here's where their hidden value comes to the fore.

The trick for midlevel managers, like project editors, is to make the bosses partners, not just critics.

By sharing those early efforts and soliciting responses to your storytelling approach as well as the findings so far, top editors become partners in reacting to the focus and approach, just as interested as you are in finding the best approach.

Moreover, if various drafts just don't work for them, there is plenty of time to change. It's easier to change drafts early, because the writers haven't as much emotional investment in drafts as they do in the real thing.

■ Avoid unnecessary meetings.

The project editor should try not to have meetings after each draft. Instead, still seek out the top editors individually for reaction. This takes up your time, but not the reporters' and mild criticisms can be muted by you until the most appropriate time for passing them on, if ever.

If you must meet, always take the reporters to the meeting. When top editors talk to subordinate editors, they aren't nearly as receptive to differing ideas as they are when reporters are present. In addition, reporters always know more about the details of the project than the project editor.

Thus, when the managing editor says, "Why didn't we develop the story about the dwarf, the giant and the anteater?", the project editor would probably mumble, "I'm not sure, but I think there's a reason we couldn't do that. I'll check and see."

If the reporters are in the meeting, one of them can say, "That's a great idea, but we've been checking it out and just found out it's not true, and I don't think we should even quote them on it."

Of course, the project editor can find that out, then return the next day, but it's better if the answer is given in response to the advice. In addition, there's reduced confusion over what's decided if all the parties are in the room. And once again, it's collegial rather than judgmental.

■ Let the bosses help.

I often would go out of my way to tell the bosses about reporting problems so they'd have an idea about what we're up against. Maybe they have a great solution. Even if they don't, they have an ongoing understanding of why we're still down in the trenches slugging it out.

In this manner, our problems are their problems; our successes are also their successes.

■ Allow enough time for writing and design.

If you spend three months getting a story and then two weeks on writing and presentation, it will look and read like it was a two-week project. Without fail.

The major reason projects don't read well is that not enough time is spent on telling them, a chore many project reporters and editors don't actually enjoy.

■ Reintroduce the concept of rewrite.

Most reporters have not actually rewritten anything since freshman composition class. There's just never any time in regular daily journalism.

During the very first week of most projects, I tell reporters that we may have to rewrite drafts. They always nod in agreement over the reasonableness of this prediction, but usually are stunned when they actually have to do it.

I once borrowed a brilliant reporter from the business desk to conduct an examination of U.S. farm policy.[7] We spent three months on the investigation.

The difficulty was how to tell a big farm project to a largely urban readership who would pick up their Sunday newspaper one morning and, surprise, here's forty zillion words on the U.S. farm program.

We knew that how we wrote the main stories of the two-day series would be critical. We rewrote—as in starting over—the main story for day one more than a dozen times as we struggled to make it interesting to an uninterested, or at least indifferent, audience. In this case the reporter was happy to do it, usually insisting himself that there was a need.

Getting Finished

■ Organizing output.

Someone's got to give the data to the artists and check it when it comes back reincarnated as charts and graphs; someone's got to sit down with the lawyers who want to know what was your state of mind for paragraphs one through four; someone's got to sit with the copyeditors to answer all their questions; someone's got to check all the facts for accuracy and fairness and make appropriate changes; someone's still got two sidebars to write and a rewrite of the second day main story to do; someone's got to sit down with the promotions department to check their house ads promoting the upcoming project; someone's got to see if the main sidebar on day one can be trimmed to 12 inches because an artist wants to tuck it into a really neat design he's been dying to try since he saw it last year in the *Seattle Times*. And someone still hasn't come up with a name for all these words that the artists can make into a logo.

Back here at Reporter Central, we're looking around to see who can do all of this and all we see is you.

Good luck. You now have four days left and you are the single reason everyone else is behind. Ready, go.

"Helter skelter" is a phrase invented by Noah Webster to describe how major projects come together at most newspapers and is the real reason that project reporters burn out on projects.

It needn't be this way.

To manage this chaos, Tim Bitney, then the *Star Tribune* assistant managing editor for graphics, design, photography and everything else that has only one or two words, and I developed a backout schedule (BS). An example is printed in Sidebar 7.1.

This is how it works.

When we agree on a target date for publication, usually a month or so in the future, I go to Tim and ask him to back us out from that date.

He has in hand a budget of stories with estimated lengths and some idea of photo and graphic effort. He produces a day-by-day list of tasks that need to be done if the project is to be ready to run on time.

His list includes when data is given to artists; rough sketches returned to reporters and proofed, then returned to artists for finishing; when rough page designs will be offered, examined and finished; virtually everything else needed to be done by artists, photographers and designers and the dates the tasks must be done by if the project is to be run on the selected date.

This is your first reality check. You may find, on doing the BS, that the job can't be done without many hours of overtime.

The second reality check occurs when the reporters and I sit down and work into Bitney's schedule all the things we must do to get done.

Once everything is included, the BS is typed up and sent to all the people involved, including the top editors. The BS also tells them when they will get things and when they must return them if the project is to run on time.[8]

In business, this is called a critical path chart. In journalism, we call it the backout schedule. Put the task list right into your computer and modify it to suit whatever project you're doing.

There always will be new barriers and other reasons that you and others will fall behind. The BS allows you to see if the changes mean missing the deadline or not. It let's you and others monitoring the project check where you are against where you need to be for the selected deadline. And it's a damned fine list of tasks.

After we designed and implemented this, the managing editor decided all major efforts around the newspaper would have backout schedules. Bitney swears it made his life easier. When Bitney's life is easier, the lives of 300 other people working in the *Star Tribune* newsroom are easier, too.

■ Looks great, but is it right?

Near the end of each project we go over every word of every line to check for accuracy, fairness and context.

We call this line-by-lining and we do a version of it on every single project.

I take a draft of the first story, starting at the top, and the reporter goes back to the original documentation to check out each fact. When we come to quotes, the reporter reads the quotes from the computer where the transcribed interviews preside.[9]

This is our last chance to make sure everything is right and it's a much more thorough method than any lawyer's. We wait until near the end because most problems arise not from the facts we use but in the words used to characterize them, as in adverbs and adjectives. How we say something is as important as what we say.

In a long project, line-by-lining will add five to ten days to the work, maybe more.

In investigative projects, we do every word. In some kinds of projects we use a modified procedure. For instance, since we weren't writing about anyone stealing federal payments in our farm project, I let the reporter check all the quotes and other facts. But he and I went over all the thousands of numbers in the series as it was numbers that girded our premise.

We are not just looking for simple things, such as, is the name spelled correctly or is the date of birth right. Here are three examples of what line-by-lining can and should do.

In the early 1980s, a prosecutor in the small, rural town of Jordan, Minn., began looking into a suspected child sexual abuse ring involving several dozen children and adults.

It was a sensational case and was covered by news media throughout the country. In the end, there was one failed prosecution of one couple and one successful prosecution of an abuser. All other charges were dropped.

State investigators conducted their own investigation next and concluded the original prosecutor had done such a poor job there was nothing for them to do at that late date.

There was even a publicly aired inquiry about whether the prosecutor should be sanctioned. She wasn't, but the prosecutor appointed to investigate that effort concluded that there was evidence of child abuse but that the Jordan prosecutor had done such a poor job that some of the guilty went free with the innocent.

During all of this, the *Star Tribune* decided to do its own investigation of what happened.

The results were ultimately presented over seven full pages, but the story could be broken in two basic parts.

Part one showed there were a lot of red flags that should have warned the Jordan prosecutor that many of the claims by children were unlikely.

Part two showed how poorly the case had been investigated, which doomed any successful prosecution. How did we know that? In part because of what some of the children told us about the prosecutor and her investigators.

Here's the objection raised in the line-by-line.

How can we, in part one, raise credibility concerns about the children and their stories and then, in part two, criticize the prosecutor based in part on what some of these same children told us? It didn't seem fair.

The fix made the story stronger.

The reporters went back to their notes and documentation and then wrote paragraphs leading into the second part to this effect: Readers were reminded that some of these children were the same children who told some of the obvious lies. However, on these points we believed them because their story was verified or corroborated in investigators' notes, sociologists' notes, psychologists' notes, state investigators' notes and interviews we conducted with others. And where we couldn't do this, those parts were dropped.

The first installment of Fatal Neglect, mentioned earlier, revolved around the case files of some 22 children who died from abuse, neglect or under suspicious circumstances during the previous two years. All of the children had been known to authorities as being in problem homes, but the system had failed to protect them. Most didn't live to their first birthday.

The project team concluded that these deaths showed a system out of control. But against what standard?

It can be argued that the death of one child is one child too many, but can we conclude the system is a failure?

During this same period, the system handled some 20,000 cases. Did some 22 deaths make the system a failure? Looked at another way, did the 20,000 or so child survivors make the system a success?

How about another measure—the success/failure rate of other states? Depending on how it is measured, Minnesota was about average or among the best.

What, then, could be reasonably concluded from the facts we'd dug up?

By taking the cases and poring over them anew, a different pattern emerged. In every single case, when the person taking care of the child wanted to avoid supervision it had been ridiculously easy for him or her to do so. The parent would move a lot. Or, in at least one case, when the social worker came to the door and was told to come back because the child was sleeping, the compliant and overworked case officer failed to return before the child's death.

Another clear pattern showed that the system never integrated observations of doctors, police and case workers until after the death, thus severely reducing the chance, in many cases, of exposing the fact that the child was in danger.

This was coupled with some underused research the team had dug up. A researcher in Chicago had made a statistical profile of the child most likely to be at risk, a profile that fit most of our children like a glove. That is, these were children who should have benefited from the most aggressive intervention, but hadn't.

This *was* a system seriously out of kilter and in need of reform.

In a project on Hmong immigrants, reporters learned that the Hmong soldiers, and their families who immigrated to the United States after we lost the war in Vietnam, were expecting to be taken care of by the U.S. government.

In that project, we decided to tell the whole story from the Hmong perspective—through their voices.

We could have reported what they said just as they said it, but we decided to find out if there was reason to believe them.

Having identified this issue in advance as a line-by-line issue, the reporters contacted former and current CIA officials, former and current State Department officials, government documents, former U.S. soldiers who'd worked with Hmong, and other sources.

We found ample evidence to believe the Hmong and even made a box out of the material to accompany the story so the reader could see the reasons to believe the Hmong.

Why agonize over conclusions?

Because conclusions about what facts mean are exactly what project reporting is all about.

A project is not just a collection of facts we've found out, but also what we think they mean. Nothing more, but certainly nothing less.

If you are uncomfortable about making conclusions, stay in the bulletin-board side of the craft, which is valuable work but different from projects.

Nor does this mean that we have the only possible version. It means only that this is the best available version that we could find, indeed, we think that anyone could find. And this is what we think it means. Where it is gray, not red or blue, say so.

No one I ever worked with likes going through the line-by-line procedure, including me, but they and I like the feeling before publication that every single thing we published has a reason to be believed. And the veterans of this procedure prepare for the line-by-line by footnoting the paragraphs in the story to the documentation so that the actual line-by-lining goes more quickly.

As with the backout schedule, this is a method that institutionalizes the possibility that things will work the way they should. In this case, it creates a process whereby all errors of fact and judgment are more likely to be caught.

Confessions and Endnotes

None of these things discussed in chapters 6 and 7 works all the time, either for me or for you. They are, however, tactics and techniques that elevate the process of producing projects to something we are managing, rather than something that is managing us.

A project—each and every one—should be the apex of our effort in journalism. It is that part of journalism that truly needs a First Amendment, that justifies our staying in a low-paying, unappreciated, burnout craft. It is precisely investigative stories that have the opportunity to benefit a public increasingly removed from managing our democracy.

Approach each one as if it is the only chance you will ever get to produce outstanding journalism, because it just may be. And if you can't approach projects this way, give us all a break and don't approach them at all.

NOTES

1. Since we don't pay readers to read and since we don't (gasp) listen to them, or anybody else, after we publish, this means that we have to actually take the time to entice readers to read this story.

2. This sentence and its derivatives have sent more reporters and project editors into alternate careers than any other journalism hazard.

3. One of the failures of some published investigative projects is the failure to throw out the bowling balls so they don't clutter up the lane.

Example of bowling balls: The person embezzled $400,000, killed his mother, married three times without benefit of a divorce and committed five other felonies to boot.

Example of bowling balls: He also has four parking tickets, once knocked down an old lady trying to be first at a Blue Light Special and is known to kick his dog when frustrated.

Reporters want to put in everything they find. I call this piling on and think the projects read better and are more focused if we can agree to throw away the bowling balls.

4. If we were to reduce to one sentence what journalism is all about, it would be this one: Reporters tell stories. Of course, we like to think of it as something more important than that, like Defending the First Amendment.

But the sad truth is, we just tell stories. They are truthful, accurate and, if anyone with the same skills and time cared to duplicate our efforts, they would arrive at the same conclusions. But this is only just another way of saying that what we do is tell stories.

In fact, they aren't even the *truth*. They are a version of the truth. We start from the reality that we weren't there to see then we go about trying to find out what happened. It is the very best version we can dig up, and we have every reason to believe it is the best version, but we should know it is only a version of the truth. Philosophers through all the ages have been telling us that the *truth* cannot be known in this life and journalism is about nothing but this life.

5. Greener won every major photography award but one for those photos.

6. This is one of the symptoms of Toxic Project Syndrome (TPS).
Other TPS symptoms include:

- A fear by reporters diverted to the project that their colleagues will say, "You took three months for that?" or "I knew that."
- A reporter fears that you, the project editor, or other top editors will totally gut the project at the last minute.
- A fear by all on the project that somehow there is a memo or document we overlooked that simply devastates the thrust of the project and which the subject of the investigation will produce the day after the project runs.
- Reporters who repeatedly and heatedly argue with you for days over a point, then, when you give in, attempt to argue with you repeatedly and heatedly to go the other way.
- Sleeping through lunch.
- Actually enjoying meetings.

There are others and the reasons are legion. However, suffice to say that TPS is a real disease and everyone will get it, some worse than others.

Here are some ways that I tried to lessen its impact.

- Daily wandering into the projects office to tell long, boring and pointless war stories so that reporters would worry more about my sanity than their's.
- Asking reporters to pick me up at home and then forcing them to go kayaking with me on the creek running behind my house.
- Sending reporters to museums or art galleries for the entire day.
- Taking reporters to movies on company time, which always produces that delicious feeling you had back in high school when you played hooky.
- And once, I even sat on a park bench to make sure a project reporter wasn't molested while he slept like a babe under a pine tree.

7. Actually, I asked him to do something simpler, like find out where all the farmers have gone. He came back after a couple of weeks and said the real story was how misguided, wasteful and doomed U.S. farm policy was.

This actually happens a lot.

Lou Kilzer and Chris Ison worked several months on a gambling probe. They then determined the actual story was about arson; they then produced a series that would win them the 1990 Pulitzer Prize for investigative reporting. We talked about the new focus and I quickly became convinced.

Later, so did my bosses.

However, they would like me to find out sooner than two months what a project is all about.

I must admit, that sounds reasonable.

In the abstract.

8. Managing your bosses is an important part of a successful project. From their perspective, an editor's most important task is to keep pressure on you to get the project into the newspaper. You know they're going to have lots to say, so the trick is to get them to say it when it's most useful. The backout schedule helps manage your bosses.

9. We don't save script notes in the projects office. After an interview the reporter transcribes it into the computer and the original notes are discarded. After they are transcribed and checked, the original notes have no value, so we don't keep them.

If you adopt this policy, you have to religiously follow it for all projects. Check with your lawyers and editors.

The Backout Schedule

by John Ullmann

The backout schedule is a useful device to see whether you can humanly make your deadline without setbacks or outrageous overtime. Type this one into your computer and modify it for your next project.

Project Backout Schedule

---

25 March, Monday

    ☐ Do all chart screening: reporters, Ullmann, design.
    (Story conference has already occurred.)

26 March, Tuesday

    ☐ Do all chart screening: reporters, Ullmann, design.

27 March, Wednesday

    ☐ Line-by-line CIA, American policy questions.

28 March, Thursday

    ☐ Reporting and writing continue.
    ☐ Bring in concept copyeditor for duration.

29 March, Friday

    ☐ Reporting and writing continue.

30 March, Saturday

    Off.

31 March, Sunday

    Off.

1 April, Monday
- ☐ Reporting and writing continue.

2 April, Tuesday
- ☐ Reporting and writing continue.

3 April, Wednesday
- ☐ All chart and map information to design by noon.
- ☐ Final rough edit of photographs.
- ☐ Name for series finalized by 3 P.M.

4 April, Thursday
- ☐ Continue work on maps and charts.
- ☐ Begin copyediting of story.
- ☐ Print photographs from final edit.
- ☐ Begin structural design of section.

5 April, Friday
- ☐ Final final-stage copyediting of story completed.
- ☐ Proofs of copy to Troik by 5 P.M. (Troik is a term of affection for executive, managing and deputy managing editors.)
- ☐ Continue work on maps and charts.
- ☐ Complete final printing of photographs.
- ☐ Continue structural design; make space request.

6 April, Saturday
- ☐ Complete maps and graphics.

7 April, Sunday
Off.

8 April, Monday
- ☐ Troik returns copy with comments by 10 A.M.
- ☐ Copy reworked and re-edited.
- ☐ Begin section layout.

☐ Write subheads for series—complete by noon.

☐ Dump test type of copy for length and positioning.

☐ Proof and check maps and graphics.

9 April, Tuesday

☐ Copy re-editing finished by noon.

☐ Make corrections on charts and maps.

☐ Continue layout of section.

☐ Start work on art elements needed for section design.

☐ Begin writing cutlines for photographs.

☐ Line-by-line.

10 April, Wednesday

☐ Continue layout of section—finish by noon.

☐ Complete roughs of layout—finish by 3 P.M.

☐ Meet with editors to go over roughs with photos and copy.

☐ Complete writing cutlines for photographs by 3 P.M.

☐ Line-by-line.

11 April, Thursday

☐ Make changes in copy as per editors suggestions by noon.

☐ Copy is typeset for final fitting—length remains exact after this point.

☐ Work on blue-line sheets for layout.

☐ Copyedit cutlines—complete by noon.

12 April, Friday

☐ Continue sizing and moving art and photos to photoplate.

☐ Continue work on blue-line sheets for layout.

☐ Headlines and miscellaneous copy written and edited.

13 April, Saturday

Off.

14 April, Sunday

Off.

15 April, Monday

☐ Final art to photoplate—finish by noon.

☐ Complete blue-lines layouts.

☐ Complete any final editing, writing, coding, etc.

16 April, Tuesday

☐ All type is dumped—early afternoon, finished by 2 P.M.

☐ Begin section makeup—afternoon and evening.

17 April, Wednesday

☐ Finish makeup of section—early afternoon.

☐ Pull proofs and distribute to editors by 5 P.M.

18 April, Thursday

☐ Editors return proofs with comments by 10 A.M.

☐ Corrections and changes worked into copy and layouts by 6 P.M.

19 April, Friday

☐ Type is redumped with corrections—complete by noon.

☐ Makeover section with final corrections—early afternoon.

☐ Pull final proofs and distribute by 5 P.M.

20 April, Saturday

☐ Pages go to photoplate.

21 April, Sunday

☐ Section appears in paper.

22 April, Monday

☐ Battlefield promotions and raises for reporters and project editor.

APPENDIX ONE

An Outside View of Investigative Reporting

In recent years there have been a number of efforts to critique the work of investigative reporters, and even the reporters themselves. In this brief appendix, the first of three, we get a taste of what someone in another profession thinks investigative reporting offers his colleagues.

One of the more interesting dissections of investigative reporting is by Egon Guba, a professor of education at Indiana University, who turned the journalism as social science discussion around and offered a fascinating treatise on what evaluators of educational programs could learn from investigative reporters, along with what they shouldn't bother with.[1]

To do that, he had to turn his very perceptive mind to analyzing what we do and how we do it. Here's an example of how he thinks as he analyzes the attitudinal barriers erected by management at many news organizations. (Notice how perceptive he is about newsroom management. We can learn from him the same way his colleagues can learn from us.)

- Just as an editor (to use that term to include all persons who have some authority over the investigative reporter) may have a "bulletin board" rather than a "watchdog" philosophy, so may an evaluation administrator prefer to emphasize description over judgment and process over impact.
- Just as an editor may permit stories that expose petty scandals but oppose those that question the basic institutional structure of the community, so may the evaluation administrator permit evaluations that expose minor program breakdowns but oppose those that insist on evaluating the objectives themselves in addition to assessing the congruence of performance and objectives.
- Just as an editor may be unmotivated toward investigative journalism because of public apathy, so the evaluation administrator may be unmo-

183

tivated because he does not perceive an audience interested in getting strong evaluation results.

- Just as an editor may seek to cover up (to avoid scandal) or overlook (in the interest of a larger social good) certain problems, so the evaluation administrator may choose to "whitewash" a program or minimize its shortcomings. . . .
- Just as editors may avoid controversy for the sake of furthering their careers, so may evaluation administrators.
- Just as editors may not have achieved their positions by coming through the ranks of investigative journalism, and so fail to understand and support it, so may evaluation administrators.

The lessons of these parallels are clear: evaluation administrators can and do heavily influence evaluation outcomes, as editors do in the case of investigative stories.[2]

NOTES

1. "Investigative Journalism," by Egon G. Guba, in "New Techniques for Evaluation," Nick L. Smith, ed. (Beverly Hills: Sage Publications, 1981), 167–262.

2. Guba, 223–24.

APPENDIX TWO

An Inside View of Investigative Reporting

Researchers at Northwestern University have produced one of the more interesting and thorough jobs of analyzing investigative reporting. Their book should be read by all reporters. Here are some excerpts.

One of the most thorough, most interesting and most often on the mark investigation of investigative reporters and their work can be found in "The Journalism of Outrage," written by a host of university professors led by David L. Protess at Northwestern University.[1]

If you've been to an IRE conference anytime since 1981, you may have been approached by Protess et al. to fill out a survey on how you do your work. More than 900 of us responded. In addition, Protess spent time with investigative print and broadcast teams as they produced six projects and answered questions about what they were doing:

The first case examines a nationally televised investigation of fraud and abuse in the federally funded home health care program (Garrick Utley, NBC News Magazine, May 7, 1981, and sparked by the Better Government Association, a Chicago investigatory group that often gives project ideas to Chicago and national media and which often aids the subsequent investigation). The second focuses on a *Chicago Sun-Times* series that disclosed problems in the reporting and prosecution of sex crimes ("Rape Epidemic: No Woman Immune," beginning July 25, 1982). The third case involves a multipart Chicago television report about repeatedly brutal police officers (Peter Karl, WMAQ-TV, February 1983). The fourth examines an investigation by the same station of the toxic waste disposal practices of a major midwestern university (Peter Karl, May 1984). The fifth involves a "60 Minutes" investigation of international child abductions (Diane Sawyer, "Missing?," early 1987,

185

sparked by both a BGA effort and an earlier WBBM-TV airing). The sixth case examines a *Philadelphia Inquirer* investigative series about kidney dialysis clinics that have become "profit machines." ("Dialysis: The Profit Machine," by Matthew Purdy, beginning May 15, 1988).

Armed with answers from years of interviewing and surveying investigative reporters—along with access to projects before, during and after the series was produced—and augmented with surveys of readers and viewers conducted before and after publication or broadcast, Protess is well-equipped to describe the craft and to come to some conclusions.[2]

Many are not anti-intuitive: Project ideas come from different places, not one; they are difficult to produce, involving many trade-offs (some of which are good and some of which are not); reactions to the series are varied as to any "results"; the public is rarely mobilized to "demand" change as a result of an expose; for various reasons, public officials usually do respond, however, sometimes effectively addressing the issues raised by the investigators.

Protess's main myth-busting effort is devoted to annihilating the linear idea that the news media expose a problem, the public gets outraged, public officials are then forced to address the problem. Anyone who's ever worked even a single project and then watched to see what's going to happen will already know this.

In the projects Protess studied, however, the news organizations often don't just sit back to see what happens.

Protess shows how reporters in these case studies often interact with public officials, talking with them before the series runs about changes and following up the project with numerous stories. Protess calls it building media and policy agendas, with the news media trying and often succeeding at being the architects, just to complete the metaphor.

For those of us who haven't worked in the competition-chocked and charged arenas of Chicago, Philadelphia and national television, and who don't have the benefit of a first-class investigative organization like the BGA to help us, the case studies will offer some areas of discomfort and large areas for second-guessing the appropriateness of the relationship reporters develop with certain segments in the government-political arena. This is especially so where the news media's effort seems too geared to bringing about results the news organization can then claim its project stimulated.[3]

This is a good book, one we all should read. In addition to the case studies and critical analysis, the book offers a first-rate chapter on the history of investigative reporting and, unlike the work discussed in Appendix Three, is full of good analysis that usually pulls back from unwarranted generalizations.[4]

Here are two examples.

These stories (case studies) suggest that the task of winnowing evidence triggers a new stage of investigative agenda building. In this stage, some problems rise in salience, whereas others decline. Significantly, the selection of problems has little to do with larger societal realities. Instead, the choice is based on the most vivid cases that fit the story line. Having begun their probe with specific wrongdoings and having later identified emerging classes of abuse, reporters return in the presentation stage to emphasize the most compelling cases they found along the way. Elsewhere, we have called this phenomenon "the logic of particularism."

Cases that survive the winnowing rarely provide inaccurate depictions of reality. Reporters' standards of thoroughness virtually ensure that each case is internally valid. Its generalizability, or external validity, may be suspect, however.

Partial exception to this rule occurred in the editing of the rape investigation and the production of the police brutality probe. In editing the newspaper series, journalists emphasized the geographic patterns of sex crimes and the underlying bureaucratic and sociological problems that produced them. Similarly, in "Beating Justice," reporters used a variety of graphic devices to show that the individual cases of brutality were part of a larger system of abuse.

However, the logic of particularism was evidenced even in these stories. Despite reporters' plans to include statistically representative victims in the rape series, they instead included depictions of sensational sex crimes, including a detailed profile of a woman who was raped twice. The police brutality series emphasized the sordid details of victimization by a handful of police officers. Indeed, the most brutal case reported was not committed by a repeat offender, which was the main angle of the series.

We do not mean to suggest here that journalists ignore the bigger picture in the winnowing process. Rather, it is a matter of emphasis. With the audience in mind, journalists' storytelling role once again becomes dominant. Consequently, in the effort to appeal to readers or viewers, cases are emphasized over classes, and the most compelling cases are chosen over undramatic ones. Patterns are identified, and journalists hope consumers of their product will not miss the larger message. But it requires inductive logic—learning by example—and a discerning audience to do so (224–25).[5] This extract is from the concluding paragraphs of their book:

In 1984, *Editor and Publisher* magazine reported the "death" of investigative reporting. This prognostication proved to be unnecessarily gloomy. Still, cutbacks in local television "I teams" and in newspaper investigative units have been widely publicized.[6]

Our surveys of investigative reporters and editors in 1986 and 1989 suggest that investigative reporting retains a core strength, although it may be shifting directions. Both surveys show that most muckrakers continue to spend as much time on investigative reporting as in the past. However, there is a trend toward doing more short-term investigative stories. This might well lead to a decline in the lengthy project stories that have been the focus of this book.

Investigative reporters also may be becoming less of an elite breed of journalist. The success of Investigative Reporters and Editors' workshops for different kinds of journalists suggests that the techniques of investigative reporting are being adapted by the professional mainstream. Thus, although separate investigative units have been disbanded, investigative practices have become more widespread. As we concluded in 1986: "The IRE survey findings point to the institutionalization of investigative journalists have merely become less visible as their efforts become more conventional. Today's muckrakers may be more akin to inveterate watchdogs than starving wolves."

The apparent trends in investigative reporting may seem somewhat contradictory. However, they have certain common elements that have significant implications for future governing practices. The decline in resources for investigative reporting, especially long-term projects, probably will mean an increase in collaboration among journalists and policy makers. Journalists will more readily seek out policy partners because they will need information more quickly, and because they will not be given the time to follow up their stories to ensure impact. Similarly, the use of investigative techniques by beat reporters, for whom transactions with officials are already routine, will further facilitate coalition journalism.

For policy makers, these trends will provide additional opportunities for image and agenda building. The institutionalization of investigative reporting creates increased potential to draw the media spotlight to their problem-solving activities. Policy makers will be able to decrease their reliance on a handful of reporters—some of whom see themselves as adversaries of officialdom—and broaden their capacity to achieve results through a diffusion of partnerships.

The implications of these developments for public policy making are significant. The expansion of the media-policy connection means journalists will play a greater role in helping set policy agendas. The actual content of stories may become even less important for policy making than the kinds of alliances that form between journalists and officials.

Second, the long-term policy impact of investigative reporting may be circumscribed by the declining commitment to crusade. Media muckrakers may be able to continue to set the deliberative agenda of policy makers. However, as they move fleetingly from one story to another, the action agenda—the substance of reform—will remain under the control of established policy-making interests.

Finally, present trends suggest the general public will play even less of an active policy-making role. American popular democracy has been victimized by twentieth-century developments in media and society. Scholarly analyses have described the American people as the "phantom public," the "captive public," the "semi-sovereign people" and the "by-stander public." Our media age has produced, in one scholar's words, a "democracy without citizens." "Manufacturing consent" is what others have called it.

There is every reason to conclude that present trends in investigative reporting will exacerbate this problem in the future. Muckraker–policy-maker reporting transactions will continue to bypass the public in the resolution of important public issues. Even where such issues are not resolved, the public will be led to *believe* they have been resolved by viewing or reading the reaction stories of reporters. Public outrage about important social problems may not have been manifested for some time; in contemporary times, outrage may prove to be irrelevant even where it does not surface.

These trends are not immutable. The historical pendulum may swing back to an era of reform at some future juncture. We have concluded that conditions will be ripe for such an era when public alienation toward authority recurs, and at the same time changes in media engender fierce competition for stories about moral disorder. If and when this does happen, conventional notions about popular democracy may once again become relevant. Until that time, investigative reporting will continue to be a catalyst for policy reform without necessarily being a vehicle for mass public mobilization or enlightenment (252–54).

NOTES

1. "The Journalism of Outrage," by David L. Protess, Fay Lomax Cook, Jack D. Doppelt, James S. Ettema, Margaret T. Gordon, Donna R. Leff and Peter Miller (New York: The Guilford Press, 1991).

2. Protess even offers a simpler definition for investigative reporting—the journalism of outrage.

3. Protess's reporter interviews, his own insights and his surveys show him that many reporters think that "results" (a surrogate for "impact" or what happened after you ran it) is an appropriate way to measure the success of a project. This is wrong. "Results" are not the job of journalists.

4. An unwarranted generalization is one I don't agree with.

5. One yearns here for an examination and analysis of the role of the project editors and their bosses to nail down who's the actual villain of, at best, unclear thinking. Who among us would argue that the role of a project is to show the patterns and causes, where we can, and that the role of anecdotes is to explicate and place the reader into the problem, to demonstrate its realness to those who are abused. The best projects to both, with the preponderance of weight on the former.

6. True, but the number of entries at IRE for its national investigative reporting contest remains about the same every year—evidence that the commitment remains strong.

APPENDIX THREE

A Critical View of
Investigative Reporting

These two university professors use a different methodology—the in-depth interview—of award-winning investigative reporters and their methodologies. You may, as I do, question some of their conclusions. As a bonus, you get a primer on story form analysis, a method of analyzing journalism now in vogue in the academy.

What are we to make of the work of professors James S. Ettema and Theodore L. Glasser?[1] These two have been interviewing award-winning investigative reporters and editors for several years, primarily interested in how we work and how we think about how we work.

Their conclusions are always well written, sometimes illuminating and sometimes just plain wrong.

To understand more fully their point of view, it is important to take a brief sidetrack to gain some insight into the study of "narrative" or storytelling, an area that's found a strong following in mass media studies. To gain the insight we need, we will find no clearer or better-told guide than that presented by Adrian Tilley in "The Media Studies Book."[2]

> To *study* narrative, then, is to pick apart storytelling, our own and that of others around us, in our personal interaction and in our relations to other agencies who are in the business of "telling tales." The media are in the forefront of narrative production and offer ripe pickings. They produce, circulate and present a vast range of narratives that share certain similarities and can be distinguished by important differences. Some characteristics they share with our own acts of storytelling but others are very different. There are differences in *forms* of narrative and differences in the *situations* in which narratives are met; between "story time" at school and being asked what we did at school today when we get home.[3]

191

To see how the study of narrative can be applied to investigative reporting (or any reporting), we need Tilley's explanations of equilibria and character as function.

First, equilibria:

> The basic formula . . . [is] . . . where a narrative consists of a fictional world in which an *initial equilibrium* is then *disrupted,* with a different and *new equilibrium* produced at the end. The initial equilibrium may be a balance of social, psychological or moral elements according to the story genre: the harmonious social and family grouping in the opening scenes of *Klute* or *The Godfather;* Josey Wales in *The Outlaw Josey Wales* tilling the soil of his land in a dappled sunlight; the rocket launch—a pinnacle of technological achievement—in the opening of *The Quatermass Experiment.* Even non-fiction titles such as "The Nine O'Clock News" begin with an initial equilibrium—the safety and reliability of reports from the world of news—soon to be disrupted by that "other world" of violence, death and politics. After a series of accounts of an event, interpretations are made by "experts" on our behalf, resolution and order re-established by a final, often lighthearted story offering relief and release in a new equilibrium.
>
> The notion of equilibrium raises questions about how social order is represented and how it functions to effect *closure* within stories. We leave the news world as we found it, with the readers at their desks as the credits roll and the music plays once more; the "other world" has been dealt with for the time being and we can proceed safely onwards. At the end of *The Outlaw Josey Wales* a new community has been created—a sharing and stable community of male and female, young and old, white and red. Threat and disruptions of that new order have been dealt with violently—in the case of the marauding Redlegs—and by negotiation— with the local Indian community. The utopian resolution of many fictions and news programmes contrasts with the more ambiguous resolutions of other examples. In the final sequence of *Klute,* Bree Daniels, a call girl who has been the victim of a psychopath's brutal campaign of fear, leaves her flat—and, apparently, her independent city existence—to share a small-town life with John Klute, the detective who has "saved" her. . . .
>
> Comparing the initial social order with the final social order is always revealing. Key questions will be: What has changed in the world of the story? What has been transformed? What has been added or lost in the process? How have the characters' relative positions of power and status changed?

Across the range of narratives, patterns emerge. Positions of dominance or submission are taken up by certain characters depending on their gender, race, class or position in a family. So, in *The Quatermass Experiment,* whilst medicine, law and order, science and the media cooperate together to prevent catastrophe, it is science which asserts its dominance and independence at the end as the Professor marches into the night towards a technological future. The film has a familiar and powerful discourse on the primacy of science as saviour of the world's troubles. Narrative analysis like this can deal with the way narratives speak *ideologically,* about organizations and relations of power.[4]

You can see how attractive, and potentially useful, is a methodology that allows for studying how we tell our stories. We need only a few more paragraphs about "character as function" to gain a fuller appreciation.

Characters are understood not for who they are or what they are like but for the structural role they play in the story. Thus, characters are rendered as hero, villain, donor (of gifts or help) or magical agent. . . . The (model) can be applied to any narrative and not just fiction; to the study of newspapers, for instance, to trace how character types and events function in news reporting. News stories feature heroes, who are seen as supporting and defending the social order, and villains seeking to disrupt and destroy it. This is at its starkest in news coverage of terrorist acts, strike pickets and moments of civil disorder. . . .[5]

The similarities here—the parallel universes—of fiction writing and the stories of investigative reporters are striking. Who among us, after getting the facts, doesn't sit down to intentionally discover a compelling way to tell them to readers, to show them to viewers. In print, we are often looking at the best writing—even among fiction—to help inform our own, borrowing approaches or even devices where they seem to fit.

And who can argue against the notion that over time the impact of investigative reporting is to uphold the existing moral order? After all, it is against the existing order as expressed by law, regulations, codes of conduct, agreements in a contract or other commonly accepted standards that we find and then make conclusions about people in violation of those standards.

It is the unusual, but not rare, investigative or public policy project that goes beyond finding the problem within the framework of existing boundaries, and asks instead that we rethink the problem in its entirety.

In "Narrative Form and Moral Force: The Realization of Innocence and Guilt Through Investigative Journalism," Ettema and Glasser up the ante.[6]

Over a number of years, Ettema and Glasser had lengthy interviews with investigative reporters who are "highly accomplished;" that is, investigative reporters who have won national awards.

The researchers are also concerned with narrative, but they seem to decide that the reporters they studied are not only adopting the form of fiction but engaged in producing it, at least in some small measure. Ettema and Glasser adopt their own story form—that of outsiders come to view the insiders, who then discover things the insiders don't know and, hence, come to conclusions they think are new, important or startling. To do this, they have to push the bubble further than it can contain itself.

For example, let's examine what these authors make of the work by William Marimow in "The K-9 Cases" of the *Philadelphia Inquirer,* which reported on the unwarranted attacks by police dogs in that city and which earned Marimow one of his two Pulitzer Prizes.[7] (Also included was Loretta Tofani's Pulitzer winner on jail rapes in Prince George's County produced while she worked at the *Washington Post,* and a Pam Zekman award-winner titled "Killing Crime: A Police Cop-out" that ran on WBBM-TV in Chicago.)

To understand what informs their analysis, one might say fully informs their analysis, we must first report some of what they demonstrate that guides their thinking:

> One important implication of (an) argument about the relationship between historical narratives and the historical facts that presumably constitute them is that the coherence which the story provides to the facts "is achieved only by a tailoring of the 'facts' to the requirements of story form." Facts are selected to fit the story but, more than that, fact and story are mutually constituted, though not necessarily consciously, by the historian.[8] . . .
>
> The point here is not to dissolve the distinction between the discourse of the real and the discourse of the imaginary or, following Lacan, the discourse of desire. Rather, the point is to highlight the extent to which narrative transforms the real into an object of desire through a formal coherence and a moral order that the real lacks.[9]
>
> Investigative journalism defends traditional virtue by telling stories of terrible vice. The value of justice, for example, is affirmed in stories of outrageous injustice. Like a number of other story forms, investigative journalism maintains and sometimes updates consensual interpretations of right and wrong, innocence and guilt, by applying them to the case at hand, though it seldom analyzes or critiques such interpretations.[10] . . .

If these stories do not usually challenge public morality, they can, as another reporter said, "amalgamate it and vocalize it." . . . These reporters are, then, the intellectual successors not only to muckrakers but to Jeremiah himself. Their moral task is to evoke outrage at the violation of dearly held values in the conduct of public affairs and implicitly invite, if not explicitly demand, a return to those values. Their venue is a kind of demonstrative discourse, as Aristotle might have described it, designed to distinguish between the honorable and dishonorable.[11] . . .

In each of these reports, we focus on the accomplishment of two specific moral tasks: the realization, through narrative, of innocence and of guilt. The narrative strategies employed to meet these tasks are strikingly similar in these reports but, of course, we claim to have found neither the essential features of all narrative nor the formula for success in this particular genre of narrative. We seek only to appreciate how narrative has been, and can be, used as a moral force in the life of the community. The moral force brought to bear through each of these reports is, in large measure, the result of skillfully crafted stories of victimization.

These reports do not merely identify individuals who apparently have been wronged but rather define them as victims who are innocent—innocent enough, at least, to make their victimization by "the system" a moral outrage.[12]

With this as a backdrop, how do they use Marimow's articles and their interview with him to bring their views on investigative reporting to fruition? Here are the relevant paragraphs:

And so it was for the victims of police dog attacks on the streets of Philadelphia. The investigation into their plight began with a tip that certain K-9 unit officers and their dogs were conducting "target practice" on the streets. It soon became clear to the reporter that attack cases came in "all shades of gray." A few cases were clearly accidental attacks on "innocent citizens," though many others were quite ambiguous. Some attacks, for example, occurred on subway platforms or outside of bars very late at night after the police had been called to the scene. The victims were sometimes young men who provoked the responding officers. But it also became clear to the reporter that innocence was an essential theme of the story: "I think the more factually innocent a person is who has suffered one of these attacks the more compelling, the more important it is that these things don't happen again. . . . It makes a situation where this could happen to you, a good citizen."

As in the jail rape story, the reporter here had definitional work to do and, as in that story, the strategy was use of ironic detail and control of point of view. . . .

Once again, the most interesting examples of the reporter's narrative craft are the cases in which innocence is most problematic. The narration of one such case begins not from the point of view of the victim but from that of witnesses. A young couple, both lawyers, walking home after a long day at the office see a swirl of activity across the street. "Still on the south side of the street, across from police, Sarah Solmssen said she saw several officers 'throwing a person against a brick wall. I saw the night-sticks, and then I started running.' By the time she had broken free of her husband's grip and crossed Spruce Street, she said she could see a K-9 dog biting the leg of a young man who was lying inert, in a semi-fetal position, on the sidewalk in front of the Engineers' Club. 'I saw the dog's jaws moving up and down three or four times,' she recalled. 'No officer was attempting to get that dog off the boy. He was just lying there motionless.' Peter Solmssen, who is 29, was slightly behind his wife, but with his height, 6-foot-2, he could see the boy on the ground, his hands cuffed behind his back, unmoving. . . ."

With an image of the attack in place, "the boy" is revealed to be a 220-pound, 17-year-old who is so drunk that later he could not clearly recall the events. It is clear, however, that he had been fighting inside the bar and that, when hauled out of the bar by relatives, as his aunt reported, "he was cussing very bad." He may or may not have tried to throw a punch at either his aunt or the officer who had responded to the report of a brawl. He was handcuffed by the officer but then, suddenly, the dog was on top of him.

Of nine cases reviewed in this story, the reporter singled out this one as the best example of his commitment to reporting "all possible points of view" and revealing "all the foibles of the victims" so that readers could make up their own minds about what happened: "I spoke to (the victim's) aunt, who'd been at the scene. I spoke to one of her friends . . . who'd been at the scene. I got the reports of the officers even though they wouldn't talk to me. And in publishing my account I stressed that [the victim] had been profane. He'd been drunk. He'd been obnoxious and even his aunt and [her friend] said that the police would have been totally justified in arresting him for disorderly conduct and that they exercised remarkable restraint. I put that in there because I'd come to the conclusion that [the victim] should have been arrested but what happened afterwards, once he'd been knocked to the ground and handcuffed, was not justifiable."

Nevertheless, in privileging the account of the Solmssens, who had come onto the scene just as the victim was being bitten by the dog, the reporter had defined the target of the dog attack not as a drunken and violent teenager, but as "the boy" handcuffed and in a "semi-fetal position."

It is important to note here that the reporter does not characterize the privileging of the Solmssens' account as a persuasive tactic. Indeed, he denies ever attempting to persuade the reader of anything. Rather, he characterizes his reliance upon their account as the use of the best available evidence, the evidence provided by those witnesses "who have nothing to protect."

And yet it is important to note that the Solmssens' account also earns its place in the story—and thus its reality—from its place in "an order of moral existence" in which innocence and guilt are principal concerns and indignation the only proper response. It can be no surprise, then, that these witnesses serve not only to define the target of the attack as "the boy" but also to vocalize indignation to the report: "Horrified by what they had seen, the Solmssens walked directly home to their townhouse on Juniper Street, less than a block from the Engineers' Club. Peter Solmssen said he wanted 'something done about' what he and his wife had just witnessed."[13]

Ettema and Glasser have more to say, but their overall conclusion is that

Notwithstanding our considerable respect for the accomplishments of these reporters, our argument is that the development, selection and assembly of facts into a story serves the moral task at hand. That task, as the reporters themselves obliquely acknowledge, is the evocation of righteous indignation—indignation at the plight of victims who are, if not entirely innocent by the standards of white middle-class newspaper readers, at least innocent enough to make what happened to them an outrageous injustice, and also indignation at the demeanor of officials who are, if not guilty of criminal behavior, at least guilty of indifference and hypocrisy.

The task is accomplished by cueing the audience's response to these characters through the emplotting of events as recognizably moralistic stories and, more specifically, through the skillful use of such story elements as point of view, ironic detail and ritual denial. [Marimow reported that the police department denied there was a problem and refused to be interviewed. Ettema and Glasser call this "a ritual denial, which journalistic convention demands be included in the story."] Innocence and guilt thus emerge from these stories as we are instructed which "images to look for in our culturally encoded experience in order to determine how we should feel about the thing represented." And so it is that these stories permit us to "judge the moral significance of human projects . . . even while we pretend to be merely describing them."[14]

Ettema and Glasser are expert storytellers themselves, especially in their preferred story form, the refereed academic journal. However, for their story to be heard (accepted and printed), it is not enough to "discover" that project stories have a moral form that resonates with other kinds of storytelling. This view has already been told, years before, and many times.

Okay, then, how about this: Journalists actually manipulate the stories to make you think one way or another. And specifically, journalists use as their tools (gasp) words. Moreover, they stretch the so-called truth to do it. And, we aren't talking about just any journalists. These are the best of the best. Think what the rest are like. And, for total, unbelievable irony, they don't even know they do it.

There are many issues raised here, but two need to be addressed.

Ettema and Glasser would have us believe they have discovered that these investigative reporters cooked the books to make people who are not innocent appear innocent so that the reader or viewer will be outraged, and to ensure that the reader or viewer will believe the reporters that there is a real problem.

The researchers' "evidence" is less than compelling. In the Marimow case, we are supposed to be discomfited because the handcuffed teenager, already subdued when attacked and bitten by a police dog, was big, drunk and abusive.

Has Marimow made someone innocent who isn't? No. In the real world, ordinary people are sometimes heroic, otherwise ordinary people sometimes perform criminal acts, and sometimes people who break laws are victimized by cops (or their dogs).

If the examples offered by Ettema and Glasser are intended to outrage us as to the skillful nature in which reporters manipulate the story, they fail to persuade.

It's never all right for dogs to bite someone already restrained, criminal or otherwise; it's never all right if some people are raped in jails, criminal or otherwise; it's never all right if cops downgrade crimes so they are never followed-up.

What about other ideas related to storytelling?

I plead guilty, and so should we all, that we are storytellers. Further, I plead guilty to being skillful. And last, I plead guilty to coming to conclusions about the situation I've investigated and with sharing those conclusions with readers and viewers.

Elsewhere in this book I argue that it is our duty to come to conclusions about the findings we investigate. It is not enough, for example, to write 50,000 words about water. What readers want to know and what we are obliged to tell them is what all our research means, if only to us. And, of course, we should offer the reader all the evidence—exculpatory and inculpatory—that we find.

NOTES

1. Ettema, who also is credited on the Protess book, teaches at Northwestern University; Glasser at Stanford University. I was one of the journalists interviewed by them, but after publication of the articles reviewed here.

2. "Chapter Three: Narrative," by Adrian Tilley, in "The Media Studies Book," edited by David Lusted (London: Routledge, 1991), 53–79.

3. Tilley, 53–54.

4. Ibid., 54–57.

5. Ibid., 58–60. In these pages, Tilley gives credit to models proposed by Tzvetan Todorov and Vladimir Propp, which I deleted there but have restored here. It is interesting to note that Todorov was writing about the gothic horror genre and Propp about folk tales.

6. "Narrative Form and Moral Force: The Realization of Innocence and Guilt Through Investigative Journalism," by James S. Ettema and Theodore L. Glasser in the *Journal of Communication,* Summer 1988, 8–26.

7. Marimow is now an editor at the *Baltimore Sun.* I did not interview Marimow, nor either author.

8. Ettema and Glasser, 10.

9. Ibid., 11.

10. Ibid.

11. Ibid., 12.

12. Ibid., 12–13.

13. Ibid., 15–17.

14. Ibid., 24.

Index